GREAT AMERICAN BRANDS

GREAT AMERICAN BRANDS

The Success Formulas that Made Them Famous

DAVID POWERS CLEARY

Fairchild Publications
New York

Designed by Elaine Golt Gongora

Edited by Angelo J. Virgona

Second Printing 1981

Standard Book Number: 87005-338-8

Library of Congress Catalog Card Number: 80-68646

Printed in the United States of America

TABLE OF CONTENTS

For Gertrude and Leo,
Marguerite and Timothy,
Virginia and Shelley,
Michael and Christopher

PREFACE

In the course of preparing a marketing plan, I once went to a large library, urgently in need of some basic background information about successful consumer brands—not just how they began, but about the marketing principles they had followed in the winning and holding of consumer trust.

Incredibly, no such book existed. There were numerous books on modern marketing theory, and there were some flimsily nostalgic collections of early advertisements. But there was nothing with a case-history kind of perspective on the building of popular brands.

That was a shame, I thought, because *brand-building* is one of the most basic functions of any producer of consumer goods, and certainly it is one of the finest things that ever happened to the consumer. Without trade-marked brands, there would be no trustworthy marketplace, no sure and simple way to know what to reach for—and what to avoid.

Out of raw necessity, I shot off some inquiries to companies whose products and promotion I admired, asking for the kind of information I could apply to my marketing problem. The answers were slow because often they could come only from a tedious searching of ancient files. But the answers did come, each a concentrated capsule from someone's hard-knocks experience. The insights they offered about the successes—and failures—of various marketing activities were often a reminder of George Santayana's haunting observation: "He who forgets the past is doomed to relive it."

It soon became apparent that I had the meager beginnings of a case-history sampler for other marketing professionals. In turn, a surprising number of the marketers who previewed the early material suggested that it also could serve a useful purpose as collateral reading for college-level students of marketing and related business subjects.

More than a few of the previewers pointed out how timelessly the trial-and-error experience of the past can relate to even the most advanced marketing concerns of today. Some highlight examples:

On building product image: Harley Procter was doing it in 1879—doing it so wisely that his original concept would go unchanged into its second century, while growing into the largest advertising program in the corporate universe. And the Coca-Cola Company, in the same early years, was beginning to shape the four elements of an image that would help make theirs the best-known product in the world.

On market segmentation and psychographics: Campbell's Soup, pioneering convenience foods at the turn of the century, not only had the marketing advantage of a precisely-defined target audience, but copy and media guidelines in direct support. And in the field of male fashion, in 1897, Hart Schaffner & Marx was going beyond demographics and learning how to aim at lifestyles, long before "psychographics" became a part of the marketing vocabulary.

On innovative merchandising: It was all the way back in 1856 that Singer introduced the trade-in allowance and the installment buying plan. And it was in 1900 that Milton Hershey coupled mass production with mass distribution, complete with a built-in promotion force that is still not universally understood. Both actions were born of imaginative thinking about special marketing problems of the day and, in both cases, *what* was done is not as instructive and memorable as *why* it was done.

On innovative advertising: William Wrigley Jr. was ridiculed, in 1907, for choosing a depression year for his most ambitious advertising campaign; so was Charles D. Armstrong, a decade later, for his "noncommercial" advertising approach; and so was Joyce Hall when, in 1951, he brazenly disregarded some cardinal rules of television. What happened, in all three cases, made marketing history and qualifies as essential background knowledge among well-read marketing people.

The profiles in this book were carefully selected to

cover a spectrum of marketing fundamentals utilizing a concise, but complete, case-history method, and—with the exception of the Ford cars story, which begins with the company's spectacular, post-World War II comeback—the stories begin with the brands' earliest days.

Because no single book could do full justice to all the great consumer brands in the American marketplace, I used the following criteria to compress the hundreds of contenders to a representative sampler group:

- The brand must be a product manufactured for the typical consumer home.
- The product must have genuine social significance— some influence, large or small, vital or quaint, on the quality of our lives.
- The maker of the brand must be the originator or principal developer of its product category. (The brand need not be the current best seller because sales rankings fluctuate from year to year and often are of no great consequence.)

For the convenience not only of the student, but of the busy professional, I have included a concise marketing insights section with each brand profile, and have provided a marketing subject index.

It is my hope, of course, that the stories will also provide some enrichment for the general reader who simply likes to be intelligently informed about consumer affairs, or who has enough of the social historian in his or her makeup to be aware that the Great Brands are a very revealing and a very solid piece of Americana. In their humble or prestigious, widely varying ways, the trademarked brands that became household words automatically became an unforgettable part of the fabric of our lives.

The reader is advised that all the brandnames profiled are trademarks protected by law.

Because virtually all the information in this work had to be dug out of old files and fading copies of company house organs, I am deeply grateful for the help of at least one person, and often as many as five or six, in every company represented in this book. I also offer my thanks to the trade journal editors, too numerous to name individually, who helped me track down the principal pioneers and developers of the major consumer brand categories.

David Powers Cleary
Tampa, 1980

ARMSTRONG FLOORS

"Let the buyer have faith."

1 In the early 1960's, as part of its continuing consumer research program, Armstrong Cork Company included a question asking respondents to name the carpet companies with which they were most familiar. When the survey results were tallied, company executives were very surprised to find that Armstrong Cork had been ranked as the fourth most recognized carpet company in the United States.

Armstrong Cork, at that time, had recently observed its one hundredth anniversary, and never in that entire century had Armstrong ever manufactured a carpet. So why had so many consumers become convinced that Armstrong made carpets?

The answer had two parts. First, of course, was the fact that Armstrong had been making linoleum, tile, and other resilient floor coverings since 1908. The second part of the answer could be traced back to two basic decisions about management philosophy, one made in 1860, the other in 1917. Both decisions were incredibly simple and logical, but they had seemed revolutionary at the time they were made.

Back in 1860, Thomas M. Armstrong, age twenty-four, had decided to supplement his wages as a shipping clerk in a Pittsburgh glass plant by investing his three hundred dollars in savings for equipment to cut cork stoppers for bottles. His new venture, which would become known as Armstrong Cork Company, had just one unique quality—a basic business principle. At a time when many businesses followed the ancient rule of *caveat emptor* ("Let the buyer beware"), Thomas Armstrong decided his guiding principle would be: "Let the buyer have faith."

By 1917, the humble cork bottle-stopper company had become even better known for its cork-backed linoleum flooring and was ready to enter the advertising pages of *The Saturday Evening Post*. The company president was

Founder Thomas M. Armstrong started his cork bottle-stopper business with three hundred dollars and a guiding principle: "Let the buyer have faith."

When the time came to apply his father's guiding principle to the company's first advertising, Charles D. Armstrong decided the advertisements should aim first to serve the reader.

Opposite: Armstrong's first national advertisement for linoleum flooring appeared in 1917 in *The Saturday Evening Post*. Along with the helpful decorating suggestions, Charles Armstrong insisted that his company's product be shown in combination with other elements of home beauty. Associates criticized the approach as "too modest and noncommercial."

now Charles D. Armstrong, who had always been guided by his father's basic rule, and who was now wondering how "Let the buyer have faith" should be applied to an advertising campaign.

Charles Armstrong felt a deep pride in his company's linoleum operations. When his father had expanded into linoleum manufacturing in 1908 as a way of utilizing the cork remnants from the bottle-stopper operations, linoleum had been in the marketplace for fifty years, but always as a starkly utilitarian product, available only in a handful of plain, rather somber colors. It had been Thomas Armstrong who organized a research group to develop what he saw as the much greater potential offered by linoleum— a way to make America's homes more attractive, more comfortable, and easier to care for. Armstrong Cork was now determined to establish a brand name in a business where brand names were virtually nonexistent and where most merchandise was bought on a cut-price basis.

The ambitious, new advertising campaign in *The Saturday Evening Post* promised to become an historic turning point in Armstrong Cork's history, and Charles Armstrong had listened carefully to many viewpoints on what should be carried on those advertising pages. His decision: Armstrong advertising would be based on the principle of service to the reader. It would offer helpful ideas that would cause readers to feel repaid for the time they had spent reading an Armstrong advertisement.

To some associates who criticized the new approach as "too modest" and "too noncommercial," Charles Armstrong doggedly maintained that the Armstrong linoleum would speak for itself in ads containing large illustrations of beautiful rooms; in addition to being an honest and accurate rendering, it would always be associated with beauty.

Within the course of the first year's campaign, readers of *The Saturday Evening Post* were looking forward to the Armstrong Cork advertisements for the latest, most imaginative ideas in home decorating.

Meanwhile, Armstrong was showing retailers how to welcome the consumer at the point of sale with informa-

Linoleum is made of powdered cork and oxidized linseed oil, pressed on burlap. Be careful you get it. For there are inferior floor coverings nowadays that look like linoleum on the surface, but which are merely imitations. Remember these two easy ways to tell genuine linoleum: First, look at the back and make sure it's burlap. Second, try to tear it. Imitations tear easily. Better still, ask for Armstrong's Linoleum by *name*.

The living-room floor is a warm brown linoleum, with a hint of tan in the carpet design. In the hallway, Parquetry Inlaid Linoleum gives the effect of hardwood. Note how the decorator has carried the linoleum design into hangings and upholstery.

Three Armstrong patterns, suitable for the interior shown above.

I N many of the finest homes in Europe, you will find linoleum in every room. Not gaudy "oilcloth" patterns, but rich, polished linoleum *floors*, in mellow tones that harmonize perfectly with rugs and walls and furniture.

Such linoleums are made right here in America by Armstrong Cork Company. And women who love beauty are laying them throughout their homes, creating floors that are at once tasteful, sanitary, economical.

Armstrong's Plain Linoleums in soft green, brown, red and gray—without any figure or pattern—make superb backgrounds for rugs. The darker shades give those low color tones necessary to make the floor the real base of the color scheme, and to harmonize with the darker woods in trim and furniture.

Send for booklet,"The House that Jack Re-Built" and the names of merchants near you who handle Armstrong's Linoleum.

Then for your guest-room, your bedroom, or nursery, there are the Armstrong carpet and matting designs—light, tastefully simple things in greens, blues, tans, and rose. Or the wonderful parquetry inlaid patterns—accurate reproductions of hardwood—for dining-room, living-room, hall, and den.

Look into this matter of linoleum floors. Have you seen the new Armstrong designs? Do you know how economical linoleum is? How absolutely sanitary? How easy to clean? How durable?

Stop thinking of linoleum as gaudy, old-fashioned. Go to some Armstrong merchant in your town and see for yourself what beautiful decorative effects you can have in floors that blend with your color scheme; floors that really *belong* to the room.

ARMSTRONG CORK COMPANY
Linoleum Department Lancaster, Pa.

Armstrong's Linoleum

For Every Room Ⓐ in the House

tive displays and kits of decorating guidance literature. As an additional way to make sure of customer satisfaction, Armstrong conducted free schools for linoleum installers.

Within a decade, beyond pushing flooring sales steadily upward, Charles Armstrong's service-to-the-reader series paid a major bonus. The research group had developed a new cork acoustical ceiling tile aimed at a vast new market. It simply moved into its rightful place in the Armstrong parade of beautiful rooms.

Several years later, when the economic freeze of the 1930's arrived, the service-to-the-reader strategy provided the company itself with some timely insulation. Armstrong Cork had been ahead of its time in cultivating the favor of America's do-it-yourselfers. During the Depression, a house was seldom spruced up unless the owner did it himself.

The Depression seemed interminable—and scarcely had it lifted before World War II put a stop to housing progress for another four years. By the end of the War, the nation had about fifteen years' worth of pent-up demand for better homes.

Fortunately, back around the turn of the century, Thomas Armstrong had decided he should use a research group in order to develop ingenious answers to two very basic questions: (1) What else can we make out of remnants of cork? and (2) To what would we turn if cork, our one raw material, suddenly became unavailable?

The R&D group had grown in direct proportion to the ingenious answers it had amassed, and it now welcomed the post-war challenge. By the end of the 1950's, more than one-third of Armstrong's sales volume was being generated by new products the company had developed during that single decade. Vinyl plastics entered the resilient flooring field with a rush. (Today, cork accounts for only three hundredths of one percent of Armstrong's raw material purchases.) Sound conditioning was brought within easy reach of the homeowner. For commercial and institutional buildings, acoustical ceilings evolved, step by step, into acoustical, ventilating ceilings with added fire protection and engineered illumination.

After finding that cork remnants from bottle stoppers could be used for making linoleum, Thomas Armstrong organized a research group to pursue other development work. Armstrong's research and development center has now guided the company into a line of some four hundred diversified products.

And, as fast as they arrived, the new products had a ready-made, rightful place in the Armstrong service-to-the-reader series of beautiful rooms.

The advertising, in turn, had cultivated such a large and loyal following that it kept raising the following question in the public mind: Why didn't Armstrong complete the beautiful room settings with carpeting and fur-

In time, service-to-the-reader advertising included promotion of guidance for the shopper at Armstrong Floor Fashion Centers which carry 18" × 24" samples of all Armstrong floors.

niture? As the survey of the early 1960's was to reveal in specific terms, many consumers already were *assuming* that Armstrong had been making carpeting all along.

In the late 1960's, Armstrong responded with new lines of carpeting and furniture. Charles Armstrong's beautiful room concept of 1917 was now much more complete—and still gathering momentum.

From its headquarters in Lancaster, Pennsylvania, the Armstrong company now runs an international business with about twenty-four thousand employees, and an annual sales volume of over one billion dollars derived from a diversified line of more than five hundred products (no longer including linoleum, which was phased out in 1974), produced in more than fifty-five manufacturing plants.

Inevitably, in an organization that no longer sees much (if any) cork, the time came for a change of corporate name. In 1980, the venerable Armstrong Cork became Armstrong World Industries, Inc.

MARKETING INSIGHTS

Without a solid foundation of consumer trust, no marketing effort can count on long-term success. Armstrong's service-to-the-reader approach in advertising was (and is) a fundamental step in the building of a trustworthy company.

Being helpful to the reader meant offering creative ideas about the entire home, not just about Armstrong products. In time, of course, the Armstrong research and development effort was destined to provide accoustical ceilings, carpeting, furniture, and many other new products to be used throughout the home.

Helpful service to the reader in advertising was then extended—in a natural, evolutionary way—to helpful decorator guidance for the shopper in Armstrong showrooms.

In its support of the marketing effort, Armstrong's research and development prowess can be capsuled in these simple terms: Armstrong, once a user only of cork, now makes more than five hundred products, and cork accounts for only about three hundredths of one percent of the company's total raw material purchases.

BIRDS EYE FROZEN FOODS

"You've got a great idea . . . if you can make it work."

2 As he neared the pivotal age of forty, Clarence Birds-eye of Gloucester, Massachusetts, looked back over his varied career as a field naturalist, fur trader, purchasing agent, fisheries investigator, and holder of several "in-between" jobs and asked himself if there was anything, in that curious mixture of experience, that could be turned into a substantial commercial success.

It was a familiar inventory; he had taken it many times. The son of a judge of the New York State Supreme Court, and the grandson of a well-to-do Connecticut inventor, Clarence Birdseye was fully aware that many of his friends expected more from him than he had delivered.

Now in 1923, as he repeated the evaluation, he concluded that he had been exposed to a major opportunity nearly a decade earlier and had passed it by. During the arctic winters in Labrador, as a fur trader, he had watched the Eskimos spread their freshly-caught fish on the snow, in temperatures of thirty to fifty degrees below zero, Fahrenheit, and had noted that, almost instantly, the fish froze solid. He also had noted that, months later, when one of those fish was thawed and cooked, it tasted like one freshly caught. And he had watched the Eskimos achieve the same results with freshly-killed caribou and geese.

The secret of the Eskimo success, Birdseye concluded, was all in the speed of the freezing. In his Labrador years, along with the quick-frozen foods, he had tasted the less satisfactory results of the more gradual freezing of fish and game at higher than sub-zero temperatures.

When Birdseye took his observations to nutritionists, they not only agreed with his comments about flavor, but pointed out that the super-fast freezing of foods, at sub-zero temperatures, could contribute importantly to the locking-in and preservation of basic nutrients. "You've got a great idea," they assured him, "if you can make it work on a practical basis."

Clarence Birdseye

Clarence Birdseye was confident he could—confident enough to borrow on his life insurance and begin formal experiments. By 1924, after many failures, he got the results he wanted by placing packages of fish between two refrigerated metal surfaces at sub-zero temperatures. He called his device a "belt froster," persuaded three backers to stake him to sixty thousand dollars, and organized the General Seafoods Corporation. By 1926, the inventor's model had grown into a twenty-ton "Quick-Freeze" machine, forty feet long; and by 1927, bulky packages of frozen fish were being shipped to the Midwest, further experiments with fruit, vegetables and meat were underway, and Clarence Birdseye was organizing the General Foods Company to act as the stockholding company for General Seafoods and to control all patents on the belt froster process.

But, at the market place, Clarence Birdseye's spectacular new products crashed into a double stone wall of resistance. Retailers balked at the need for special refrigerating equipment. Consumers balked at what they perceived as just another "cold storage" product—usually of such doubtful quality that many states required markets to post a warning sign, "We sell cold storage foods," if they carried any such items.

As the winter of 1928 approached, most of the 1,666,033 pounds of seafood frozen during the previous summer was still unsold. For want of marketing capability, Birdseye's company was about to fail. He already had tried to interest leading meat packers and canners in his venture, and they had turned him down. Now, in desperation, he looked for help from any company with a strong reputation for marketing savvy. Ultimately, in the Postum Cereal Company, he found a willing collaborator.

Since its beginnings in 1895 with a new cereal beverage, the Postum organization had introduced Grape-Nuts, one of the first ready-to-eat breakfast cereals, and later had entered into a series of consolidations with such other old-line, independent companies as Jell-O, Minute Tapioca, Walter Baker Chocolate, Franklin Baker Coconut, and Maxwell House Coffee. Postum had never launched a product quite like quick-frozen foods, but was confident it could do the job and, in June of 1929, Postum purchased the assets of Birdseye's General Foods Company and rechristened itself General Foods Corporation. The sale included all patents covering the quick-freeze process as well as the "Birds Eye" trademark (born of a name Clarence had always pronounced *BIRDS-ee).*

The long-awaited "breakthrough" introduction of Birds Eye frozen foods was set for March 6, 1930, in Springfield, Massachusetts, and marketers everywhere would soon agree that nothing had ever equaled it for thoroughness and sustained salesmanship.

In eighteen selected Springfield grocery stores, General Foods installed—free—new Birds Eye storage cases, especially built at fifteen hundred dollars each. A corps of demonstrators urged shoppers to taste free samples of chicken, haddock, sirloin steak, and strawberries. "Traveling" electric signs were rotated among the stores. Birds Eye speakers appeared in domestic science classes, women's clubs, and public utility showrooms. Birds Eye salesmen interviewed customers in their homes to get detailed reactions. Backed all the while by strong advertising, the campaign continued for forty weeks.

At the end of forty weeks, the General Foods marketers concluded that frozen foods had strong potential—if the company could solve many newly-observed problems of refrigeration, transportation, and the selection of foods most suitable for quick-freezing.

Four long years after the big sale to Postum, Birds Eye had processed nearly twenty-three million pounds of a full line of products, developed super-insulated railroad cars, built a fleet of special Birds Eye trawlers, established the first frozen food laboratories—and still had only 516 retail outlets, most of them in New England. The company's goal of national distribution was beginning to look hopeless.

In 1933, the marketers made an abrupt switch in strategy. Instead of aiming first at retail outlets, they would concentrate on big-quantity sales to the huge institutional market: hospitals, schools, hotels, restaurants. Refrigeration problems would be more manageable, quality could be better controlled, and consumers of the food

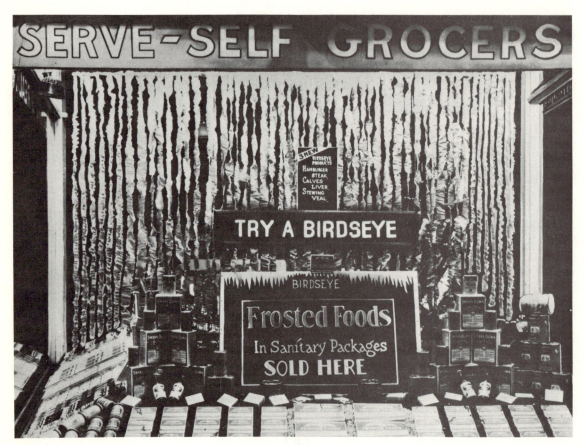

Grocer's display of Birds Eye
Frosted Foods during the
Springfield (Mass.) introduction of 1930. Signs empha-
sized "sanitary"!

would be better pleased. It would build volume nationwide and also do a national "sampling" job. At the same
time, Birds Eye developed a new kind of freezer case, to
be made available to retailers at low monthly rentals.

By the fall of 1934, in Syracuse, New York, Birds Eye
was able to test its new strategy of institutional distribution followed by retail distribution, all carried out by a
specially-trained task force. Results were excellent, and
the task force repeated their procedure in city after city.
But it was not until 1937 that Birds Eye operations were
in the black, and not until 1940 that national distribution
was within the company's reach.

In its final drive for national distribution, in 1940, Birds Eye got an unexpected boost from the nation's defense mobilization effort. By year's end, every fourth housewife had become a defense worker and "convenience" foods suddenly came of age. But the boom soon created a new problem: a host of fly-by-night operators entered the frozen foods business and began to undermine its carefully-built reputation of quality.

Then came Pearl Harbor—and another series of surprises for the frozen foods industry. Processors were suddenly threatened with cutback status as a "nonessential" industry. They promptly responded that "to can twenty million pounds of vegetables would require twenty-six hundred tons of vital steel." The U.S. Government not only agreed, but immediately ordered quick–frozen foods to be listed on the OPA (Office of Price Administration) charts posted in all food stores—and thus completed the job of making the entire nation frozen-food conscious. Meanwhile, the GI's of World War II were getting accustomed to the best in frozen foods quality, carefully maintained by the Army's portable refrigerated warehouses and the Navy's refrigerated ships.

The demand for frozen food was now at an all-time high and still climbing steadily. Canners and packers who had been serving as Birds Eye co-packers began establishing their own brands. Meat packers entered the business, and so did farm cooperatives. The TVA (Tennessee Valley Authority), working with the University of Tennessee, turned to frozen foods as an outlet for Tennessee's produce and developed a refrigerated barge to transport frozen foods throughout inland waters.

Birds Eye management responded to the proliferating competition by turning from co-packers to the building of its own new plants and the acquiring of new subsidiaries. Then, as the level of technology approached parity throughout the industry, Birds Eye called on the General Foods Kitchens to come up with a steady flow of new recipes and new combinations to maintain Birds Eye's edge as the brand with "the extra measure of flavor."

For years after he sold his company to Postum, Clarence Birdseye served as director of the pioneer frozen

food laboratories he had established in Gloucester, concentrating his talents on nutrition and leaving the distribution problems to someone else. And long before his death in 1956, he was busily applying his inventiveness to still other new fields.

Among his later developments: paper made from sugar cane fibers, and a light bulb with an inside-silvered reflector. Both products, at the retail level, could simply be unwrapped and put on a shelf.

MARKETING INSIGHTS

Clarence Birdseye knew that the quick-freezing of fresh fish at sub-zero temperatures could offer the consumer an important bonus in both flavor and nutrition. But as a marketing venture, his idea bumped immediately into two major roadblocks: grocers resisted the need for expensive refrigerating equipment; consumers resisted the product as "just another inferior cold storage food."

The company first tried marketing through retail grocery stores, with disappointing results, then switched to the institutional/commercial market and began to succeed. The institutional/commercial market—hospitals, schools, hotels, restaurants—made refrigeration problems more manageable, thus leading to better pleased consumers. It also served as a national "sampling" effort.

At the same time, along with improving their product, Birds Eye research and development people created a new kind of freezer case that could be made available to retailers at a low monthly rental.

Birds Eye marketing, begun in 1930, did not reach national distribution until 1940—at which point the mobilization for World War II brought two major boosts: the armed services began exposing millions of GI's to a variety of quick-frozen foods, and defense-plant work turned millions of housewives into buyers of "convenience foods," quick-frozen included.

Inevitably, the success of quick-frozen foods generated a multitude of competitors. Birds Eye maintained its market leadership by developing a steadily broader choice of imaginative recipes and combinations.

BISSELL CARPET SWEEPERS

"To live up to our ideals, we must keep clean."

3 Name the dirt that is the most difficult to pick up from a carpet: Would you say lint, ashtray spills, dog hair, pins, leaves from plants, thread ends, crumbs, or what? Everyone has his or her own nonfavorite.

To Anna Bissell, the problem was something rarely seen in any home. Almost daily in their little crockery shop in Grand Rapids, Michigan, she and her husband, Melville, would open a new shipment of china or glasses, packed in masses of protective sawdust—and then spend the final part of the day sweeping up the tiny, bouncy, sticky particles from the shop's carpet. When even a newly-invented product called a "carpet sweeper" failed to do the job, Melville R. Bissell, whose hobby was tinkering with mechanical objects, decided to develop a new and better sweeper of his own design.

The original Bissell Carpet Sweeper (1876) was built for a market of one: Anna Bissell. Then, a customer of the Bissell crockery shop saw the device in action and asked where she could buy one. The question was soon being repeated, and Melville Bissell began asking himself if this device met a need important enough to warrant its commercial manufacture. He decided, after some reflection, that it did—and that the need was not just physical, but psychological.

Years later, a close associate recalled: "Mr. Bissell began with a conviction that the American people were clean in mind and body, and that to live up to our ideals, we must keep clean—we must have clean houses, clean bodies, clean minds. That was the basis of his faith in his business and of his hopes for its success. Then there was the added opportunity of making that cleanliness easier of attainment, to reduce the strain and drudgery of the housewife."

The floor above the crockery shop soon became a factory. Melville supervised the metalworking and woodworking; Anna delivered materials to the homes of the

Melville R. Bissell, inventor of the Bissell carpet sweeper.

Anna Bissell, one of America's first female corporate chief executives.

Grand Rapids residents who made the vitally important brushes; then each took a turn at canvassing stores that sold housewares. As storekeepers, they had decided early to concentrate on retail distribution rather than selling door-to-door; but it was many months before Anna Bissell was able to report the firm's first large order from a single store. She did decide, however, that selling was an activity she enjoyed.

By 1883, the Bissells were ready to build a factory designed expressly for the manufacture of carpet sweepers. During that year, they acquired the young Michigan Carpet Sweeper Company and the Grand Rapids Carpet Sweeper Company—mostly to gain the management talent of such persons as Walter J. Drew and C. B. Judd—and now had the organization and volume to support an ambitious, new, all-brick plant, five stories tall, and fully equipped with the latest machinery.

But the new manufacturing operation was barely running smoothly before a fire in an adjoining factory went out of control and reduced the Bissell plant to rubble. Melville Bissell was forced to mortgage not only his home but his personal property—even his highly prized harness horses—to get the company back into production.

Disaster soon struck again when a new Bissell model proved to be defective. Melville Bissell made the hard decision to recall the entire output—worth a then astronomical thirty-five thousand dollars—and destroy it.

Within the retail trade and among its customers (predominantly homemakers), the Bissell reputation for integrity and reliability was now so dominant that no other company ventured to compete. But the progress had been grueling. In March of 1889, Melville Bissell, at the age of forty-five, came down with pneumonia and was dead within a week.

Anna Bissell, at the urging of her associates, now assumed her husband's management responsibilities—and did so well, as one of America's first female corporate chief executives, that she would continue as the guiding force in Bissell management well into the 1920's.

To protect and strengthen the Bissell name, Anna Bis-

Left: The first Bissell carpet sweeper, patented in 1876. Handmade of solid walnut, with hog bristle brushes, it promised a "lifetime of hard usage." **Right:** Today's Bissell carpet sweeper co-exists successfully with all the electric vacuum cleaners.

sell set down strict guidelines on trademark and patent procedures. She then proceeded to establish Bissell on the international scene. Queen Victoria accelerated the momentum when she endorsed Bissells for her palace, and English housewives soon learned to refer to the daily sweeping as "Bisselling" their carpets. Turkish sultans and Arabian sheiks decided Bissells were best for their priceless Oriental carpets, and even the world's more modest homes could afford the little work-saver.

Meanwhile, in Grand Rapids, Anna Bissell was permitting a young Bissell bookkeeper to try out his theory that Bissell sales pamphlets should be stripped of their usual mechanical detail (because "women don't care about machinery") and instead filled with "woman talk" about "golden maple, opulent walnut, and rich mahogany." Male executives snorted that the kind of wood contributed nothing to the sweeper's performance—but the pamphlets were soon generating more orders than were being written by the firm's fourteen road salesmen. The young bookkeeper, Claude C. Hopkins, was thus encouraged to write an imaginative pamphlet about a limited collection of carpet sweepers made up in a rare, exotic wood called vermilion, a strangely beautiful wood found deep in the jungles of India, from whence it was lugged by elephants to the banks of the fabled Ganges and then rafted to market.

Early Bissell animated, life-size display went through all the motions of sweeping, "to the wonderment of beholders."

Bissell established itself early
in retail outlets and offered
dealers a variety of displays.

Male Bissell executives balked, but Anna Bissell nod-
ded her approval, and the pamphlet earned more money
for Bissell in just six weeks than the company had made
in any previous year.

At Bissell, Claude Hopkins also seems to have been the
first to promote a household appliance as a Christmas
gift. At any rate, he was destined soon to leave Grand
Rapids for an advertising career in Chicago, where he
became one of advertising's early "greats" and a
multimillionaire.

Throughout the early 1900's, Bissell went rolling along
as the undisputed leader in carpet care. When Irving J.
Bissell, third son of the company's founder, decided in
1910 to design and build Michigan's first airplane, the
Bissell factory gladly took time out to build most of the
airplane's parts, including the engine.

Then, in the next decade, a revolutionary new kind of
competition moved into the marketplace. To those fortunate enough to live in homes having electricity, the electric vacuum cleaner now offered the ultimate in easy carpet care, and there were those in the trade who predicted
deep trouble for Bissell.

To Anna Bissell and her associates, there were at least
three good reasons for not reacting defensively to the
new competition. First, Anna Bissell was convinced that
it would take more than a few years for the average consumer to overcome his or her fear of electrical machinery.

Second, the electric vacuum cleaner was cumbersome to handle and could be harsh on carpets, particularly Orientals. Finally, and most important of all, the electric vacuum cleaner required door-to-door salesmanship for demonstration and explanation, whereas the simple Bissell sweeper was well-established in high volume retail stores.

Ultimately, some of the growing number of brands of vacuum cleaners would win a place in retail channels, and Bissell itself would be obliged to make a token electric cleaner. But not until the early 1930's did the electrics become firmly established in retail stores—just in time for the pressures of the Depression to start forcing some of them out of business. With Melville R. Bissell, Jr. now in charge, the Bissell company decided to withdraw from the electric category and concentrate on doing what it did best: the design, manufacture, and marketing of lightweight carpet sweepers. Instead of becoming "just another vacuum cleaner," Bissell would continue as the preeminent carpet sweeper.

There was no reason, Bissell concluded, why the carpet sweeper could not coexist successfully with the electric vacuum cleaners. The electrics could win favor for heavy-duty cleaning; but the lightweight Bissells would be unequaled for in-between cleanups, for versatility on a variety of floor surfaces, and for gentleness on costly Orientals and other sensitive carpets.

In 1953, Melville R. Bissell, III, succeeded his uncle in the presidency and expanded the emphasis on marketing. The Bissell company, he decided, should mean not just "carpet sweepers," but "floor care" and ultimately "home care." The company would offer more service to homemakers, including special aids to home economics teachers. And, in its product line, as part of the expanded "home care" strategy, Bissell introduced Bissell Rug Shampoo and the lightweight Shampoomaster. During a ten-year period, 1957–67, the Shampoomaster would be featured ahead of the carpet sweeper.

But as the Bissell company neared its 1976 centennial, now under the direction of John M. Bissell, the carpet sweeper was reinstated as the company's number one product, surrounded by a growing array of carpet care, fabric care, and general home care products, including vacuum cleaners.

As the company began its second century, it would note that the work force had grown to more than fourteen hundred in manufacturing alone, and that its headquarters in Grand Rapids was rivaled by modern manufacturing complexes in Canada, France, Germany, Ireland, Switzerland, and the United Kingdom.

And the writers of Bissell Carpet Sweeper advertising would be able to point out, as competitively as ever: "Quietly, efficiently whisks up dirt, grit, pet hair from any surface from polished hardwood to medium shag carpeting. No electric cord, so the Bissell is useful everywhere in the home, around the pool, on the patio, at the cottage."

MARKETING INSIGHTS

What should a pioneer product do when it suddenly is confronted by an army of competitors offering newer technology? That was the Bissell situation when electric vacuum cleaners moved into the marketplace.

At first, the Bissell company noted that many consumers had a strong fear of electricity; and that the selling of vacuum cleaners required house-to-house demonstrations, whereas Bissell Carpet Sweepers were selling in steady volume through retail stores.

Later, as the electrics slowly established themselves with consumers and with the retail outlets, Bissell offered a token vacuum cleaner—but decided that its major product should continue to be *THE carpet sweeper* instead of just another vacuum cleaner.

By positioning its product as the handy, cordless, gentle picker-upper—the product to be used in-between the heavy-duty vacuumings—Bissell co-existed successfully with the electrics.

Bissell also is noteworthy for its pioneer efforts in making household appliances more beautiful; for its early use of what Bissell considered woman-oriented language in its advertising; and for its early, voluntary recall of a defective product model.

BLACK & DECKER POWER TOOLS

"No idea is worth anything unless you have the guts to back it up."

4 It was early in World War II that Black & Decker formed its Post-War Planning Committee. And the planning task force had barely outlined its marketing research objectives when one member's eye was caught by an item in the news: workers in defense plants, in growing numbers, were stealing the portable power tools and taking them home.

The sketchy, unexpected report was a highly relevant bit of marketing research information. It was in the war plants that a whole generation of Americans was being introduced to power tools of all kinds, and no company was more synonymous with *portable* power tools than The Black & Decker Mfg. Co. of Towson, Maryland.

Back in 1914, in the course of its business of developing special machinery for industry, Black & Decker had designed a portable electric drill with a pistol grip and a trigger switch. It introduced a new kind of handiness and accuracy, was awarded a United States patent for its pistol grip and its switch, and ultimately became the world's most copied power tool design. It was built especially for professionals.

The Post-War Planning Committee, headed by Alonzo ("Al") G. Decker, Jr., had a keen awareness of the traps as well as the opportunities that lay ahead. The son of a co-founder of the company, Al Decker had started out on the shop floor—"like everybody else"—during his high school summers. Years later, after college and a successful term as a Black & Decker sales engineer in the United States and overseas, Al Decker—"like a lot of other people"—was laid off during the Depression. When he finally was rehired by Black & Decker, it was as a laborer at twenty-five cents an hour because the budget was short of money for engineers.

Al Decker had listened to all his father's stories about the company history: how the two co-founders had met as employees of the Rowland Telegraph Company; how

S. Duncan Black

they had left in 1910, in their twenties, to start a new company of their own; how Al's father had been able to borrow his share of the twelve hundred dollar investment from his father-in-law, whereas S. Duncan Black, to raise *his* six hundred dollar share, had been obliged to sell his prized 1907 Maxwell automobile.

S. Duncan Black and Alonzo G. Decker, in their original downtown Baltimore plant, had built a milk bottle-cap machine and a candy-dipping machine; a postage stamp slitting and coiling machine and a cotton picker; a shock absorber for the automotive industry and machinery for the U.S. Mint. Not until 1916 would their products be sufficiently standardized to start carrying the Black & Decker trademark.

Then, with their new and growing line of power tools, they went out to call on industry, and they learned to do it well. By 1925, they were demonstrating their products to plant operating personnel throughout the United States with Black & Decker "Schoolrooms on Wheels"— not just trucks, but special buses built by Pierce Arrow. By 1929, they were impressing their customers with a six-passenger Travel-Air monoplane, fitted out as a flying showroom of power tools.

Al Decker would also remember that, when the company veered away from its industrial markets, it had run into problems. In 1930, for example, as its first venture in the consumer field, Black & Decker had introduced the Cinderella washing machine. And if the Cinderella had failed to live up to its name because of the bad timing of its introduction (the beginning of the Depression), there was still another, earlier example: the one-half inch BB special drill. Black & Decker had introduced it as "the first all sleeve-bearing power tool at a popular price" with the hope that it would popularize power tools in even small industrial operations. But the price had not been low enough.

As Al Decker and his post-war planners moved through their painstaking collection and evaluation of facts, five basic conclusions began to take shape: (1) the defense plants were serving as a massive power tool demonstration program; (2) at the end of the War, with proper promotion, a substantial home market would develop for power tools; (3) Black & Decker performance had earned the respect of a large segment of the future home market; (4) unfortunately for Black & Decker, almost any other manufacturer could turn out a pistol-grip-and-trigger-switch tool that would *look* like Black & Decker; and (5) ultimately, Black & Decker could not count on sales leadership unless it could first achieve *cost* leadership.

Could the post-war Black & Decker products be backed by the kind of productivity programs that would ensure cost leadership? Al Decker's "up-from-the-shop-floor" committee said it could be done. In a company that had always taken great pride in the way it knew its people, their families, and their backgrounds, that was assurance enough.

Alonzo G. Decker, Sr.

Al Decker, who went on later to become chairman of the board, never thought his market planners were taking any unnecessary risks. He had a different view. "No idea is worth anything," Al Decker observed, "unless you have the guts to back it up."

In 1946, Black & Decker introduced the world's first line of popularly-priced drills and accessories for the home and do-it-yourself power tool market. It was followed by Black & Decker jig saws, sanders, and circular saws.

The prices were right. Black & Decker met the competition head-on, dollar for dollar—and then, during a period of generally rising costs, Black & Decker initiated a series of price reductions.

In 1957, Black & Decker moved into another new market with portable electric lawn edgers and hedge trimmers, followed later by electric power lawn mowers.

In 1961, Black & Decker introduced the world's first cordless electric drill, powered by self-contained nickel-cadmium cells, and thus launched the second generation of portable power tools for the do-it-yourselfer. This would soon be followed by Black & Decker's cordless hedge trimmer. Do-it-yourselfers who already owned power tools now had good reasons for buying the newer and better models.

The original Black & Decker pistol grip and trigger switch drill, developed in 1914.

The world's first popular-priced drill for the do-it-yourselfer, introduced in 1946 and priced at $16.95. By the late 1970's, its much-improved successor was selling for less than $10.00.

At his company's Museum of Progress tool exhibition, Alonzo G. Decker, Jr. holds a modern power jig saw while demonstrating an antique pedal-power jig saw for Francis P. Lucier, Black & Decker chief executive officer.

The Black & Decker cordless drill, introduced in 1961.

HOME-UTILITY ELECTRIC TOOLS

$16.95 ¼-INCH CAPACITY IN STEEL Portable Electric Drill

Again, in 1973, Black & Decker brought established owners back for new models by introducing at no increase in price the first line of double-insulated, consumer, indoor power tools, and by reducing the price of the company's cordless drill by thirty-three percent. In the same year, Black & Decker introduced its innovative Workmate portable vise and workcenter and then capped the busy season by acquiring the McCulloch Corporation, a pioneer maker of small gasoline engines and gasoline chain saws.

And the prices continued to be right. Black & Decker's first drill for the do-it-yourselfer had been priced at $16.95 in 1946. By the late 1970's, the same size drill, vastly improved—and in the face of severe inflation— was priced below $10.00.

All the while, Black & Decker continued to serve its industrial customers throughout the world and to build its consumer markets overseas. In 1975, for the first time, Black & Decker sales outside the United States exceeded U.S. sales, and the world market is growing. Worldwide, Black & Decker now has thirty-one manufacturing plants and some twenty thousand employees, compared with the company's five plants and fewer than two thousand employees at the time the Post-War Planning Committee began its work.

And there is still another market, *beyond* the Earth, in which Black & Decker has done some exploratory work. When America's astronauts needed lunar drills for taking core samples from the moon, it was Black & Decker that developed the cordless powerhead.

MARKETING INSIGHTS
Black & Decker had long been building power tools for industry. When World War II introduced a generation of Americans to power tools, it paved the way for Black & Decker's entry into the do-it-yourself home market.

The postwar market was a hungry one, "ready to buy almost anything." But Black & Decker took the long view, and it did not move until its factory *cost* leadership assured decisive, marketplace *price* leadership.

Beginning with a portable drill, Black & Decker's workshop tools were expanded to a complete line. Its production and marketing expertise then led B & D into the related field of power gardening tools.

Later, as its markets matured and neared saturation, Black & Decker was ready with new, improved products that gave customers the incentive to come back for the newer models.

Apollo Lunar Drill, used on Apollo 15 mission in 1971 and subsequent missions 16 and 17. Black & Decker developed the no-torque, cordless power head.

BUDWEISER BEER

"Making friends is our business."

Adolphus Busch, founder of Anheuser-Busch and father of Budweiser and Michelob beer.

5 Eberhard Anheuser, at the time young Adolphus Busch came to court his daughter, was wishing he had never heard of the beer business. A while back, out of friendship and against his business judgment, he had given Georg Schneider a modest loan to strengthen Schneider's faltering young brewery. Now in 1855, just three years later, the brewery had begun floundering again, and Anheuser, having paid off the other creditors as the first step in straightening out the mess, was suddenly the reluctant owner of The Bavarian Brewery of St. Louis, a city to which the massive fifty-year flow of German immigrants had shrunk to a trickle, leaving it with an overabundance of local breweries.

To further complicate Anheuser's life, Adolphus Busch, age twenty-two, and about to marry Lilly Anheuser, was a newly-arrived Bavarian immigrant who could offer an employer very little beyond a robust constitution, an earnest willingness to work, and a conspicuous talent for winning new friends. Perhaps, thought Anheuser, the new son-in-law should be given a chance to prove himself as a salesman for The Bavarian Brewery. Nothing young Busch might do could possibly make matters any worse.

The hunch was sound. Although Eberhard Anheuser had a lingering apprehension about Busch's approach to business because it sounded much too simple, he had to admit that it was working. "Our business," Busch kept telling his father-in-law, "is not just making beer. No. Making *friends* is our business."

The young Bavarian not only was meeting and winning new friends, he was devising imaginative ways of keeping them from forgetting him. Instead of leaving business cards, for example, he gave each customer a handy pocket knife, emblazoned with the name of his company and with an intriguing little peephole at one end. A glance through the peephole revealed the image of Adolphus Busch himself.

Adolphus Busch's "calling card," a pocket knife-cork-screw. A look in the peep hole at right revealed the image of Adolphus himself.

At the same time, Busch was enhancing the brewery's reputation with showy draft horses and gleaming wagons, was turning the brewery into a showplace, and had issued a standing invitation to customers and the general public to "come visit us." And once again, Anheuser was surprised by the excellent responses to what he considered simple ideas. Slowly, and always based on the results he was delivering, Adolphus Busch rose to become president of The Bavarian Brewery and then founder of Anheuser-Busch.

By 1876, fifteen years after his marriage to Lilly Anheuser, Adolphus Busch was ready to revolutionize his business with two major concepts. One was ancient; the other was radically new.

The ancient concept involved applying the centuries-old European Kraeusening (pronounced *croy-zen-ing*) process to the brewing of his beer. In the Kraeusening process, a small amount of freshly-yeasted wort (a dilute solution of sugars obtained from malt) from the fermentation cycle is added to a batch of beer when it is beginning to lager or age. The added wort creates a second fermentation and produces a beer with natural carbonation. As a further step, Busch introduced beechwood chips to the ageing cycle to enhance the clarity and taste of the beer.

The second—and radically new—concept involved the marketing of beer on a national scale. Transportation-minded St. Louis, once the great river port of the central plains, was now rivaling Chicago as a railroad hub, inviting St. Louis industry to think in national distribution terms. Shipping beer, of course, meant protecting it against flavor-destroying heat and oxidation and Busch was confident he could solve that problem by applying the relatively new pasteurization process to his beer, by setting up an ambitious network of railside ice houses, and by acquiring a fleet of refrigerated rail cars.

His new brand of beer—America's first national beer—

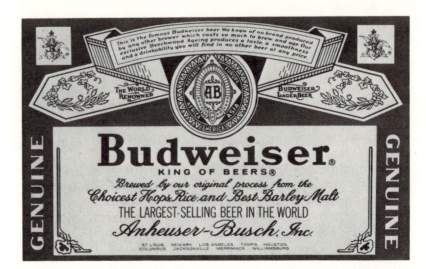

The Budweiser label made advertising history in the mid-1960's, when it appeared, all by itself, as a two-page spread in magazines.

he called "Budweiser," and he brewed it to the highest standards of quality known to the brewing art. He began with the best barley malt, the "soul" of beer. He chose costly rice, instead of the usual corn, as his "adjunct" or taste-perfecting agent. His hops, the "seasoning" in beer, were the choicest ones from Germany and the western United States. He avoided any use of extracts, artificial ingredients, and chemical preservatives. After this brew had received its time-consuming Kraeusening and beechwood ageing, it was proclaimed on its label to be a beer that offered "a taste, a smoothness and a drinkability you will find in no other beer at any price."

Budweiser—named for the town where its recipe was born, Budweis, in what is now Czechoslovakia—was so wisely conceived that never, from 1876 forward, would Anheuser-Busch ever make a change in its formula. The ponderous brewery wagons would give way to trucks, the old wooden barrels and vats would yield to stainless steel, and the movement of materials would in time be guided by computers; but the ingredients and brewing of Budweiser would remain the same.

At the great World's Fair of 1876—Philadelphia's U.S. Centennial Exposition—Budweiser was selected, over even the most distinguished European beers, as the finest

beer of its time, and it would go on to win the same
honor in Paris, Amsterdam, Vienna, and other international expositions.

The year 1876 would become historic for still another
and very different event: the massacre at the Little Big
Horn of General George Custer and his Seventh Cavalry
command. Adolphus Busch, noting the public's unusual
fascination with the battle, commissioned artist F. Otto
Becker to paint "Custer's Last Fight," and offered large
reproductions to taverns throughout the United States.
Before the requests from tavern keepers had all been
filled, more than one million prints had been distributed.
"Custer's Last Fight" would become the first of many
now famous paintings commissioned to promote
Anheuser-Busch and Budweiser.

The simple belief that "making friends is our business"
was working. Budweiser, a premium beer, would soon be
outselling the so-called "popular-priced" beers. Budweiser not only was becoming a household word, but was
the title of some popular songs of the day. In time, Adolphus Busch began to wonder if there was a market for an
even finer companion to Budweiser. He had in mind a
"draft beer for connoisseurs," using an extra measure of
the very finest imported hops. Again, he was right. The
new connoisseur's beer, for which he coined the name
Michelob, quickly won and held its own select circle of
customers. Together, the two brands made doubly sure
that Anheuser-Busch would stand out in the public mind
as the number one quality name in beer—and volume
followed. By the twenty-fifth anniversary of Budweiser
in 1901, annual Anheuser-Busch shipments had reached
the million barrel mark.

When Adolphus Busch died in 1913, he left behind a
record of almost magical successes. Unfortunately for his
son August, Sr., who now became the new chief executive officer, the amazing luck of Anheuser-Busch was
about to change, and drastically. Instead of going on to
steadily greater glory, the company would soon be lucky
to stay alive.

In March 1913, over President William Howard Taft's
veto, Congress passed the Webb-Kenyon Act, "divesting

intoxicating liquors of their interstate character in certain cases," and stimulating state prohibition. During the following year, state constitutional amendments were adopted by popular vote in Arizona, Colorado and Oregon, and statutory prohibition was adopted in Washington and Virginia. Ten additional states would follow within the next two years, and there would be persistent talk about the need for a national prohibition law.

With the outbreak of World War I in August 1914, food shortages were almost immediate, and Washington was soon hinting that the consumption of precious grains by America's brewers and distillers faced an ultimate cut-off.

August A. Busch watched his national market shrink state by state and wondered into what a giant brewery could be converted in the event of a total ban on beer.

In 1917, Congress passed a resolution for the submission of the Prohibition Amendment to the U.S. Constitution. By January 16, 1919, it had been ratified by three-fourths of all the states and would be implemented one year later. Thus began what has been called "the greatest social experiment of modern times." It would last for fourteen years.

Under federal law, the business Anheuser-Busch had been building for nearly three-quarters of a century was now denied the right to exist. The company turned to the production of corn products and bakers' yeast, then added commercial refrigeration units, and even truck bodies. Earlier—in 1916, with state prohibition laws closing in around it—the company had perfected a malt-derived nonalcoholic beverage it called Bevo, and had introduced it with high hopes. But Bevo, the beer substitute, was only a fleeting success.

With his father's stubborn optimism, August A. Busch kept his picturesque brewery in showplace condition and talked with his son, August Busch, Jr., about ways of bringing their beer back to the public with a majestic flourish when sooner or later Prohibition and all its problems would come to an end. More and more, in quest of an idea for celebrating the repeal of Prohibition, August Busch, Sr. found himself turning to the memories of his boyhood. Perhaps the most vivid one of all was the sight

Public tours are a daily feature at the seventy-block Anheuser-Busch, Inc., brewery in St. Louis. The Brew House (with clock tower), in operation since 1892, is one of three officially designated National Landmark buildings within the brewery complex.

of the giant brewery horses pulling their ponderous wagons through the streets of St. Louis. People along the sidewalks always paused to watch them go by—and the most impressive of all teams were the big Clydesdales with feathered hair on their legs and a showy kind of high hoof action, whether trotting or walking. What more dramatic symbol could there be for the return of "The King of Beers" than an eight-horse team of Clydesdales drawing an antique Anheuser-Busch wagon?

To August A. Busch, Jr., the Clydesdale idea was a unique combination of early American romance and relevant showmanship. He sought out sources of carefully matched teams, from bay to black in color, with prominent white markings, conspicuous feather, and a high-stepping gait. He supervised the sprucing up of a museum-piece Anheuser-Busch wagon. Almost at the moment of the repeal of Prohibition in December 1933, while the sidewalks swelled with crowds, an eight-horse Clydesdale hitch was ready to parade up Fifth Avenue in New York City, heading for the Empire State Building to

Above: With the repeal of Prohibition in December 1933, August A. Busch, Sr. (*center*) and his sons, Adolphus III (*left*) and August Jr. (*right*), celebrate the resumption of the brewing of beer in the St. Louis plant. **Right:** The famous Budweiser Clydesdales have now become three separate eight-horse hitches, making about three hundred appearances a year. The driver of the antique Budweiser beer wagon has a seventy-pound handful of reins.

deliver a case of Budweiser to a tireless crusader for repeal, former New York Governor Alfred E. Smith.

It was an unforgettable use of romantic business symbolism. Public reaction to the Clydesdales that day encouraged Anheuser-Busch to establish a breeding farm for the perpetuation of the ancient Scottish horse that had once carried the Crusaders into battle. By 1980, Grant's Farm near St. Louis would have approximately one hundred purebreds, the largest collection of Clydesdales in America, and there would be three separate, meticulously matched eight-horse hitches ready to meet the public. One team would be based at Grant's Farm, one in

stables adjoining the Anheuser-Busch brewery at Merrimack, New Hampshire, and the third on the West Coast.

August A. Busch, Sr., who had guided the company
through the bleak fourteen years of Prohibition, would
die the year after its repeal. It would be up to his son,
August A. Busch, Jr., to lead the company through its
next historic era, the building of a national brewery network: Newark; Los Angeles; Tampa; Houston; Columbus,
Ohio; Jacksonville; Merrimack, New Hampshire; Williamsburg, Virginia; Fairfield, California.

Anheuser-Busch could now invite the public to "come
visit us" in ten separate locations coast to coast, and some
of those places began to add some extra attractions to
beckon the tourist. In Tampa, for example, an exhibit of
exotic birds near the brewery would soon grow into a
unique African zoological and theme park through
which the visitor could ride in air-conditioned monorail
comfort.

In 1950, Anheuser-Busch became the first brewer to
sponsor a network program on the infant, unproved medium of television. The results were dramatic. In the fif-
ty-one markets receiving the "Ken Murray Variety
Show," beer sales were soon growing at twice the rate of
the non-TV markets.

With the power of television pushing Budweiser to
new heights, the next step was to launch a product in the
so-called "popular-priced" field. In 1955, Anheuser-
Busch introduced Busch Beer. It soon ranked as the first
successful new brand in the beer industry since the repeal of Prohibition. Six years later, Michelob would be
offered for the first time in bottles and cans to further expand and strengthen the company's position in the top
quality field.

But never would Michelob and Busch be allowed to
overshadow the Budweiser brand. In the mid-1960's, for
example, the company ran the Budweiser label—all by
itself—as a two-page spread in *Life* and other magazines.
The bold and forthright message on the label told the
whole Budweiser story: "This is the famous Budweiser
beer. We know of no brand produced by any other
brewer which costs so much to brew and age. Our exclu-

August A. Busch, Jr. takes
time out to watch the company's St. Louis Cardinals play.

Certified brewmaster August
A. Busch III, chairman and
president of Anheuser-Busch,
Inc., examines a handful of
natural hops.

sive Beechwood Ageing produces a taste, a smoothness and a drinkability you will find in no other beer at any price."

When the "label" advertisement appeared, even history-proud Anheuser-Busch was surprised by the results. Many readers seized the spread as a bit of Americana to be framed and hung on the wall. Others converted it into book jackets and place mats. Suddenly the nation had a new pop art form and a new advertising medium. Budweiser labels would soon be appearing on caps and T-shirts, sailboat spinnakers, and even, in giant size, on the bottoms of swimming pools.

When, in 1974, August A. Busch III succeeded his father to become the fourth-generation head of the family-controlled business, it was a time for looking backward as well as forward. Anheuser-Busch was busily preparing to celebrate the centennial of Budweiser in 1976, and company history was undergoing an in-depth review. The record offered a treasure of material for centennial promotion. It also offered abundant evidence that the principles established by Adolphus Busch in 1876 had been so sound that they richly deserved even stronger application a century later.

The "come visit us" policy had been making friends at all breweries and most spectacularly at "The Dark Continent," the Busch Gardens theme park in Tampa. August A. Busch III soon launched a major family entertainment and real estate complex near the company's brewery at Williamsburg, Virginia. Its seventeenth century European theme park, "The Old Country"—complete with *schuhplatt* singer and dancer shows in a huge replica of a Munich Oktoberfest hall—would soon be attracting more than two million visitors a year, all of whom would receive a monorail ride through the adjacent Anheuser-Busch brewery as part of their tour. Other hospitality centers, beginning with the historic parent brewery in St. Louis, would combine to push the annual visitor total far beyond the seven million mark.

It was also time for a comparable, updated application of the Adolphus Busch maxim: "Making friends is our business." In the new age of market segmentation, An-

Left: *Schuhplatt* dancers and a large "oompah" band entertain visitors to the seventeenth century European theme park, "The Old Country," at Williamsburg, Virginia. **Right:** Volleyball action during the Budweiser College Super Sports competition, the largest college-oriented promotion ever sponsored by a brewery.

heuser-Busch continued its long-established, promotional association with baseball, football, basketball, boxing, hockey, golf, and tennis—and expanded into soccer, fishing, sailing, rugby, auto racing, running, and jogging.

In the important young adult market, the company launched new programs ranging from concerts to raft races to ecology. On college campuses, the Budweiser College Super Sports competition—a program of decathlon-style games—became the largest college-oriented promotion ever sponsored by a brewery.

From its many friends among the young actives, Anheuser-Busch began hearing requests, in the 1970's, for a lower-calorie, less-filling beer. The company responded with not just one beer, but two: Natural Light and Michelob Light. The lighter beer held the promise of a fitter figure, and the young female segment of the market was among the first to respond. Women beer drinkers, who had accounted for about twenty percent of all beer sold, were soon accounting for more than forty percent of all the lighter, lower-calorie beer. Anheuser-Busch promptly moved into women's magazines to promote its two special-segment products.

By the beginning of the 1980's, the two light beers would help build Anheuser-Busch to a volume of more than forty-five million barrels a year, a work force of nearly thirteen thousand, and a distribution force of approximately one thousand independent wholesalers.

In the midst of the light-beer introductions and all the promotional fanfare, however, Budweiser continued unchanged from the day in 1876 when Adolphus Busch first brewed it. And one of Bud's most successful promotional vehicles continued literally to be a vehicle—an antique Anheuser-Busch brewery wagon bossed by a driver whose hands manipulated seventy pounds of leather reins, keeping eight ton-size Clydesdales in perfect formation while each of their thirty-two feathered hoofs clopped the pavement with a custom-forged, four-pound shoe. By the beginning of the 1980's, the company's three eight-horse Clydesdale hitches were making about three hundred appearances a year at state fairs, shopping centers, rodeos, festivals, and in nationally televised parades viewed by scores of millions. First seen in 1852, the Anheuser-Busch horses were doing their part to prove that the simple, practical, customer-pleasing concepts of Adolphus Busch had never gone out of style.

MARKETING INSIGHTS
Adolphus Busch followed three basic guidelines: (1) he wanted his beer to be the world standard of excellence; (2) he viewed his business not just as the making of beer, but as the making of friends; and (3) he believed his friends should have a standing invitation to visit his business.

Simple though they may seem, those guidelines set the direction of his company for more than a century and helped make it the world leader of its field.

From the day of its original brewing in 1876, Budweiser Beer has never changed; but the process of winning and hosting friends would in time be accelerated by such new forces as television, a Budweiser-in-

The Python, at "The Dark
Continent," Busch Gardens,
Tampa, Florida, takes riders
through two 360-degree
loops and travels at speeds
up to 50 m.p.h.

spired boom in pop art, and some of the nation's most
unique theme parks.

Beer marketed originally to the German immigrant
population of St. Louis would move into the age of market segmentation and psychographics and be aimed selectively at sports enthusiasts, ecology buffs, concert lovers,
and just about everybody who enjoyed good showmanship.

In the alcoholic beverage industry, which once had
generated enough public disgust to bring on Prohibition,
the makers of Budweiser have applied relevant, romantic
symbols of beer-making to build an image of pride-in-
quality and wholesome fun, and have carried out a commitment to make beer synonymous with responsible,
moderate drinking.

In its advertising, the makers of Budweiser do not hold
out a promise of a more exciting life, or more attractive-
ness to the opposite sex, or better acceptance by one's
peers, or any other kind of success.

Budweiser advertising simply says, in effect: "If you
drink beer, this one is the best." Following specific
guidelines, it is aimed primarily at "male beer drinkers
who are currently drinking other brands more often than
Budweiser," but also is designed to "reinforce the belief
of the regular Budweiser drinker that Bud is best."

BUSTER BROWN SHOES

*"Kids of six today are smarter
than they used to be at twelve."*

Buster Brown and his dog Tige, created in 1902 and still going strong as the Buster Brown logotype.

6 In May of 1902, New York City's newspaper readers were introduced to a spectacular new art form. Not only was it the first full-page, full-color comic strip, but it starred the first successful comic character created in America: Buster Brown. Syndicates would soon carry the strip nationally and cartoonist Richard F. Outcault would become the Walt Disney of his day.

Buster Brown, in his modish Lord Fauntleroy suit, was the incongruous source of endless mischief, in which his sister Mary Jane and his dog Tige were lively co-conspirators. The impish three were very real to Outcault because they were inspired by his own son and daughter and their Boston bulldog—and they were equally real to the nation's growing new legion of comic strip followers, including John A. Bush, a rising young sales executive in the Brown Shoe Company of St. Louis.

To Bush, the little comic strip character seemed to have been born to be the living, selling trademark for his company's line of shoes for boys and girls.

Would his company go along with this new idea? They would. Founder George Warren Brown had left New England, traditional home of the shoe industry, to pioneer shoemaking in the Middle West in 1878, and his company prided itself on its forward thinking. Bush was equally successful in his talks with Richard Outcault, and a new collection of Buster Brown Shoes was ready for prominent display at the St. Louis World's Fair of 1904. So dramatic was the introduction that the company won the only Double Grand Prize awarded to a shoe exhibitor at the Fair.

Young John Bush had overlooked just one point: he had not contracted for *exclusive* rights to Buster Brown. Cartoonist Outcault, now aware of the merchandising value of a comic strip character, had rented a booth of his own at the Fair, and Buster Brown would soon appear as the licensed trademark on candy, chewing gum, soda pop, soap, raisins, apples, bread, textiles, horse shoes, egg-dye (for the Easter trade), waffle irons, pocketbooks, cigars, bourbon—and some thirty additional products.

Undaunted, Bush went a step beyond the others and hired a midget to tour the country and appear—complete with Lord Fauntleroy suit, Dutch boy wig, and trained dog—in department stores, shoe stores, and rented theaters. In time, there would be a succession of six Buster Brown midgets—and four-foot, two-inch Ed Ansley, the most famous one of all, would devote twenty-eight years of his life to traveling fifty thousand miles a year, ultimately visiting every county in the United States, drawing crowds as vast as twenty-five thousand, and appearing in ceremonies as exalted as receiving a large silver key to the city of Boston from Mayor James M. Curley. Along the way, he "wore out" five dogs.

The "act" consisted mostly of the appearance, *live,* of Buster Brown, resplendent in scarlet jacket and knee breeches, billowing collar and bow tie, and scarlet, flat, broad-brimmed hat. Then came the traditional greeting:

John A. Bush

"I'm Buster Brown; I live in a shoe.
(WOOF! WOOF!) That's my dog Tige; he lives there too."

The act continued with the awarding of modest prizes to children who stepped up to the stage and showed the Buster Brown label in their shoes, plus some dog tricks and informal banter between Buster Brown and his audience. In the days when rural folk often dropped in at the town barber shop to "watch a haircut," the appearance of Buster Brown was one of the big events of the season.

Ultimately, the comic strip audience would turn from Buster Brown to the Katzenjammer Kids and then Dick Tracy. And radio would bring a whole new kind of entertainment, and no more need to leave home for it. But Ed Ansley continued to draw audiences until his retirement in 1938, and they continued to be his friends until his death, at age eighty-three, in 1972. After one of his final interviews, he observed, "Kids are still swell; and they're a lot smarter. With all their television, radio and newspa-

Ed Ansley, most famous of
the Buster Brown midgets,
with one of his series of Tiges
at a typical show on the road.

pers, kids of six today are smarter than they used to be at twelve."

John A. Bush went on to become president of Brown Shoe Company, Inc., and later, in 1948, was named chairman of the board—and his comic strip discovery was still showing no signs of wearing out.

In the early 1940's, "Smilin' " Ed McConnell became Buster Brown on radio and then, in 1951, on television. A quarter-century later, the young viewers of the Saturday morning cartoon shows were still tuning in promptly to watch Buster Brown, now back in comic strip form, and to hear the familiar greeting: "I'm Buster Brown, I live in a shoe. (WOOF! WOOF!) That's my dog Tige; he lives there too."

Year after year, brand awareness surveys continue to show that Buster Brown, after three-quarters of a century as a living trademark, is still number one in the field. Other research shows that children are the predominant influence in the shoe brand decision—beginning at the age of five.

Today, Brown Shoe Company is a member company of Brown Group, Inc., a diversified manufacturer and retailer of footwear, recreational products, fabrics and specialty apparel, with sales of more than $840 million, and approximately twenty-five thousand employees. Buster Brown continues to tailor its shoes for the pre-teen market.

And what happens later? When those youngsters grow up and become parents, do they buy Buster Brown shoes for *their* children? "Yes," says Brown Shoe Company, "we've studied that, too. That's the 'carryover power' of the brand, and it has contributed very importantly to our continued growth."

MARKETING INSIGHTS
Buster Brown, a cartoonist's creation of 1902, was the Mickey Mouse of its day. Thus, John A. Bush of the Brown Shoe Company became one of the first to demonstrate how a synthetic personality of that sort could help build a brand.

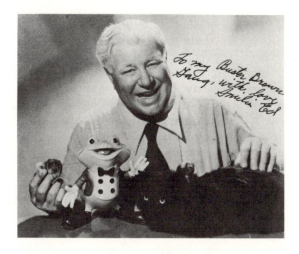

Smilin' Ed McConnell became Buster Brown on radio, then on TV.

In the course of doing so, he also became one of the first to discover the penalty of not getting exclusive rights to such a character. His shoes for children were soon sharing their Buster Brown symbol with such alien-to-children products as cigars and whiskey. Happily for Brown Shoe Company, Bush had the imagination to make his comic-strip character "come alive" in the person of a touring midget attired in a Buster Brown costume and accompanied by a dog, Tige. It was masterful showmanship.

Along with his resourceful use of a living trademark, Bush was an important pioneer in the art of advertising to children. At the turn of the century, more than a few of his colleagues must have argued that shoes for children were selected by parents, so why waste advertising dollars on youngsters? Decades later, Brown Shoe Company's marketing research would find that children are the predominant influence in the shoe brand selection—beginning at the age of five.

During those decades, Brown Shoe Company did a skillful job of keeping its Buster Brown symbol up-to-date and in tune with the audience as Buster Brown moved from road show to radio to television—all the while setting a wholesome as well as an intelligent example of how to advertise to children.

CAMEL CIGARETTES
"Don't look for premiums or coupons. . . ."

Richard Joshua Reynolds

7 What was to become the most combative chapter in American marketing history began, in a strangely paradoxical way, in the hushed dignity of the U.S. State Department auditorium. There in Washington, on Saturday, January 11, 1964, U.S. Surgeon-General Luther L. Terry and members of his eleven-person advisory committee made a detailed presentation to the press of "Smoking and Health" and distributed copies of the 387-page document to be quoted from over all the newswires of the world. Thus, the government of the United States made its official declaration of war on the nation's oldest industry, charging that cigarette smoking was causally related to lung cancers in males, was one of the most important of the causes of chronic bronchitis in the United States, may have been a contributor to other diseases, and was "a health hazard of sufficient importance . . . to warrant remedial action."

To the six major U.S. cigarette producers, the official declaration of war came as no surprise. Since the early 1950's there had been a fairly steady flow of ominous health reports, alerting the industry to expect another cycle of the recurring anti-tobacco sentiment it had encountered since the day it became the Colonies' first exporter in 1613.

The two principal leaders of the industry in 1964—R. J. Reynolds and American Tobacco—were relatively well-prepared for battle, because they had been waging a running feud with each other ever since the days when James Buchanan Duke and Richard Joshua Reynolds were squaring off to see who was going to be the number one seller of cut-plug chewing tobacco throughout the South. Both had grown up on tobacco farms, both had peddled the leaf by the wagonload, and both were so physically imposing as to command ready respect among customers and growers alike.

Duke, the younger of the two by seven years, would be

the first to be acclaimed a tycoon as he expanded a business founded in 1865 by his father. Reynolds, having left his father's place at age twenty-four to start his own factory operation in 1875, was a steady but slower success. Duke would be producing machine-made cigarettes by 1884; Reynolds would not make a cigarette until 1913.

By 1910, Duke's many American Tobacco Company brands accounted for more than eighty percent of the total industry—an achievement that was blasted the following year when the U.S. Supreme Court ruled that Duke's combine had violated anti-trust laws and must be dissolved. Meanwhile, Reynolds, the most outspoken critic of Duke's monopolistic ways, had been concentrating on running *"the* tobacco factory of the South" and had added some smoking tobaccos to his varied lines of cut-plug chewing tobaccos.

To one of the smoking tobaccos, a Kentucky burley, Reynolds had applied some special marketing touches: he developed a metal package that could be hermetically sealed to protect the moistness of the tobacco and serve later as a humidor. He then reviewed a list of possible names and chose one that was at once familiar, respected, and relevant: "Prince Albert." The ever-popular Prince of Wales was not only the new King Edward VII of Great Britain, he was also the avid-smoker son of Queen Victoria, whose contempt for tobacco had inspired the creation of scores of anti-tobacco societies throughout her realm. Prince Albert smoking tobacco, introduced in 1907 and packed first in cloth bags selling for a nickel to promote widespread trial, was both an overnight and a national success.

RJR, a man known increasingly by his initials, now turned his thoughts to the idea of a cigarette product and spent a good part of the next six years pondering ways of launching a new product with sureness and safety in a field his old rival, Duke, had expanded more than twenty years earlier. Although most cigarette smokers of the time still rolled their own, there were at least fifty manufactured brands competing for the available business. Reynolds was impressed, however, by the fact that the manufactured brands offered a limited choice; they were all made of straight tobaccos, mostly either Virginia or Turkish, neither of which had proved very popular when offered to the roll-your-own buyer. There should be a market, Reynolds concluded, for a *blended* cigarette that would combine the best appeals of the American tobaccos and the highly aromatic Turkish tobacco. With typical thoroughness, RJR then proceeded to check out his thinking with an actual test in the marketplace of four separate brands.

The first brand, "Reyno," a straight Virginia cigarette, offered the spectacular value of ten boxed cigarettes for a nickel. The second, "Osman," was a distinctive blend of all-Turkish tobaccos. The third, "Red Kamel," was a Turkish straight with the fancy touch of cork tips. The fourth brand was a blend of burley and bright, with some Turkish leaf for taste and aroma, and a generous amount of sweetening. This fourth brand, which RJR decided should be priced at ten cents for a pack of twenty (versus fifteen cents for most other brands of the day), he called "Camel." The name was oriental, in keeping with the current vogue, and was easy to say and remember.

RJR had taken special pains with the Camel package design. The timely arrival in Winston-Salem of the Barnum & Bailey Circus, complete with a photogenic old dromedary named "Old Joe," had proved adequate guidance on the animal RJR had in mind; but he continued to fuss with a special "value" statement he wanted to include on the package. Its ultimate wording was: "Don't look for premiums or coupons, as the cost of the tobaccos blended in Camel Cigarettes prohibits the use of them."

When the new cigarette was ready for the market in 1913, Reynolds leapfrogged the regional marketing patterns of the day and went into national distribution, backed by a two-page spread in *The Saturday Evening Post.* During 1914, Reynolds sold 425 million Camel cigarettes. In 1915, sales rocketed to 2.4 billion—with a massive, additional 10 billion to come in 1916.

Frantically, to meet the new Camel competition, American Tobacco readied a new cigarette, for which it revived a brand name it had once used on a cut plug during the California gold rush: "Lucky Strike." Liggett & Myers, for its part, was improving its own well-established brand,

In an early market test (1913), R. J. Reynolds introduced his new Camel Cigarettes, using a blend of domestic and Turkish tobaccos, and these three other test brands: Reyno, a straight Virginia; Osman, a blend of Turkish tobaccos; and Red Kamel, a straight Turkish. The new Camel brand decisively outsold the others, persuading Reynolds to move directly into national distribution.

Camel Cigarettes

Turkish and Domestic Blend

Don't look for premiums in any form, as the cost of tobaccos blended in CAMEL Cigarettes prohibits the use of them

If your dealer can't supply you, send 10c for one package or $1.00 for a carton of ten packages (200 cigarettes), sent postage prepaid. If after smoking one package you are not delighted with CAMELS, return the other nine packages and we will refund your money.

Do you like good Turkish cigarettes? Do you like good Domestic cigarettes? In either case, you will immediately like the rare combination of the flavor and fragrance of both as found in Camel Cigarettes. These are an expert blend of the choicest grades of Turkish and Domestic tobaccos, voted by men who have tried them as far superior to either kind smoked straight. No cigaretty after-taste. They do not dry the throat or parch the tongue.

You will find *Turkish and Domestic Blend* printed on the Camel package. This means exactly that—the finest Turkish and Domestic tobaccos expertly blended.

Because of the superior quality of tobaccos used in Camels we cannot give premiums in any form with them. The goodness of this smoke is its own premium. Money cannot buy a more delightful cigarette. 20 for 10c everywhere.

R. J. REYNOLDS TOBACCO CO., Winston-Salem, N. C.

With this two-page announcement spread in *The Saturday Evening Post*, in 1914, Camel Cigarettes broke with the regional marketing patterns of the day and moved directly into national distribution. It featured a version of the statement R. J. Reynolds had written for the back of the package—"Don't look for premiums in any form, as the cost of tobaccos blended in Camel Cigarettes prohibits the use of them."

named for the fashion-setting symbol of gracious living, Lord Chesterfield. Those Camel competitors appeared, along with a variety of others, in 1916; but the Camel momentum was unstoppable. By 1921, Camel cigarettes hit the eighteen-billion mark, accounting for about half the market total, and cigarettes, for the first time, became the best-selling of all tobacco products.

In the same year, Reynolds made national use of a slogan that was born when an out-of-cigarettes golfer asked a friendly bystander for one, adding: "I'd walk a mile for a Camel." The friendly bystander just happened to be a man concerned with Camel advertising.

Duke, who died in 1925 after a last hurrah as chairman of the British-American Tobacco Company, lived to see the full sweep of the Reynolds triumph. RJR, who died at sixty-eight in 1918, did not.

Meanwhile, at Duke's old American Tobacco Company, George Washington Hill, son of a close Duke colleague, had taken over the management reins and was building a reputation for being an advertising genius. World War I had introduced a generation of young Americans to cigarettes, and the product, once relatively limited and fashionable, was now commonplace. Mass-selling Camel was often referred to as "the truck driver's cigarette." Hill aimed for something much smarter. His flamboyant campaigns—"Reach for a Lucky instead of a sweet" . . . "With men who know tobacco best, it's Luckies two to one," and many more—coupled with the showmanship of the chant of the tobacco auctioneer, and the popularity of the "Lucky Strike Hit Parade" shows on radio and television, assured George Washington Hill of a prominent place in marketing history. More to the point, his approach helped move Lucky Strike into first place in the industry by 1929.

To a complacent Reynolds company, no longer headed by RJR, the surge of Lucky Strike was disturbing. Then, by 1933, Chesterfield, too, had passed Camel, and Reynolds Tobacco was feeling the additional competitive bite of new Depression-born discount brands, and a revival of consumer use of roll-your-own cigarettes. Against the new competitive forces, the 1931 introduction of Camel cellophane packaging—an important industry first—had fallen woefully short of reversing the market trend.

The Reynolds response was slow in coming; but it came. And it consisted mostly of a simple but massive increase in advertising and other promotion. In 1934, for example, advertising costs amounted to slightly over eighty percent of the company's net earnings. By 1935, Camel was back in the number one position.

Cigarettes had been promoted originally with picture cards showing pretty girls, often scantily clad. George Washington Hill had introduced unique-sounding but hollow product claims, like "It's toasted," which applied, of course, to all flue-cured tobacco. Liggett & Myers, by 1926, had introduced the "nice girl" in cigarette advertising, to enhance social acceptability and expand the market. Reynolds took a different tack: it associated Camel, year after year, with famous athletes.

When the cigarette industry was struck by the post-World War II health scare, Camel, the choice of so many athletes, was slow to feel any crimp in its sales. Along with its wholesome reputation, Camel was being helped by the fact that the post-war years brought more than a health controversy; they also brought television, and

Camel was soon being featured on leading prime-time shows, with special emphasis on sportscasts. Camel, after World War II, held its number one position for fifteen years.

The filters that mushroomed in those postwar years had an ancient pedigree. Back in 1854, when British soldiers in the Crimea captured some Russian officers and thus acquired the Empire's first cigarettes, the slender cylinders had cardboard mouthpieces, stuffed with cotton. A similar mouthpiece popped up long after, in 1932, when Benson & Hedges introduced the Parliament cigarette. Brown & Williamson Tobacco Company, the wholly-owned U.S. subsidiary of British-American Tobacco, introduced the Viceroy cigarette, with a sturdy filter tip, in 1936. A filter was a simple and practical way to keep tobacco particles out of the mouth. In Europe, after World War II, it was also a good way to conserve scarce tobacco.

Then came the health scare, and the makers of certain filter-tip cigarettes began to make health-protection claims for their products. The public, largely through the advertisements of the cigarette makers, became aware of the evils of "tar" while learning more about the long-familiar threat of nicotine. Filters, during the decade of the 1950's, exploded from less than 1.5 percent of the cigarette market to more than half the total.

In 1955, the Federal Trade Commission stepped in, forbade all further health claims, direct or indirect, by cigarette advertisers, and published a set of Cigarette Advertising Guides. Later, in 1959, the FTC notified the tobacco industry that "all representations of low or reduced tar or nicotine . . . will be construed as health claims." (Note: The 1959 position was reversed in 1966, after various health organizations and certain scientists advised the FTC that they thought disclosure of tar and nicotine content would be a good idea, definitely in the public interest.)

Filter cigarettes were bland, compared with the "regulars"; so makers of the filter-tips were soon rewarding the consumer with the longer smoke of the king-size cigarette—a length pioneered by the original Pall Mall of 1907.

"I'd walk a mile for a Camel"—the actual, unsolicited comment of a Camel smoker—was launched as a slogan in 1921 and was still being used in recent years.

Amid the enthusiasm for the new filters and kings, there was also considerable speculation that "cooler" smoke could be beneficial—and Brown & Williamson's Kool, which had been a lonely menthol pioneer since 1933, was suddenly surrounded by imitators.

Reynolds, the maker of Camel, watched the mushrooming of kings, filters, and menthols—and made not the slightest change in Camel. In 1949, Reynolds introduced Cavalier in the king-size category, but later withdrew it. As for filters, a Reynolds man once remarked: "A filter, to a tobacco man in this country, was like ketchup to a French chef."

When, in 1954, Reynolds introduced its first filter cigarette, the company avoided any loss of Camel identity by calling the new brand "Winston." It was aimed at consumers who now favored a filter, but also wanted some taste, and Reynolds said a lot in a short introductory line: "Made by the makers of Camels. . . ." Winston disregarded any aspects of health protection, promising only to be a filter cigarette with flavor. Within two years, it was the best-selling filter. Then, ten years later, when filters dominated the industry, Winston became the number one seller among all brands.

In 1956, to buttress its position in the new health-minded market, Reynolds introduced Salem, the first filter-tip menthol cigarette, promoting it with a spectacular new springtime-green, springtime-fresh look and sound that started new trends in "image" advertising.

Not until 1966 would Reynolds introduce a filter companion to its regular Camel cigarette.

By now, government intervention in the smoking and health controversy was bringing stern and specific measures to bear on the cigarette industry. The Cigarette Labeling Act, passed in 1965, called for a new health caution notice on all cigarette packs. In mid-1967, the Federal Communications Commission (FCC) ruled that stations which aired cigarette commercials must, under the "fairness doctrine," broadcast anti-smoking announcements—at no charge—for anti-tobacco organizations. Later that year, the Federal Trade Commission (FTC) published results of its first semi-annual test of the "tar" and

"Camel"
-the greatest
tobacco word
of all time

This early Camel poster reflected R. J. Reynolds' belief that the most important thing about a cigarette was its tobacco. (*Courtesy of Friendship Library, Fairleigh Dickinson University*)

nicotine content of U.S. cigarettes. And the biggest blow of all, to the tobacco industry, was still to come.

In 1969, the tobacco industry had offered to cancel all radio and TV advertising, a major consideration, because about one-third of the industry advertising budget was in television. In 1970, the government formalized the industry offer and imposed a ban, to become effective January 2, 1971.

Anti-tobacco pressure has continued, with legislative and citizen proposals for bans on smoking in public places and on air carriers; demands for smoker segregation in offices; a proposal to disallow business expense deductions for cigarette advertising; proposals to prohibit smoking in bus depots and in railroad dining cars; a ban on smoking in federally-owned caves; a proposal to prohibit airline flight crews from smoking during the hours prior to flight; a proposal for a tax on cigarette advertisements; a proposal to give employees time off from work for stop-smoking programs, with a federal subsidy to help cover the cost to employers; a proposal to ban the use of people in cigarette advertisements.

During the decade of the 1970's, in the marketing stam-

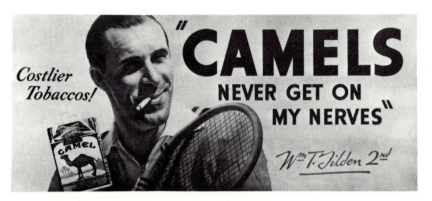

Costlier Tobaccos!

"CAMELS NEVER GET ON MY NERVES"

Wm. T. Tilden 2nd

To calm the public's concern about the possible health hazards of smoking, the makers of Camels identified their product with famous athletes in a strong, continuing way. Here, "Big Bill" Tilden, seven-times national men's singles champion during the 1920's, testifies that "Camels never get on my nerves." (*Courtesy of Friendship Library, Fairleigh Dickinson University*)

pede to provide the consumer with what could be called a "reasonably safe cigarette," the tobacco industry introduced more than one hundred new brands or variations on existing brands. During the decade's second half alone, low-tar brands (defined as having no more than fifteen milligrams of tar) soared from ten percent of the industry in 1975 to fifty-nine percent of the total at the close of 1979. As for nicotine, 101 brands (out of 176 on the market) had less than one milligram of nicotine at the close of 1979.

In January of 1979, U.S. Surgeon-General Julius Richmond issued a twelve hundred-page report on smoking and health. Although the document reiterated much of the 1964 report, it noted: "In the fifteen years that have elapsed since the original Report of the Advisory Committee on Smoking and Health to the Surgeon General, there have been many new scientific studies on the relationship between tobacco consumption and health. There are now more than thirty thousand articles in the world literature on this subject." Among the new conclusions in the 1979 report: (1) smoking is a major contributor to coronary heart disease; (2) women who smoke develop lung disease just as do men who smoke; (3) certain occupations, such as asbestos and textiles, pose greater risks to workers who smoke; (4) smoke is causally related to cancers of the larynx, esophagus, and mouth; and (5) maternal smoking harms the unborn child. The report also

Famous women athletes soon joined the men in the Camel sports series. Aquaplane expert Gloria Wheeden made this appearance in 1940 to agree, "Camels never get on my nerves." (*Courtesy of Friendship Library, Fairleigh Dickinson University*)

While sport celebrities were endorsing Camels, the makers of Chesterfields took a loftier approach with this endorsement by the distinguished Byrd Expedition to Antarctica in the late 1920's. (*Courtesy of Friendship Library, Fairleigh Dickinson University*)

dealt with smoking among children and adolescents.

Progress of the anti-smoking effort over the fifteen-year period since the first Surgeon-General's report is highlighted by these figures from the government's Health Interview Survey, showing estimates of the percentage of current, regular cigarette smokers, seventeen years and over, in the United States:

Year	Total	Male	Female
1965	41.7%	51.1%	33.3%
1979	32.3	36.9	28.2

In the frenzied field of cigarette marketing, at the end

In the 1950's, cigarette advertisers were well-advised to avoid specific health terms in favor of such noncontroversial words as "mild." This poster appeared in 1952. (*Courtesy of Friendship Library, Fairleigh Dickinson University*)

of the 1970's, there was a new industry leader. Marlboro Cigarettes, once aimed at women, had been reintroduced in 1955 by Philip Morris and given a rugged new masculine image. The lean, weatherbeaten Marlboro cowboy had now ridden into the industry's number one position. In his laconic, cowboy way, he had never made any speeches or any specific promises. A typical Marlboro invitation to the reader: "Come to Marlboro Country."

At R. J. Reynolds Tobacco Company, at the end of the 1970's, Winston and Salem had been joined by Doral, Vantage, Tempo, More, Now, Real—and Camel Lights. Following the ban on broadcast advertising, the company had turned to sponsoring auto racing and rodeo events, major bowling tournaments, and programs for recreational skiers. Back in the mid-1950's, after achieving a one-third share of the U.S. tobacco market, the company had begun diversifying its operations into other fields ranging from food to packaging materials to transportation. By 1980, R. J. Reynolds Industries Inc., the parent of R. J. Reynolds Tobacco Company, showed annual sales and revenues of more than four billion dollars and had more than thirty-three thousand employees.

MARKETING INSIGHTS
Richard Joshua Reynolds was a tobacco man with shrewd marketing instincts. In the Camel cigarette, he developed

Come to **Marlboro Country.**

17 mg "tar," 1.0 mg nicotine
av. per cigarette, FTC Report May '78

Warning: The Surgeon General Has Determined
That Cigarette Smoking Is Dangerous to Your Health

In an industry represented by "image" advertising, Marlboro's cowboy (America's number one "folk hero") ultimately outpointed all other "macho" symbols. By the end of the 1970's, Marlboro had become the best-selling U.S. cigarette.

a unique product. He gave it a highly practical name, and a package design that reflected the appeal of golden-brown tobacco. To the package, he added a masterful, twenty-one word statement about his product's quality and value. He then devised an imaginative market test to determine consumer reaction to his product. Given a positive report, he moved boldly into national distribution—and number one position. Not until long after RJR's death would any competitor succeed in overtaking his Camel cigarette.

Cigarettes offer a classic example of a "brand differentiation" problem. Not only do they look alike; they also smell and taste so much alike that seasoned smokers, in blindfold tests, cannot tell them apart with any reliable degree of accuracy. The character, image, and public perceptions of a cigarette are (or can be) fashioned entirely by its maker.

The Camel cigarette was one of the first simple, look-alike products to acquire a strong, exclusive character by being associated closely and consistently with a certain type of user. The Camel cigarette became synonymous with the "regular guy"—and ultimately with the sports hero. It was a doubly practical approach. The "regular guy" was a heavy user; and certainly the sports hero helped neutralize what every athletic coach was saying about cigarettes being "bad for the wind."

In the early days of the smoking and health controversy, one cigarette maker (not Reynolds) conducted a survey among cigarette smokers, probing their fears and asking for their opinions about what a truly "safe" cigarette would offer. To the sponsor's surprise, a high percentage of the respondents said a truly "safe" cigarette already existed in the marketplace: it was the Camel brand, the cigarette chosen by athletes who had to take care of their health.

America's smoking and health controversy, born in the early 1950's, soon became open warfare between the United States government and a major industry. The government moved in to control and resolve a health crisis; the industry fought back to ensure its survival. The issues involved were far too serious and complex to be covered completely or realistically here.

Because our concern here is with marketing fundamentals, let it simply be noted that the cigarette industry, during the smoking and health controversy, was characterized by an almost unbelievable proliferation of brands. At the start of hostilities, the nation's cigarette smokers gave most of their business to Camel, Lucky Strike, Chesterfield, Pall Mall, and Old Gold. All leading brands were easily accommodated by the eight-column vending machine of the day. A quarter-century later, the smoker was completely encircled and bombarded by the promotional efforts of 176 different brands and types of cigarettes.

Never had the cigarette marketplace known such competition. And never had it known such confusion. At the height of both, a lone cowboy rode through the scene, carrying his brand to the number one industry position.

In a marketing category long conditioned to the simplest forms of image advertising, the lone cowboy did not have to explain a thing. Sometimes he did not even mention "smoke" or even "taste." Sometimes, all he had to say was, "Come to Marlboro Country."

CAMPBELL'S SOUP

"We blend the best with careful pains
  In skillful combination,
And everything we make contains
  Our business reputation."

8 Scholarly, young John T. Dorrance of Philadelphia
was a very practical kind of gourmet. When he finished
his studies in Europe and was awarded his Ph.D. in
chemistry, he wrote his uncle, Arthur Dorrance, that he
planned to spend some time working in the kitchens of
Parisian restaurants before he returned home. His interest, he explained, was not just in discussing recipes with
famous chefs, but in seeing how they made their soups.

John T. Dorrance *(Courtesy of
The Historical Society of Pennsylvania)*

Uncle Arthur, several years earlier, had become a partner of Joseph Campbell in the Jos. Campbell Preserve Co.
of Camden, New Jersey, a canning and packing firm with
an eighteen-year-old reputation among the carriage trade
for the excellence of its tomatoes, vegetables, salad dressings, jellies, mince meat, condiments, and ketchup. The
company was small; but elderly Mr. Campbell was planning to retire, Arthur Dorrance had become president,
and he had assured his nephew that Jos. Campbell Pre-
serves represented a good career opportunity for a bright
young chemist. At the same time, Uncle Arthur had made
it clear that the salary could not exceed seven dollars per
week.

Young Dr. John T. Dorrance, back from Europe, turned
down several attractive college teaching offers in favor of
the seven dollars per week. To pleased, but surprised
Uncle Arthur, he explained: "I think there is a big market
for a new kind of soup. Not just canned soup, but condensed canned soup. It would cost less to ship, would
take less room in the store, and could be sold for less to
the housewife. She would then just open the can and add
water as she heated the soup. With that kind of convenience, why would anybody go to the bother of making
her own soup?"

The "Campbell Kids," created by Grace Gebbie Drayton, appeared in 1904 and later inspired a national boom in Campbell Kids dolls.

Uncle Arthur had no concern about the practicality of the idea. After all, it was now 1897, almost a century since Nicolas Appert of France had perfected a method of canning food to preserve it, and nearly half a century since Gail Borden had introduced condensed milk. "But," scowled Uncle Arthur, "I have to ask myself if *our* kind of customer would think of it as *quality*." Uncle Arthur would soon have a chance to sample the new condensed soup and would agree it would not hurt the company's reputation and should be taken to market.

Consumer reaction was both immediate and good. Campbell's condensed soup was hailed as a revolutionary new kind of convenience food. So brisk was the demand for the new soup that the Dorrances decided it deserved its own special label. They called an office conference and began with the choice of colors. Someone promptly suggested red and white. "Any special reasons?" the suggester was asked. "Were you thinking, perhaps, about white for purity and red for all the tomato products we handle?" "No, "he said." I was just thinking about the colors of Cornell. Very simple, but very striking. I've always thought so."

The new red and white label was introduced in 1898,

and now Dr. Dorrance said the company should make plans for an advertising program. Another office conference was called. Swift agreement was reached that all Campbell's Soup advertising should be addressed to women. But in what medium? "Trolley car posters," said one positive voice. "Why trolley cars?" someone asked. "Because women are not walkers. They are frequent riders in the street cars. Where you have car lines in the cities, you'll find that women use them a great deal."

The company budgeted $4,264 for the introductory 1899 effort, enough to put car cards into one-third of New York City's surface cars. The cards would carry a friendly jingle (like the one at the opening of this story) and pictures of the product and the red-and-white can. Within three years, the introductory effort had become a program covering 378 cities, and the Campbell's Soup purchases of up to forty-five thousand cards per month made the company the number one target of every major lithographic printer and his salesmen.

One such salesman, hoping to stand out from the crowd, asked his artist wife, Grace Gebbie Drayton, to do some sketches of children he could take along with his card samples on his next Campbell's call. She had a flair for drawing what she called "round roly-polies."

At about the same time, the writer of the card jingles, Charles N. Snyder, was recommending to Dr. Dorrance that some friendly human character be added to the cards. Out of some advertising discussions had come agreement that "the best way to reach the housewife is through 'child appeal.'"

Grace Gebbie Drayton thus became suddenly famous as the creator of the "Campbell Kids." The stylized cherubs made their bow in 1904, and soon brought such a demand for Campbell's car cards that the company felt compelled to charge for the postage. Kindergartens wanted them; mothers put them up in the nursery; even coeds in college thought the Campbell Kids were an ideal way to brighten up a room. By 1909, Grace Drayton's cherubs had inspired a national boom in Campbell Kids dolls and, by 1911, were helping Campbell's Soup to move into California and thus achieve national distribution.

In this hard-working, single-column advertisement in a 1909 issue of *The Saturday Evening Post*, the maker of "the soups for all occasions" gave extensive details of their quality processing, offered menu suggestions, listed all twenty-one varieties, and still found room for a verse alongside a picture of a Campbell Kid.

The power of the Campbell Kids was a surprise to grocers, advertising experts, even to Campbell executives—and most of all to Grace Drayton, who thought of them as pure fun. "I draw fast," she once said, "because I can't wait to see them myself."

Dr. John Dorrance, the practical gourmet, entered his condensed soups at the Paris Exposition of 1900 and won a gold medallion for excellence, a medallion the labels have carried ever since. But he also, by 1904, had broadened his basic product line by introducing Campbell's Pork and Beans, and had extended the variety of his soups from the original tomato to a choice of about twenty; and would later acquire the Franco-American Food Company, well-known for gourmet foods and soups.

He also established a tradition of advertising to women in a wholesome, positive, happy way—never boring and always in good taste. And, though Campbell's Soup was often called "conservative" in its advertising programming, it was widely referred to, in time, as "America's most *consistent* advertiser."

Dr. John T. Dorrance died in 1930 and was succeeded as president by his brother, Arthur C. Dorrance. In 1946, Arthur C. Dorrance died; but John T. Dorrance, Jr. joined the company and went on to become chairman of the board in 1962.

Among the world's prepared foods, few are more basic and commonplace than soup. At the same time, few are more versatile. Along with adding varieties to its condensed soup line, Campbell's has added in recent years the Chunky line of ready-to-serve soups and a semi-condensed Soup-for-One line. Now, in answer to the often heard question, "What should I fix for the next meal?" Campbell's offers cooking soups, lunch soups, main dish ideas, and pour-ons to go with rice or noodles.

In the scientific tradition of Dr. Dorrance, Campbell's was the first to establish a formal agricultural research department, opened in 1939, and later added an Institute for Food Research. As one example of basic research, Campbell's scientists found long ago that chicken contains more than one hundred flavor components; then, in a quest for natural methods of enhancing the flavor of the soup, they began experiments with flavor precursors that held the promise of being obtained genetically or through feeding. Vegetable research includes the development of varieties that will ripen all at one time, not over an extended period; new varieties that will hold up better during processing; and new varieties that are better adapted to mechanical harvesting. Campbell research also involves a continuous study of how to cope with insect pests without harm to natural resources or human health.

The company describes itself in these terms: "The Company is a major manufacturer of prepared convenience foods for human consumption and considers itself to be engaged in that one general line of business. In recent years, the Company has entered into several small operations in the candy, pet food, restaurant, garden center, mail order, and technical service businesses."

Today, at twenty-nine plant locations in the United States, five in Canada, and at others in Australia, Belgium, England, France, Italy and Mexico, the Campbell Soup Company makes more than four hundred special recipe convenience foods. Its approximately thirty-three thousand employees are involved in a food production spectrum that ranges from the fields of the Campbell contract farmers to the shelves of the supermarkets, and on to the mobile van units in which current and new products undergo continuous consumer testing.

And not the least of Campbell's diverse activities takes place in the company's Art and Design Center, whose responsibilities include the custody of the Campbell Kids.

For their first twenty years, the Campbell Kids were the exclusive creations of Grace Drayton. After she passed from the scene, the Kids became the wards of a series of two advertising agencies and four art studios, and their fortunes varied with the changing times. During the depression of the 1930's, for example, the Kids were ruled out as being too chucklesome for the grim economic environment, and they were similarly subdued during the dark years of World War II. Then, by the end of the War, they were judged by some skeptics to be old-fashioned and obsolete.

After World War II, some critics said the Campbell Kids were obsolete. But television brought them back. To be sure they are drawn properly, they are now the wards of the Campbell Art and Design Center.

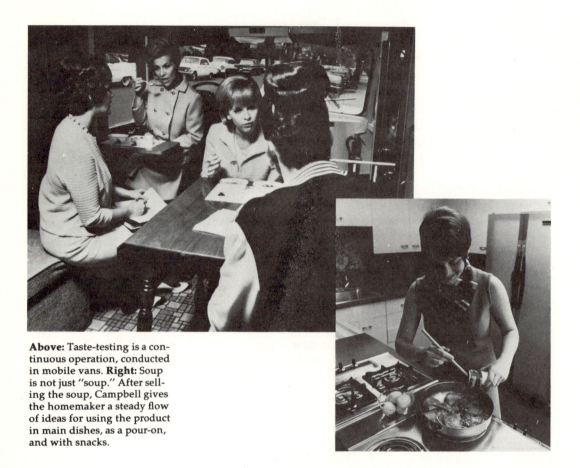

Above: Taste-testing is a continuous operation, conducted in mobile vans. **Right:** Soup is not just "soup." After selling the soup, Campbell gives the homemaker a steady flow of ideas for using the product in main dishes, as a pour-on, and with snacks.

Suddenly, with the coming of television in the early 1950's, there was a renewed call for the Campbell Kids. A distinguished art studio was commissioned to give them a proper facelift, covering eyelashes, chubbiness, knee-caps, chin, eye position, nose, and neck. But as each new artist did a rendering of the Kids, the company could detect a slight but steady tampering with their ideal character.

Thus, in recent years, the Kids have been entrusted only to the Art and Design Center. The time had come, the company decided, for the Campbell Kids to be under as strict a set of quality controls as everything else.

As part of its involvement in agriculture, Campbell raises tomato plants for the farmers around the country who grow for Campbell.

MARKETING INSIGHTS

Campbell's condensed canned soup was one of the first major convenience foods, and Campbell was one of the first to define its market and the best ways of reaching it: "Advertise to women, using trolley car posters and child appeals." Later, in line with good market segmentation practice, Campbell would recognize the needs of singles and newly-marrieds as well as mothers and other mature homemakers.

The line of condensed canned soups grew to dozens of varieties to which Campbell later added a special ready-to-serve Chunky line and a semi-condensed Soup-for-One line.

All the while, Campbell's Soup advertising was characterized by a high level of service to the reader, constantly offering new answers to the perennial question: "What should I make for the next meal?" Campbell's offered a wide variety of suggestions about lunch soups, cooking soups, main dishes, and so on.

Campbell advertising also has been characterized by its dual reminder power. Appearing on a high-frequency basis, it reminds shoppers to pick up the product at the supermarket; it also reminds many customers that they already have the product in their pantries—in the home, but out of sight—and have been forgetting to use it. Until a product is *used*—not merely purchased—there is a block in the purchase cycle.

COCA-COLA

"There is no limit to what a man can do or where he can go, if he doesn't mind who gets the credit."

9 One May morning in 1886, Dr. John Stith Pemberton walked into the Joe Jacobs Drug Store at Atlanta's Five Points, slid a jug across the counter of Willis Venable's leased soda fountain, and asked for two drinks, each mixed in the exact proportion of one ounce of the syrup contained in the jug to five ounces of water and ice.

Venable snapped to and mixed with a flourish. After all, John Pemberton was not just a highly respected pharmaceutical chemist; he was also a man who had served with distinction as a Confederate cavalry officer. Pemberton asked Venable to sample the mixture. Venable, according to legend, was soon smacking his lips and suggesting a refill.

On the second mixing, he made an error, for which he promptly apologized: he had drawn soda water, not tap water, over the sweet, brown syrup. Pemberton waved a reassuring hand and said it would not make a bit of difference.

But it did, and the difference was dramatic. Pemberton watched the look of pleasant surprise flash over Venable's face and concluded he had a successful product.

In response to Venable's questions, Pemberton explained that his new "proprietary elixir" contained the properties of the coca plant and of cola nuts. The extract of coca leaf had a unique flavor; the cola nut, like the coffee bean, contained caffeine. Pemberton added that his bookkeeper, Frank Robinson, had suggested that the product be called Coca-Cola, a name that was at once catchy, alliterative, and descriptive of the content. Robinson, a penmanship buff, had even suggested a way of lettering "Coca-Cola" in a distinctively flowing script.

On May 8, 1886, Coca-Cola went on sale in the Joe Jacobs Drug Store at Five Points. On May 29, Pemberton told the whole city about it with an advertisement in *The Atlanta Journal*, proclaiming Coca-Cola as "Delicious! Refreshing! Exhilarating! Invigorating." The same issue

of the *Journal* carried an advertisement for a formidable, well-established competitor: "The marvelous Moxie Nerve Food—on draught at H. C. Beerman's Soda Water Palace."

Coca-Cola, Dr. Pemberton's "proprietary elixir," came into a market in which soft drinks were nothing new. Soda water had been introduced in 1807 and soon was being offered with lemon flavoring. (Other fruit flavors had faced fermentation and spoilage problems.) Charles E. Hires had exhibited his package of dried roots and herbs, for the making of "Hires root beer," at Philadelphia's Centennial Exposition of 1876 and, by 1884, was a national advertiser, selling both household extracts and fountain concentrates. And ginger ale had become the most successful soft drink of all, with hundreds of local producers throughout the United States.

Dr. Pemberton's new formula, developed in his kitchen and prepared in a cast iron kettle over an open fire in his backyard, was not just a latecomer to the soft drink scene; it was also a product that defied description.

Acceptance came slowly, and only with a heavy outpouring of free sample drinks. The cola nut, from faraway Africa, lacked the familiarity enjoyed by its chocolate cousin; and South America's coca, which would later be extolled by Mark Twain as a "vegetable product with miraculous powers," was hard to explain to the Atlantans of 1886. By the end of the year, John Pemberton noted that, with modest help from several investors, he had invested $73.96 in advertising, but had sold only fifty gallons of syrup, at $1.00 per gallon. Two years later, just before his death, Dr. Pemberton sold out his interest in Coca-Cola for $1,750.

The new principal owner, Asa G. Candler, wholesale druggist and old Pemberton friend, was not sure until 1891 that Coca-Cola was a viable product. He then took steps to buy out the other investors for twenty-three hundred dollars and pick up the entire physical assets of the venture in a small wagon drawn by a single horse. In 1892, he formed "The Coca-Cola Company," as a Georgia corporation, and by the end of the next year had registered "Coca-Cola" as a trademark and was ready to pay

The first advertisement for Coca-Cola, May 29, 1886.

From left to right: Dr. J. S. Pemberton, originator of the formula for Coca-Cola; Asa G. Candler, founder of The Coca-Cola Company; Benjamin Franklin Thomas, who conceived the idea of the Coca-Cola Bottling business; Ernest Woodruff, head of the group that purchased The Coca-Cola Company from the Candler family in 1919 for twenty-five million dollars; Robert W. Woodruff, who made The Coca-Cola Company a global business.

the company's first dividend of twenty dollars per share, equal to twenty percent of the book value of a share of stock. His principal manufacturing facilities were a fifteen hundred-gallon wooden tank and a one hundred-gallon copper kettle, and only he and associate Frank Robinson knew the formula. It would be passed on to successive managements by word of mouth and would become known as the "most closely guarded secret in American industry." Despite occasional rumors, cocaine, according to company sources, was never an ingredient in the formula for Coca-Cola.

Druggist Candler adopted Pemberton's words, "Delicious and Refreshing," and began pursuing the goal of selling Coca-Cola syrup to every soda fountain in America. He curried the favor of the fountain operators not only with signs, but with souvenir fans, calendars, clocks, coin purses, serving trays, Tiffany-style lamps, and a host of other merchandising pieces, many of which would in time become collectors' items. He continued an early-day sampling program and gave away countless thousands of coupons for a free glass of Coca-Cola.

By 1895, Coca-Cola was on sale in every state of the Union, and Candler was convinced that the future of Coca-Cola was at the soda fountain. When, in 1899, Benjamin Franklin Thomas and Joseph B. Whitehead came

calling from Chattanooga, suggesting that Coca-Cola should also be bottled on a large scale (it had been bottled in one locality as early as 1894), Candler was definitely negative, but he at least agreed to hear them out.

Thomas offered persuasive facts. During his Spanish-American War service, he had been introduced to a bottled soft drink in Cuba, and had witnessed its wide acceptance by the American troops. Now, he continued, Americans were flocking to baseball parks, creating a major market for a bottled thirst-quencher.

What Candler then agreed to has since been called "fabulous," but it simply reflected his view, at the time, of the potential for a bottled soft drink: he granted Thomas and Whitehead "the exclusive rights to bottle Coca-Cola within the continental limits of the United States, with the exception of New England, Mississippi, and Texas" (where certain wholesaler rights had been granted earlier). Thomas and Whitehead promptly returned to Chattanooga, invested five thousand dollars in a bottling plant, and by year's end, the franchised bottling industry was born. The Thomas operation would continue until 1975, when The Coca-Cola Company would acquire its contract rights for approximately thirty-five million dollars.

Candler, the thoroughgoing merchandiser, promptly

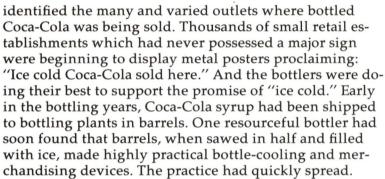

Evolution of the world's best known package: bottle at far left was used in 1894 by Joseph A. Biedenharn, Vicksburg, Mississippi, to bottle Coca-Cola for local customers; the second bottle was used in 1899 by the bottlers of Coca-Cola; classic contour design (*fifth from left*) appeared in 1915 and underwent only slight modifications thereafter. Bottle at far right, an experimental plastic package, appeared in 1975.

identified the many and varied outlets where bottled Coca-Cola was being sold. Thousands of small retail establishments which had never possessed a major sign were beginning to display metal posters proclaiming: "Ice cold Coca-Cola sold here." And the bottlers were doing their best to support the promise of "ice cold." Early in the bottling years, Coca-Cola syrup had been shipped to bottling plants in barrels. One resourceful bottler had soon found that barrels, when sawed in half and filled with ice, made highly practical bottle-cooling and merchandising devices. The practice had quickly spread.

By 1903, Asa Candler was a millionaire; by 1914, his fortune had soared to fifty million dollars and a share of Coca-Cola stock, which still had a par value of one hundred dollars, was worth approximately seventeen thousand dollars. And the momentum of Coca-Cola continued to quicken.

In his national advertising, on outdoor posters and in magazines, Candler never lost sight of the early slogan, "Delicious and Refreshing." The product was described at one time as "The Great National Temperance Beverage," and at another as "a glass of liquid laughter." But its basic promise was always refreshment and nothing more.

With Candler's approval, the bottlers of Coca-Cola sought still another way of promoting their unique product—something as exclusive as the Coca-Cola glasses used at soda fountains. The bottle for Coca-Cola, they de-

cided, should be so distinctively shaped that anyone
would be able to identify it "when it was felt in the
dark." By 1915, they had their answer, the company's
first classic contour design. Conceived by Alexander
Samuelson, a Swedish glass blower employed by the Root
Glass Company of Terre Haute, Indiana, the graceful bottle was later registered as a trademark of The Coca-Cola
Company.

Asa Candler, in 1916, was ready to retire from active
participation in the company and run successfully for
Mayor of Atlanta. Three years later, Candler family members in control of The Coca-Cola Company decided to
sell. The buyer was a group of Atlanta businessmen
headed by banker Ernest W. Woodruff. The price was
twenty-five million dollars—ten million dollars in cash
and fifteen million dollars in preferred stock. The business was reincorporated as a Delaware corporation and
the common stock was put on public sale.

The 1919 sale of The Coca-Cola Company to the Ernest
Woodruff group was the largest business transaction ever
consummated in the South. The company by then was
selling twenty million gallons of syrup a year; seventy
thousand soda fountains were dispensing it; fifteen
hundred bottlers were distributing it to retail outlets.
Coca-Cola, under Asa Candler, had become the most successful product of its kind in the history of commerce,
and stockholders throughout the South were launching
and revitalizing a host of other southern industries with
Coca-Cola money.

To Atlanta observers, Ernest Woodruff was the ideal
choice to lead The Coca-Cola Company through its next
great era. Long a principal of the Trust Company of Georgia, Ernest Woodruff had also been a prime mover in the
development of the Atlantic Ice and Coal Corporation,
the Atlantic Steel Company, and the Continental Gin
Company, and was regarded as one of the major builders
of the city of Atlanta. Unfortunately, he entered the
Coca-Cola picture just as post-war inflation jumped the
price of sugar four hundred percent—thus leading to a
battle with bottlers over the fixed price of syrup in their
contracts—while, at the same time, a deteriorating sales

Poster of 1901 featured popular singer Hilda Clark.

force had caused sales to plummet. By 1923, Coca-Cola stock had fallen from forty dollars a share to about nineteen dollars, and Ernest Woodruff decided the time had come to ask his son Robert to take over the presidency of The Coca-Cola Company.

It was a decision loaded with mingled emotions for both father and son. As a college freshman, much to his father's displeasure, Robert had turned his back on any higher education; and he had further antagonized his father by flatly rejecting his advice to consider a career in banking. Instead, after a few preliminary jobs, he became a truck salesman for the White Motor Company. Then, as if to prove his father completely wrong, Robert proceeded to rise by age thirty-three to the position of vice president in charge of sales at White, with a salary of eighty-five thousand dollars—with still another promotion about to come. Just before receiving his father's call to join Coca-Cola, Robert Woodruff was elected president of White Motor Company.

To respond to his father's call would mean taking a pay cut of fifty thousand dollars. It also would mean commuting to Cleveland for an extended period while somebody else was groomed for the White presidency. Robert

Woodruff weighed all aspects of the problem as objectively as he could and told his father he would come to The Coca-Cola Company.

In time, Robert Winship Woodruff would become known as "Mr. Coke" and later, because of his extensive, but never publicized philanthropy, as "Mr. Anonymous." But first he became known as a highly effective listener. Nobody in the company was beyond reach of the Woodruff requests for opinions, and every opinion was treated with respect. Periodically, the distillation of many opinions would emerge from the laconic leader as another policy decree. A plaque in his office carried this basic piece of Woodruff philosophy: "There is no limit to what a man can do or where he can go, if he doesn't mind who gets the credit."

Woodruff believed in concentrating on a simple product line. When he became president, there was Coca-Cola syrup to be sold by the gallon and there was Coca-Cola in the 6.5-ounce bottles, and he kept it that way for thirty years. Not until 1954 would the company start expanding into a variety of larger bottle sizes.

Unlike Asa Candler, who had always been biased in favor of syrup sales at soda fountains, Robert Woodruff decided early to put more promotion behind the bottle: "The package that can travel anywhere." In the early 1920's, the company had originated the six-bottle carton for easier shopping, and also was developing steadily better coolers to step up bottle sales. By 1929, Coca-Cola offered bottlers its first "official" cooler, and the first practical coin-operated coolers would soon follow.

Meanwhile, the soda fountain people were getting special training in the selling and serving of Coca-Cola, and, by the early 1930's, the fountains were being automated by new dispensers that mixed syrup and carbonated water at the pull of a handle.

All this while, what preoccupied Robert Woodruff above everything else was not what was happening in bottle or fountain sales, but what the company was doing to advance itself in the *world* market. His first major project, after becoming president, had been the setting up, in 1926, of a Foreign Department, based in New York City

Ceramic syrup urn,
1895, set elegant tone
for dispensing Coca-Cola.

Serving tray of 1909 featured
The Coca-Cola Girl, painted
by artist Hamilton King.

The first six-pack
carton, 1924.

Cardboard window display, 1923.

Cardboard cutout and fan, 1911.

Glascock Cooler, 1930's.

Early bottlers sawed syrup barrels in half to create the first point-of-sale coolers of Coca-Cola in bottles.

This fountain dispenser of 1933 mixed syrup and carbonated water at the pull of a handle.

Mills Vendor, 1940's.

On May 15, 1950, "the world's favorite soft drink" became the first consumer product ever to be featured on a cover of *Time* magazine.

and charged with making Coca-Cola as important overseas as it was in the United States.

Step one in carrying out that mission was to develop a syrup concentrate to reduce shipping costs. (Ultimately, the syrup would be manufactured abroad in twenty-nine separate plants.) Step two was to solve the problem of the world sugar supply. Under Robert Woodruff's direction, chemists developed a process for making beet sugar suitable for use in Coca-Cola syrup.

Step three—the most important one of all—was Robert Woodruff's economic concept of The Coca-Cola Company. To him, it was basically just a cooperative effort by a variety of independent local business people. That was the concept he would apply to the overseas expansion program.

Coca-Cola's progress abroad was swift and solid. Then came World War II, and Coca-Cola's export people suddenly had to start doing everything a lot faster. The first speed-up order came in 1941, direct from Robert Woodruff, who had served as a Major in the Ordnance Department in World War I. The Woodruff edict: "See that every man in an American uniform is able to get a bottle of Coca-Cola for five cents, wherever he is and whatever it costs the company."

The second speed-up message arrived in the form of a June 29, 1943 telegram from the North Africa Headquarters of General Dwight D. Eisenhower, requesting sufficient machinery to operate ten Coca-Cola bottling plants. A Coca-Cola engineer flew to Algiers to open those plants, and they became the forerunners of sixty-four others shipped to Europe and the Pacific during World War II and set up as close as possible to combat areas.

Ultimately, of the world's ten largest Coca-Cola bottling plants, seven would be overseas, and foreign operations would represent over sixty percent of the total soft drink sales of The Coca-Cola Company; and the familiar red and white sign of Coca-Cola would beckon the thirsty not only in the United States, but in 135 foreign countries, almost as many as are members of the United Nations. And the quest for additional world markets never slackens. When, for example, the United States made its historic resumption of trade with the People's Republic of China in 1979, Coca-Cola was the first American consumer product to go on sale there, and soon was backed by a major bottling plant in Shanghai.

Approximately 550 U.S. bottlers, and more than 900 overseas, have built their independent businesses by meeting the demand. And to keep building that demand, the company has invested more money in advertising than has ever been concentrated on a single product. Since 1886, more than one billion dollars has been spent on advertising by the entire soft drink industry, and Coca-Cola has accounted for nearly three-fourths of the total.

Robert W. Woodruff retired as an officer of the company in 1955, but he continued a major leadership role as a director and chairman of the board's finance committee.

In the course of promoting itself, The Coca-Cola Company has also expanded the soft drink industry and has watched once-minor competitors grow into major ones. By 1960, in addition to meeting its cola-type competitors, the company was launching new products to compete directly with the non-cola competition: Fanta, 1960; Sprite, 1961; Fresca, 1966; Mr. Pibb, 1972; Mello Yello, 1978. A low-calorie cola, TAB, was introduced in 1963. In the midst of this expanded line, the original brand, Coca-Cola, continues to account for over seventy percent of all company soft drink sales.

As further diversification, the company in recent years has expanded its line with Minute Maid concentrated citrus juices, Hi-C fruit drinks and drink mixes, Duncan Foods, Taylor and other wines, and Aqua-Chem, a water-conditioning firm. Still another product is Samson, a high-protein drink now sold overseas as a diet supplement. In all, since 1960, the company has developed 250 products.

Coca-Cola—also trademarked as "Coke"—is the same everywhere. In its many and varied bottler operations throughout the world, The Coca-Cola Company has long had the technology to bring local water to absolute neutral, absolute purity, before it is mixed with the unique Coca-Cola syrup. But the customers are something else—

Coca-Cola weather display at
Columbus Circle, New York
City, 1930's.

there is no such thing as a homogeneous market, and,
since 1964, the company has applied the principles of
segmentation in its marketing effort, aiming at subgroups
with similar motivations.

The segmentation approach was initiated, in radio
commercials, by simply selecting entertainers who were a
good personality match for the audience. Subsequent
commercials, for television, included the various types of
persons—all in the seventeen to thirty-four age group—
who represented the best types of customers and prospects. Then, as a further refinement of segmentation, the
advertising aimed at youth featured romance or humor in
product-oriented situations, and the advertising to
women was value-oriented, with the soft drink featured
along with food.

Under J. Paul Austin, chairman of the board and chief
executive officer since 1966, The Coca-Cola Company,
worldwide, ended the 1970's with sales of more than $4.3
billion and was the employer of more than thirty-six
thousand people. But the backbone of the business continues to be "the package that can travel anywhere"—the

classic-contoured bottle of Coca-Cola. It is now being asked for in some 135 countries, and in more than eighty different languages, to make it the best known package on earth.

Meanwhile, back in Atlanta, more than a few applications have arrived for the first Coca-Cola franchises on the moon.

MARKETING INSIGHTS

What does it take to become the best known trademarked product in the entire world?

Coca-Cola began in the most basic of ways: it was aimed at the universal need to quench thirst, and it offered a unique flavor—a flavor, it should be noted, that could not be described; it had to be sampled.

The promise of the product was uniquely simple: "Delicious and refreshing." But never has a company worked more meticulously, year after year, to enhance the uniqueness of its product and keep faith with the product promise. Coca-Cola was given its own distinctive glass—and a bottle so uniquely designed, for both look and feel, that it could be recognized in the dark.

Upholding the promise of refreshment meant creating new ways of serving the product ice cold—and of making it available almost everywhere, complete with a distinctive sign to mark its location.

Coca-Cola began as only a thirst-quencher; but its makers were soon positioning it as a symbol of America itself—an integral part of our society's happiest, most rewarding activities—backed by advertising that was keyed to America's mood.

The advertising and other promotion of Coca-Cola was given a very specific objective: make the product an inherent part of people's lives and habits—a means of contributing to their pleasure. Advertising, the company believed, should be an extension of the product itself and should have the properties of the product itself. Every advertisement for Coca-Cola should be a pleasurable experience, and it should reflect quality by being quality.

In communicating the uniqueness of Coca-Cola, its marketers concentrated on four specific elements which,

The Coca-Cola Company, early in its career, initiated what must qualify as the world's most democratic, most ubiquitous outdoor sign program. A multitude of retailers, representing almost every business field, got their first sign with the help of The Coca-Cola Company.

according to marketing research, helped identify the brand to consumers: (1) the familiar script lettering of the Coca-Cola trademark; (2) the trademark "Coke"; (3) the bright red color; (4) the unique contour of the bottle.

Those four elements—plus the unique flavor—are the foundation of the Coca-Cola *image*, which the company defines as "a composite of all communication. It is not only what you say, but how you say it, how you look, how you act, and how consistent you are in all you do and say."

To stand out clearly in today's often-cluttered complex of promotion, the advertising for Coca-Cola strives for "one sound, one sight, one sell." Typical evidence of the effectiveness of that approach: within three months of the introduction of one new advertising theme for Coca-Cola, approximately seventy percent of all Americans were able to repeat it accurately.

In applying the principles of market segmentation, the company decided in the mid-1960's to use television as an all-family medium, radio to appeal primarily to youth, and print (magazines, outdoor, and point-of-purchase materials) to cover all audiences with the sensory appeals of color, sparkle, and "the thirst-quenching, refreshing look."

Early in the 1970's, The Coca-Cola Company aired a television commercial in which a young choral group began: "I'd like to teach the world to sing in perfect harmony. . . . I'd like to buy the world a Coke to keep it company." The music went beyond the conventional "jingle" and was described as a "song-form commercial, designed to paint a picture in music—a picture appropriate to the use of Coca-Cola, but in which not every word sung is about the product."

With characteristic thoroughness, The Coca-Cola Company recognizes that the image of Coca-Cola is influenced by far more than the product itself and its promotional elements. Thus, with painstaking care, the Coca-Cola "look" is applied to uniforms, emblems, point-of-purchase materials, vending machines, cases, stationery, checks, and business forms—and the worldwide fleet of trucks.

The world is now being invited to "Drink Coca-Cola" in some 135 countries, speaking more than eighty different languages.

COLUMBIA BICYCLES

"Could it have become 'the first General Motors'?"

10 Among all the vehicles competing for efficiency honors in today's energy-conscious marketplace, the winner and still champion is the chain-driven bicycle, invented by England's H. J. Lawson in 1876 and basically unchanged for more than a century. In terms of calories consumed per mile, say the experts, the efficiency of a bicyclist is comparable to that of an automobile attaining one thousand passenger miles per gallon.

By sheer coincidence, it was in 1876 that Boston's Albert Augustus Pope saw his first bicycle—at the Philadelphia Centennial—and decided it should become his future business. What Pope saw, of course, was not the Lawson design, but its predecessor, the High Wheel Ordinary, with a front wheel that stood five feet high and a tiny rear wheel one foot in diameter. But to Pope, a manufacturer of small metal articles who was looking for a more challenging product, the High Wheel Ordinary seemed to be a dramatic answer. In 1887, his Pope Manufacturing Company launched the bicycle industry in the United States with its Columbia High Wheel Ordinary. About a decade later, Pope was first again with an American chain-driven bicycle.

The chain-driven bicycle would come to be known as a brilliant example of engineering, with its wheels and sprockets running in perfect alignment, and with all bearings parallel to one another and to the direction of travel. But first, the bicycle faced rough-ride and road problems. Not until 1889 would John B. Dunlop of Belfast, Ireland, revolutionize bicycle riding with his pneumatic tire, and never would the road problems be completely solved.

Albert Pope had been an officer in the Civil War. Now, as "Founder of the American Bicycle Industry," he would also acquire the honorary title of "Colonel" and become a leading crusader for better roads. During a long, sustained campaign, he launched educational programs, ar-

Colonel Albert A. Pope (*Courtesy of American Bicyclist and Motorcyclist*)

The original Columbia High Wheel Ordinary, 1877.

ranged for the construction of a model section of modern road in Boston, set up special courses in road engineering at the Massachusetts Institute of Technology—and in time acquired still another honorary title: "Father of Good Roads."

After more than a decade of pioneering effort, the American bicycle suddenly became a national favorite. By the beginning of the 1890's, the fad had extended to England—and England's bicycle makers, unable to keep up with the demand, watched helplessly as American manufacturers established a substantial export market there. American bicycle makers had never anticipated such an explosive boom.

Neither had the nation's leading economists. They voiced alarm over the way the mushrooming bicycle industry was diverting money away from other industries. Hundreds of new bicycle manufacturers sprang up nationally, and almost every large and medium-size city had more than one local manufacturer. Local legislators concocted new ordinances to stem the industry's explosive growth.

Then, with almost equal swiftness, the bicycle industry neared a saturation level with the public—and the public was beginning to hear of another spectacular invention: the automobile.

Colonel Pope, one of the first to see the potential of the modern bicycle, was also one of the first to feel the attraction of the automobile. In his Hartford plant, he developed the Pope-Hartford, soon to be followed by the Pope-Toledo (from a plant in Toledo, Ohio), and the Columbia automobile.

Not unmindful that motorcycles, too, might be strong contenders in the gasoline age, he also went to market with the Pope and the Columbia motorcycles. By the early 1900's, the Columbia Bicycle was being phased out of the Hartford plant and relocated in Westfield, Massachusetts, in a new plant the people of Westfield— through citizen subscription—had built for the manufacture of the Lozier automobile. The people of Westfield had wanted to expand employment, but the Lozier had been fated to become one of the automobile industry's more than two thousand failures.

As America moved into the twentieth century, Colonel Albert Pope, who had spearheaded the efforts to make it "a nation on two wheels," was now determined to lead the transformation to gasoline power. His expanding operations would soon include Hagerstown, Maryland, as well as Hartford, Toledo, and Westfield.

To this day, transportation industry old-timers still reflect on Colonel Pope's company and ask: "Could it have become 'the first General Motors'?" What happened?

What happened was that Colonel Pope's bankers came to the conclusion that the gasoline-powered vehicle was an extravagant, ill-fated fad. By 1920, the Pope automobile and motorcycle ventures had passed from the scene.

Meanwhile, in Westfield, where most local families, at one time or another, have had at least one member working at the factory the old-timers still call "The Pope," the makers of the Columbia Bicycle pushed on with their work, undaunted by the changes in corporate names.

Among its contributions to cycling history, Columbia offers a long list of "firsts," beginning with the first coaster brake, first diamond frame, and first tandem bicycle of early years, and continuing into modern times with the first streamlined bicycle with curved upper and lower frame tubes.

Early Columbia tricycle.

Company ownership was transferred early in the century to the Westfield Manufacturing Company. At that point, out of the hundreds of bicycle makers of the prosperous 1890's, fewer than fifty had attained substantial size, and only about a score had established national distribution.

The lean years continued. Ultimately, in 1953, the Columbia Bicycle makers would capitalize on their long experience with tubular frame technology and extend their operations into the manufacturing of tubular frame school furniture. And, at about the same time, Columbia and other members of the bicycle industry would get some unexpected help: President Dwight D. Eisenhower would launch a national physical fitness program.

Eisenhower's physical fitness program would soon mesh with other national developments to pave the way for another bicycle boom. The nation had more leisure time; amateur bicycle racing and intercollegiate bicycle

Above: Early Columbia Safety, with chain drive and pneumatic tires. **Right:** The Columbia Commuter Moped.

events were making a comeback; parking congestion was becoming an acute problem; environmentalists were launching anti-pollution campaigns. And then came the energy crunch.

To meet today's specialized demands, the Columbia Manufacturing Company produces a broad and varied line of cycles, ranging from ten-speed derailleurs to tracksters, from middleweights to tandems, from three-wheelers to unicycles—plus cycle exercisers—and has a work force of about one thousand people. In 1976, Columbia also became the first American manufacturer of motorized bicycles (mopeds).

Now a division of Cleveland's MTD Products Inc., the world's largest maker of power lawn equipment and a major producer of sports-leisure vehicles, Columbia anticipates increasing competition, especially from imports. After all, bicycles have always been the most numerous class of vehicles on the roads of England, France, Germany, Holland, Belgium, and Italy; and the bicycle makers of those countries are impressive competition.

At the same time, bicycle ownership has reached a level of more than seventy bicycles for every one thousand people—compared with twenty-seven per thousand in the booming 1890's.

And the problem of bikeways continues to be a matter of concern, just as it was in the days of Colonel Pope's "good roads" campaigns.

But now, well over a century since the first Columbia made its appearance in Boston, its makers are confident that, whatever the next marketing problem may be, it at least will not catch them unprepared.

MARKETING INSIGHTS

Ever since he invented the wheel, man has continuously sought better forms of transportation—and seldom has progress come easily.

Albert Pope, America's first bicycle maker—like the automobile makers who came later—would have to crusade for better roads to make his product usable. Having achieved his road goals, he would then face a mushrooming of competition—first from other bicycle makers, then from motorcycles and automobiles. To keep pace with the new competition, bicycle-maker Pope for a time was also a maker of motorcycles and automobiles.

Pope's Columbia bicycles survived the early competitive years by offering more reliability, more comfort, and more ease-of-control features than the other bicycles. Columbia would then get a timely boost from outside sources: the nation's new interest in physical fitness, the new concern about air pollution—and finally, the energy crunch.

To make the most of new developments in all the different segments of the bicycle market, Columbia expanded its line to include every popular type of unit from unicycles to cycle exercisers to ten-speed derailleurs to mopeds.

Meanwhile, as insulation against the peak-and-valley trends of the bicycle business, the company has capitalized on its tubular metal expertise by diversifying into the fields of school furniture and playground equipment.

EVINRUDE
OUTBOARD MOTORS
"I'll take care of your books, Ole."

Ole Evinrude

Bess Evinrude

11 He was a big, bashful Norwegian, a master pattern maker turned inventor. She was a spunky, petite Irish girl with dark hair and deep blue eyes, working after business school to help support her six orphaned brothers and sisters. They had been exchanging shy glances for months, in that little Milwaukee shop of Clemick & Evinrude, but they had never spoken.

Now they were alone in the heavy silence of a small company that had failed. Clemick & Evinrude, makers of small gasoline engines, had completed a government contract and no more orders were in sight. Big Ole Evinrude was discouraged, and he showed it. He had been able to organize a new venture, to be called the Motor Car Power Equipment Company; but now he faced the problem of the office work. To Ole Evinrude, that was formidable. As a Wisconsin farm boy, he had only completed the third grade, and everything he had learned later, in night school, was confined to subjects like algebra. He looked almost enviously at little Bess Emily Cary. She had finished the eighth grade; she could even handle correspondence and keep books. But Ole did not know how to broach the subject; he could only fidget with the carpenter's rule he always carried, and ponder the situation in gloomy silence.

Bess had a twinkle in her eye when she finally said, "I'll take care of your books, Ole." It was all that needed saying. Ole Evinrude did not know how to thank her, and she did not expect him to try. The Motor Car Power Equipment Company was now officially organized.

Outside that grimy little shop, it was an age of glittering promise for men who had a talent for engines; and Ole Evinrude, it was said, could make an engine do things it never knew it could do. Across the lake, in Michigan, Ransom Olds and Henry Ford were already

well established in the new automobile industry, and Ole
Evinrude's idea seemed even more practical than theirs.
His light engine could be installed on any buggy you al-
ready owned.

He and Bess worked so hard, it used to worry their
friends. A typical day ended at midnight. And when the
two took a Sunday off, their recreational routine seemed
equally monotonous: Ole always headed for a lake,
weather permitting, and Bess would tag along, always
trying to show more enthusiasm for the water than she
really felt.

On one sweltering Sunday afternoon in August, pic-
nicking with friends on an island two miles from shore,
Bess had a brief lapse of enthusiasm. "Oh," she said wist-
fully, "what I'd give for a big dish of ice cream!"

Ole Evinrude immediately insisted on rowing to shore
for ice cream. Two miles, for him, seemed easy. But on
the way back, he was suddenly bucking a stiff breeze, the
ice cream was melting, and he knew he was about to look
like a big oaf again. For the first time in his life, he hated
rowing a boat. If only someone could build an engine
light enough to put on the back of a rowboat. . . .

While Bess and the other couple sipped the liquid ice
cream, Ole was forming a mental picture of what might
be needed to propel a rowboat.

Ralph S. Evinrude, chairman
of Outboard Marine Corporation.

The idea was not new. William Steinway, the piano
maker, had teamed with Gottlieb Daimler, father of the
gasoline engine, to produce an engine for boats as early
as 1893; but it had been too ponderous to be practical. Another inventor, Cameron Waterman, would introduce a
true outboard motor in 1906, but his "Porto" would be
equally impractical.

Ole and Bess were married in 1906, and their friends
would always have one big reason for remembering it:
bashful Ole, terrified by the prospect of appearing in a
formal wedding, came early for Bess and stole her away
for a private ceremony. When guests arrived for the
scheduled wedding, they were told it already had taken
place.

It had been a cheerless time for a wedding. Ole's Motor
Car Power Equipment Company had failed for lack of

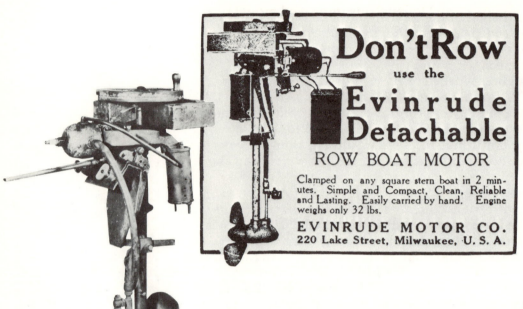

Don't Row
use the
Evinrude
Detachable
ROW BOAT MOTOR

Clamped on any square stern boat in 2 minutes. Simple and Compact, Clean, Reliable and Lasting. Easily carried by hand. Engine weighs only 32 lbs.

EVINRUDE MOTOR CO.
220 Lake Street, Milwaukee, U.S.A.

Left: Ole Evinrude's "coffee grinder" of 1909 was the first practical outboard motor. Despite its crude appearance, it introduced a basic mechanical design that remains unchanged in today's high-performance outboards. **Right:** This 1909 ad shows how Bess Evinrude introduced the "Evinrude Detachable Row Boat Motor." Ole had decided a fair price would be a dollar a pound.

capital, and he had taken the only pattern maker's job he could find. After hours, he turned occasionally, and half-heartedly, to the making of the outboard motor—and frequently interrupted his work to do favors for friends, like helping young Bill Harley and Arthur Davidson develop an air-cooled engine for their new motorcycle.

Finally, one night in 1909, it was finished—a strange contraption with a single horizontal cylinder, a vertical crankshaft and driveshaft, and a small propeller attached to a lower gear unit. Ole rushed it to Bess for her opinion. She looked more puzzled than impressed. "Ole," she said, gently but firmly, "that thing looks like a coffee grinder."

But he hurried down to the Kinnickinnic River the next morning, rented a boat for fifty cents, and amazed the deckhands on the coal boats along the docks by buzzing past them at a full five miles an hour. Mechanically, the motor was a good one. Now he would please Bess with a neater-looking design.

Ole built Evinrude Motor No. 2, and Bess gave it her full approval. Ole was delighted. He also admitted, now, that Motor No. 2 started a lot easier than Motor No. 1. He already had promised to lend this improved model to a friend, and he would not even need to offer any special warnings or instructions.

After using the motor, the friend came back with orders for ten of them, cash in hand. What was the price? Ole reflected. The motor weighed thirty-two pounds. He decided a fair price would be thirty-two dollars—a dollar a pound!

The weeks and months became busier than ever. Bess was now a mother as well as a wife; but somehow she found the time to study the literature for the "Porto" motor that had failed. Its makers had used the slogan, "Don't be afraid of it!" That was cue enough for Bess. She sat down and wrote an advertisement with the bold headline: "DON'T ROW . . . use the Evinrude Detachable Row Boat Motor."

The orders rolled in, and spunky Bess Evinrude was back in an office again, keeping the books and signing "B. Evinrude" to a stream of letters to prospective dealers and distributors. The company was a success; by 1914, the Evinrude outboard motor was internationally famous. But the load had been too heavy for Bess. Her courage and drive had always outrun her health, and now it failed.

Big, soft-hearted Ole Evinrude, the man who had rowed the four miles for some ice cream, the man who was always doing favors for friends, trusted his instincts about the right thing to do. He sold the company and packed the family Packard for an extended camping trip. He and their son Ralph would take Bess wherever she would feel better again.

The footloose retirement lasted for five years, and the results were spectacular. Bess regained her health, and Ole began to talk, restlessly, about some revolutionary new approaches to the making of an outboard motor. When Bess announced that it was time to get back to work again, Ole promptly took his designs to the man who had bought his company and offered to help put them into production.

But the man was not interested. "All right," said Bess. "We'll organize another company."

The Elto of 1921. Bess coined its name from the first letters of Evinrude's Light Twin Outboard. Made of aluminum, it weighed half as much as the original Evinrude single-cylinder engine and developed fifty percent more power.

She already had the name for it: ELTO, from the first letters of Evinrude Light Twin Outboard, a two-cylinder engine—now made of aluminum— which weighed half as much as the original single-cylinder engine and developed fifty percent more power. It also used the first exhaust discharge through a hollow propeller, for extra quietness.

Ole and Bess formed the new company in 1920 and began making new outboard history, year after year, with new streamlining of the lower unit, a new water cooling system, the first remote control steering, and a spectacular new line of four-cylinder "Quads." In 1929, Elto became the keystone in a merger of the Elto company, Lockwood-Ash Motor Company, and the "old" Evinrude Company to form Outboard Motors Corporation, with Ole Evinrude as its first president. In time, with Ralph Evinrude as president, and later chairman, O.M.C. (now Outboard Marine Corporation) would build a new headquarters in Waukegan, Illinois, and other plants in Canada, Belgium, Hong Kong, and Australia, as well as in Milwaukee. By the 1980's, O.M.C. would employ more than thirteen thousand people and be doing a sales volume of nearly six hundred million dollars.

For Ole Evinrude, the big merger of 1929 was a time to be proud. Nevertheless, it was not a happy time; Bess, once again, was in poor health. Although she had retired from the business the year before, letters were still pouring into the company, addressed to "Mr. B. Evinrude"; and visitors still arrived daily, asking to see the "B. Evinrude" who had written them so persuasively about Evinrude products.

Ole Evinrude, whose place was in the shop, whose hands could make an engine do things it never knew it could do, had given the world a simple, reliable motor they could trust in any weather. And when the world wanted something bigger and faster, his head and his hands knew how to make it. Now his work was just about finished.

Bess Evinrude died in May of 1933. She would have been forty-eight in September.

Ole went back to work for a while in the big plant in

With a fastest lap speed of 101.18 m.p.h., Team Evinrude driver Jimbo McConnell collected four separate records in 1978 with an Evinrude V-6.

Milwaukee. He still carried his carpenter's rule, and the young engineers always marveled at the way he could calculate, with his big thumb, to the thousandth of an inch on it. Weekends, he would work on the engines on his boat, or drive as far as two hundred miles to attend a church *lutfisk* supper. But he was more shy than ever now, and he even admitted at times that he felt "a little tired."

Ole died the following year, just fourteen months after Bess. He was fifty-seven.

The American outboard motor has touched the lives of millions of people throughout the world. It appears and reappears in stories about fishing and hunting, racing and exploration; and about the many ways in which it has improved the lifestyles of remote communities in faraway lands. But the best one of all is still the original, tender love story of a big, bashful man named Ole Evinrude and a little slip of a girl named Bess, who believed with all her heart in what he was trying to do.

MARKETING INSIGHTS

Ole Evinrude invented a solution to a consumer need. His basic mechanical design was so sound, it remained unchanged in even the high-performance outboards of today. Then he followed the traditional evolutionary pattern for his type of product: he improved the product's appearance; he found a way to make the same product lighter and more powerful; he expanded the product line and added new quietness and ease of control.

Bess Evinrude, meanwhile, had launched the product with one of the most effective and efficient of all advertising approaches: she spotlighted a consumer problem and offered a positive answer to that problem.

The original outboard of 1909 had a simple, single market: anybody with a rowboat who would like to have a portable motor. In today's age of market segmentation, Evinrude must aim its marketing efforts at such well-defined segments as lake and river fishermen who want a small motor for trolling; ocean fishermen who want off-shore power and speed; water skiers and speed enthusiasts who want top performance; owners of luxury cruising boats who want an extra measure of quiet stamina; explorers who want total reliability under the most rigorous sea and weather conditions.

And, because the product needs periodic servicing, the success of the marketing effort depends very importantly on the quality of the dealers the company selects and trains.

FORD CARS

"Somewhere along the line,
  there's always something more.
Our job is to find it, refine it,
  and get the public accustomed to it."

12 Historic though it was, the Ford Motor Company board of directors meeting of September 24, 1945, involved only eight people and, at least until its closing moments, was almost humdrum. If it had not been forced by two Ford women, the meeting might never have been held at all.

The first woman was Clara Bryant Ford, a quiet homebody who normally never got involved in company affairs; it was only out of deep anguish that she had once asked a Ford executive, "Who is this man Bennett who has so much control over my husband and is ruining my son's health?" She was now firm and outspoken in her belief that her eldest grandson was fully qualified to be made president of the company. The second woman, Eleanor Clay Ford, was an equally shy and private person; but she was also the daughter, widow, and sister-in-law of successful business executives and she had come right to the point: "If this is not done," she said, "I shall sell my stock." In stubborn but aging Henry Ford, who all his life had been hatefully suspicious of Wall Street and all its stock transactions, Mrs. Edsel Ford had suddenly snapped all final resistance.

The meeting agenda called only for the submission of a letter of resignation from Henry Ford and his formal designation of Henry Ford II as his successor, while the Ford women, Harry Bennett, and three other company executives looked on. Suddenly, Harry Bennett was on his feet. Striding to the door, he turned to Henry Ford II and snarled, "You're taking over a billion-dollar organization that you haven't contributed a thing to."

Within ten minutes after the meeting, Henry Ford II had performed his first official act, and Harry Bennett was no longer with Ford Motor Company.

Henry Ford in 1914.

To the 160,000 people of Ford, the Bennett news was a bright, electrifying omen. Since his early days as a Ford family bodyguard responsible for protecting the grandchildren against kidnapppers, ex-fighter Bennett had built a secret-police-like "Service Department" with about eight hundred armed toughs and somewhere over eight thousand paid informers throughout the work force. He protected the company against threats like unions. At the same time, he became Henry Ford's personal bodyguard, confidant, and trusted deputy. Nobody, not even son Edsel, could see Henry Ford without Bennett's permission and, increasingly, the answer was a flat "No." And no one knew for sure whether Bennett's orders came from Henry Ford or were Bennett's own. Ultimately, the orders that ran Ford Motor Company were Bennett's.

But for Henry II, his first official act was only a beginning. Beyond Bennett, other problems faced the company: obsolescent plants, no adequate new-model plans, and a seemingly unstanchable hemorrhaging of company funds. With paralyzing regularity, each and every month, the company Henry Ford had founded in 1903 was losing ten million dollars. Moreover, under Bennett's tyranny, the heads of engineering, styling, and purchasing had decided to clear out their desks and leave. Aside from Mead Bricker, head of production, the management echelon was a wasteland.

Fortunately for Henry II, John Bugas, the ex-FBI chief in Detroit who had been hired—then fired in a fit of pique—by Bennett, was still on the premises, ideally qualified to rid the company of the Bennett age of terrorism. Before the job was finished, he would root out more than a thousand of Bennett's enforcers.

Henry Ford II, age twenty-eight, with a background of grubby summers as a Ford shop worker, four years of engineering and sociology at Yale, and only a little over two years in Ford management, could now begin the search for a new top manager. Ernest Kanzler, Edsel Ford's brother-in-law and one-time business associate, had suggested that Ernest R. Breech would be a good choice. Beginning with a CPA background, Breech had

Eleanor Clay Ford (*left*) with
Clara and Henry Ford in
1944. (*Courtesy of Ford
Archives/Henry Ford Museum,
Dearborn, Michigan*)

revitalized one General Motors subsidiary, then had built
a brilliant record as president of Bendix Aviation Corp.,
partly owned by GM.

Breech was the essence of cordiality when young Ford
came to his office because he thought the discussion
would be about Bendix parts. Ford Motor Company was
an important customer. (Privately, Breech admitted later,
he viewed the company with a mixture of pity and contempt.) When the conversation turned to the possibility
of his joining Ford Motor Company, Breech suddenly became a completely expressionless listener and finally,
with guarded reluctance, would only agree to visit the
Ford plant and proving grounds.

At the proving grounds, in the midst of young Henry's
animated description of Ford engineering progress, ex-
CPA Breech abruptly asked to see the company's books.
He promptly discovered that a Ford comptroller did not
even know what he meant by "standard volume," that
the Ford financial record had not been audited for forty-
three years, and that much of the company's most vital
financial information had been kept by secretive Henry
Ford in scribbled notes on the backs of envelopes. Breech
was aghast. But he was also convinced that no company

Harry Bennett, Henry Ford's
trusted lieutenant. After the
death of his son Edsel, Henry
Ford had made a codicil to
his will which in effect
would have given Bennett
virtual control of the Ford
Motor Company. Unfortu-
nately for Bennett, the aging
Ford did not sign the codicil.

Henry Ford's first car, the Quadricycle, completed June 4, 1896.

BOSS OF THE ROAD

The Latest and Best

THIS new light touring car fills the demand for an automobile between a runabout and a heavy touring car. It is positively the most perfect machine on the market, having overcome all draw-backs such as smell, noise, jolt, etc., common to all other makes of Auto Carriages. It is so simple that a boy of 15 can run it.

The FORDMOBILE with detachable tonneau, $850

For beauty of finish it is unequaled—and we promise IMMEDIATE DELIVERY. We haven't space enough to enter into its mechanical detail, but if you are interested in the NEWEST and MOST ADVANCED AUTO manufactured to-day write us for particulars.

FORD MOTOR COMPANY
689 Mack Avenue   Detroit, Mich.

In September 1903, the newly-organized Ford Motor Company ran this announcement advertisement in *The Saturday Evening Post* proclaiming that the Fordmobile "is positively the most perfect machine on the market, having overcome all draw-backs such as smell, noise, jolt, etc., common to all other makes of Auto Carriages. It is so simple that a boy of 15 can run it."

Early dealerships, like this one in western Pennsylvania (circa 1904–05), carried automobiles made by several manufacturers. This one gave the Ford name big play on its building and put a Ford Model A in the center of its lineup of new offerings.

In 1909, a year after its introduction, the Ford Model T chalked up spectacular proof of its ruggedness by winning a grueling, twenty-day, New York-to-Seattle race. C. J. Smith, a Ford engineer, and driver Bert Scott capped the event with this victory lap around the University of Washington track.

In 1913, Henry Ford revolutionized industry with the moving assembly line. On the early line pictured here, the chassis (shown receiving its engine) was pushed by hand from assembly point to assembly point. The wheels on the car's left side rolled against guides, and the right rear wheel was mounted on a dolly. Mass production techniques helped cut the base price of the Model T from $850 in 1908 to $265 by 1923.

Henry Ford and his "999" race car, with Barney Oldfield driving, 1902.

This 1931 photo shows how a Ford salesman was expected to present the four-door Ford Model A to a customer. Some 4.5 million Model A's were sold between late 1927 and the end of 1931.

Ford Motor Company's top executives on April 1, 1947 (*from left to right*): John R. Davis, John S. Bugas, Benson Ford, Henry Ford II, Ernest R. Breech, Albert J. Browning, Harold T. Youngren, Lewis D. Crusoe.

in history had ever presented such a spectacular challenge to a prospective manager. He joined Ford as executive vice president on July 1, 1946, and promptly set to work to "GM-ize" the company both in management organization and with additional ex-GM executives.

When Breech was ready to talk organization, he would receive his first pleasant surprise at Ford: a freshly-prepared, highly detailed reorganization document was set down before him, and it was excellent. It had come out of a team effort, Breech was told, by the new "Thornton Group," still referred to by many at Ford as the "quiz kids" because of all their questions, but now known increasingly as the "whiz kids" on the strength of their solid contributions. Henry II had hired them in February on an "all-ten-or-nobody" basis, fresh out of the Army Air Force Office of Statistical Control, and his judgment of them was being confirmed in a spectacular way. Six of the ten, aged twenty-six to thirty-four, would ultimately rise to vice presidential level, and two others, Robert S. McNamara and Arjay Miller, would become Ford presidents.

With a sweeping reorganization under way, Henry II and Breech could turn to an equally urgent crisis: the OPA pricing problem.

At the end of World War II—despite all the wartime increases in labor rates—the federal Office of Price Administration had decreed that the 1946 cars (basically 1942 models) should be priced no higher than original tags of four years earlier. The Ford of 1946, which cost $1,041 to build, thus could sell for no more than $728. Armed with new and specific information from their new, recently-hired financial vice president, Messrs. Ford and Breech went to Washington and pleaded their case before the OPA. They failed to get the full amount of relief they wanted; but at least they got a grudging portion. After losing fifty million dollars on car sales in the first seven months of 1946, the company ended the year in the black, with a net profit of two thousand dollars.

Meanwhile, the "whiz kids" had revised all the 1947-model planning. If they had not, the company would have faced certain bankruptcy.

And the company was still waiting for its first all-new postwar car. Henry II had decided that it must have completely new styling, an upgraded V-8 engine, a new frame, new brakes, and a complete change from the transverse leaf suspension system inherited from the Model T.

The father of the Model T did not live to see the change. As the snow thawed in early April of 1947, the overflowing Rouge River flooded the private power plant of the old Ford mansion, "Fairlane." Henry Ford, who had been a Detroit Edison Company engineer before he turned to automobiles, felt a sudden call to action. According to a friend of the family, he shuffled through the icy floodwater to inspect the crippled power plant and make his own estimate of the extent of the damage. It would be the last self-reliant act of a man who had never known how to quit. On April 7, 1947, the man who had done more than anyone else to put the world on wheels was dead at eighty-three, leaving it to future historians to examine his accomplishments, eccentricities, shortcomings, and his usually-anonymous kindnesses, and draw any conclusions they pleased. He had never asked the world for any favors.

The all-new, 1949 Ford, whose styling concept

Henry II had approved in September 1946, would normally have called for a three-year development program. But there was no time for a normal pace. On June 18, 1948, the sleek, slab-sided '49 Ford went on display at New York's Waldorf-Astoria Hotel and, during that first day, the orders topped one hundred thousand. Production in calendar 1949 went beyond eight hundred thousand, and company profit for the year (with the Ford car accounting for about ninety percent of it) totalled $265 million. During the same year, the new Ford Division was organized to assemble and market all Ford-nameplate products.

Henry Ford II had also wanted a new *compact* as a companion to the '49 Ford; but Dearborn was too busy for it. The proposed design for a compact wound up as a product for the Ford operation in France to build.

Again in 1952, after interim facelifts, Ford Motor Company would introduce completely new cars—this time with the first "corporate look" extending from the Fords through Mercurys and Lincolns. To be directly competitive with General Motors, the Ford car was aimed squarely at Chevrolet; the Mercury at the Olds 88; the Lincoln at Cadillac and the Olds 98. The industry referred to them as "Ford's first GM-ized cars."

Within the next two years, with this "GM-ized" approach, Ford Motor Company would move past Chrysler Corporation into second place in the industry, would introduce a new Ford LTD with the highest level of luxury ever seen in the low-priced field, and would outsell Chevrolet for the first time in twenty years.

During the same period, Ford organized its first styling department. Founder Henry Ford had believed that styling was as frivolously unimportant to a car as it was to a farm tractor. It remained for Edsel not only to insist on a Model A, introduced in 1927, but to make it Ford's first stylish car. Edsel continued to prove his talents for directing tasteful design in such cars as the trend-setting Lincoln Zephyr of 1936 and the classic Lincoln Continental of 1939; but he had never been able to persuade his father that styling should become an official part of the business. Now, in the 1950's, it became a critical essential, not only to advance the Ford car in its own field, but to establish clear-cut identities for other nameplates to come.

Ford Motor Company, its management had decided, would have to stop being synonymous with a single line of low-priced cars. If it wanted to succeed against General Motors, Ford would have to cover the market like General Motors with the overlapping price classes of its five separate car divisions.

For its long-term good, the Ford car needed a stronger corporate parent. Ford Motor Company's three car lines (Ford, Mercury, Lincoln) were up against GM's five (Chevrolet, Pontiac, Buick, Oldsmobile, Cadillac). Even Henry Ford, Sr. had expressed a belief that Mercury should have been given a companion car to cover another price class in the increasingly broad medium-priced field. After all, GM was getting about forty-five percent of its business from the medium-priced field, and the Chrysler Corporation was getting forty-seven percent. Within those two corporations, the buyers of Chevrolets and Plymouths could graduate to something better and still remain in the corporate family. In contrast, Ford Motor Company was getting a scant seventeen percent of its business from the medium-priced field. Ford, the industry often noted, had long been busy "growing customers for General Motors."

Henry Ford II

Henry Ford II, in the fall of 1948, had initiated a program aimed at launching a second nameplate in the medium-priced field. "When a company has two or more entries in that field," he said, "the result is to strengthen the sales of *all* its car lines."

He set his sights on a 1952-model introduction, but the Korean War blocked his plan. The first full-size clay model was not unveiled until mid-August 1955, with the first cars scheduled to arrive in dealer showrooms in September 1957. Over the objections of Henry II—and his brothers Benson and William Clay Ford, both of whom were now active in Ford management—the project managers had named the car "Edsel."

It was the industry's first completely new line of cars, with a brand-new nameplate, in nineteen years, and the public crowded to see it. Then, to Ford's great chagrin,

First Edsel, 1958 model.

public reaction to the Edsel slowly turned to apathy laced with ridicule. Two years and two months later, after production of only 110,847 units, the career of the Edsel came to an abrupt end. Cost of the venture: $250 million in invested capital, plus $200 million lost during production, for a total of $450 million. To the Edsel buyers who now possessed orphans, Ford contritely mailed certificates each good for three hundred dollars against the purchase of any other Ford company product.

What had gone wrong? To this day, industry observers do not all agree, but they offer at least four possibilities (and whatever combinations you would like to make of them): (1) between the start and finish of the Edsel program, car-buying patterns had undergone a revolutionary change, with compacts quadrupling their sales, with imports soaring from fewer than fifty thousand a year to more than six hundred thousand, and with the medium-priced field sliding from 36.7 percent to 24.9 percent of the total car market; (2) Edsel styling, which had impressed so many viewers of the clay model as nothing short of "sensational," had been modified, in the interest of production economics, by the application of Mercury and Ford components; (3) workmanship of the early production cars was sloppy; and (4) the Edsel arrived just as the surprisingly sudden recession of 1958 chopped the total car market down to nearly half its former size.

For whatever the reason, the Edsel fiasco was there for the whole world to see—and many of the onlookers promptly put it down as a classic case of upper echelon mismanagement. Actually, the Edsel venture had these important payoffs for Ford: the availability of Edsel production facilities not only advanced the introduction of the compact Falcon by a full year, but made it possible for Ford to meet the heavy post-1958 recession demand, extending into 1962, for Ford and Mercury cars. Further, because Edsel commitments had been made in 1956, the facilities that served so well in the 1959–62 period had all been acquired with cheaper 1956 dollars. As a miscellaneous final note, Edsel engine tooling, not applicable to Falcon, Ford or Mercury, was put to good use in a Ford tractor plant in Europe.

Meanwhile, Ford Motor Company had shaken up the entire industry with its introduction of two Thunderbirds. The first, a 1955 two-passenger model, became America's first volume-built "personal" car, attracted buyers away from even the highest-priced competition, and soon won a place in the auto history books as a classic collector's item. The second "T-Bird," a 1958 four-passenger model, was sold as "the first personal luxury car." Together, the two Thunderbirds shook the foundations of the industry's traditional price class compartments, which traced all the way back to the time when big cars were more reliable and more comfortable than small cars. Rather than becoming just two more cars in the massive medium-priced field, the T-Birds created a distinctive new "personal car" market for Ford.

The 1950's had begun with the still pent-up demand of the war years, followed by a period of affluence. Reflecting and to some extent leading the public mood, cars became bigger with much more chrome. New superhighways invited the creation of new brute-powered engines. Status symbolism ran riot. And everybody, it seemed, had the comfortable conviction that cheap gasoline, at about thirty cents a gallon, would flow forever.

But even while his company was following General Motors' lead, Henry Ford II was looking over and beyond GM at another interesting part of the world. He would soon stick his neck out by predicting that the European Economic Community—the Common Market—would soon overtake and surpass the United States as a market for cars. In time, he ventured, U.S. designs and European designs would converge and create some new concept of a "world" car.

Under the influence of General Motors, which sold more than half the total, U.S. cars had been growing steadily larger. More and more, Ford Motor Company was being penalized by its small-car image and by its limited representation in the medium-priced field.

Back when assembly lines and other automation brought dramatic economies to car production, Henry Ford, who started it all, had elected to go the route of "the same car for less money," ultimately bringing the price of the Model T from its original 1908 price tag of $850 to an all-time low in 1923 of $265. With that approach, Ford by 1921 was selling more than half of all the cars sold in the United States. But Ford sales, after peaking in 1923 with 1.8 million cars, had gone into a rapid decline as Chevrolet announced a new six and Chrysler Corporation readied its new Plymouth. Just plain transportation at a bargain price, Ford found out, was not enough. General Motors had seen a more rewarding future in going the route of "more car for the same (or a little more) money." In time, GM would be able to point proudly to the fact that its newest Chevrolet package was larger, roomier, and more powerful than its Cadillac of not too many years earlier.

The motoring public compared the two approaches and elected to go with General Motors. Ultimately, GM would be building and selling more cars each year than all other makers combined. Among the many benefits of this domination, to GM, was a basic kind of sales leverage: by flooding the market each year with the General Motors' corporate concept of what the year's styling keynotes ought to be, GM could make the offering of minority manufacturers look tame, strange, or out-of-date. Only occasionally, as in the case of the Chrysler tail fins, would GM acknowledge—and promptly adopt—the styling leadership of a smaller competitor.

When, in the late 1950's, the smaller, simpler, less-gaudy European cars began surging into the U.S. market—from lands that had long ago accepted congested traffic and high-priced gasoline as a way of life—the U.S. market began a slow turn in the direction of the traditionally Ford kind of car.

Ford, in the fall of 1959—with an assist from the Edsel production facilities—was ready to meet the imports head-on with its 1960 Falcon. Henry Ford II now had the compact he had wanted for 1949. The tastefully clean Falcon, with sturdy, welded one-piece construction and its own new six-cylinder engine, went on to set a new record for the sales of a new nameplate in its first year and achieved clear-cut domination of the compact field.

As a second shake-up of industry styling patterns, Ford followed the Falcon with a 1961 Econoline van. Painters and plumbers—then campers—then the youthful "Keep on Truckin' " generation—would soon climb aboard, ultimately making it even more popular than sports cars.

As a third trend-maker, Ford introduced the 1962 Fairlane, sized midway between the compact and the standard-size Ford. It was initially referred to as "super compact" or "in-between," but the official designation became "intermediate"—and "intermediate" was solidly established as a new industry price class.

When Ernest Breech resigned from the Ford presidency in July 1960, saying his work was finished, though he would continue as a director, he had assured himself of a place in the record books as the principal strategist of the most spectacular comeback in all industrial history. Of the man who had persuaded him to accept the Ford challenge, Henry Ford II, Breech said, "He has the business acumen of his grandfather and the humaneness of his father."

Breech was succeeded as president by Robert S. McNamara. But McNamara was gone within a month to serve as President John F. Kennedy's Secretary of Defense. Henry Ford II reassumed the presidency just in time to face another major issue: racing.

To the company, the subject was far from new. Henry Ford, the founder, had always believed that "a car should sell itself" and, in his day, the most effective way was with racing victories. The ex-farm boy had learned how to build and drive racing cars; had then taught Barney Oldfield, famous bicycle racer, how to operate a gas-powered vehicle; and the two of them, with their "999" racer, had set out to make "Ford" a nationally known word. By the morning of January 12, 1904, on the ice of Lake St. Clair, Henry Ford was ready for the most ambitious of all his racing efforts.

The start was bad. At about sixty miles an hour and accelerating fast, "999" hit a hump in the ice, sailed into the air, then came crashing down into a wild, sickening swerve. Ford fought his tiller, regained control as he entered the measured mile, and roared through the frosty air to a new world speed record of 91.39 m.p.h. The event promptly dominated the sports sections of every U.S. newspaper, and more people bought Ford cars.

In the 1950's, the automobile industry was suddenly involved, like it or not, in stock car racing. It all could be traced back to the time, years before, when moonshiners began souping up their cars to out-run the revenuers. Inevitably, as something to do for excitement on a Sunday, the moonshiners with the best hot-rods were competing in public on local tracks; and soon the perennial winners were suggesting to Detroit that hot-rod sponsorship might be the key to a lot of publicity. The industry agreed—all but General Motors, which had too little to gain and too much to lose by laying its reputation on the line in those wild, unpredictable, unprofessional races.

America's most vocal advocates of highway safety soon allied themselves with GM. In 1957, to silence the critics, automakers adopted an antiracing resolution, though with far less than industrywide enthusiasm. Racing victories translated immediately into better sales—as Pontiac, first to violate the ban, would soon reaffirm.

Henry Ford II, closely watching the Pontiac experi-

The Ford GT Mark II scores a 1-2-3 finish in the 1966 twenty-four hours of LeMans.

ence, decided his company should withdraw from the industry agreement. Ford Motor Company's long involvement in Europe's highly respected motor-sports programs had been too successful, he felt, to be limited to Europe. In 1962, Ford mounted the most ambitious high-performance program in industry history, and the results came fast.

At the Daytona 500, in 1963, Fords finished 1-2-3-4-5. At Indianapolis, in 1965, Lotus-Ford cars recorded a 1-2-3-4 sweep of the great "500" and set a new Indy record of 150.686 m.p.h. At Le Mans, France, the next year, three Ford GT sports cars finished 1-2-3 in the twenty-four hour endurance race. The basic Ford Grand Prix engine ultimately won 110 Grand Prix events to become the all-time leader in that field, later won eight world championships—then, turbocharged for America, went on to dominate the Indianapolis 500 from that time forward. Not until the late 1960's did the checkered flag come down for the last time for the U.S. Fords. Their motor-sports involvement continued in Europe; but in the United States, the nation's now critical concern about exhaust emissions made racing a symbol of arrogant disregard for the public welfare. By then, however, Ford had made its point about performance.

And never, during that period, had Ford staked all its

success on racing. In mid-1964, another new Ford styling concept came riding into the auto market over a route smoothly paved by the Thunderbirds and the racing victories. Ford called it the Mustang, a "low-priced, four-passenger sports car." It drew 100,000 orders within its first one hundred days and went on to first-year sales of 418,812. The Mustang would be followed by two additional "pony" cars, the Maverick of 1969 and the Pinto, Ford's first modern-day subcompact.

Back at the start of postwar production, the Ford car was at the bottom of the nameplate ladder, with three medium-priced classes above it. Now the medium-priced classes were being squeezed, and the standard-size Ford had three new price classes *below* it. Thus Ford's razzle-dazzle decade of the 1960's was coming to a triumphant close in the United States—and something even more important was happening in Europe.

Out of Henry Ford II's growing interest in Europe, the company in 1960 had bought full ownership of its partly-controlled Ford Ltd. at Dagenham, England, a place Henry II had visited as a boy when his father, Edsel, took him over for the laying of the cornerstone. By 1962, Ford was teaming Dagenham with its operation in Cologne, Germany, in the development of dual-source cars for the Common Market. By 1967, Ford of Europe, Inc. became a reality and, in the following year, the Escort would become the first new Ford car to be shared by the English and German plants. It was successful; but it was also criticized as being an "Anglo-Saxon" rather than a truly "European" car. A year later, Europeans greeted the sporty new Ford Capri as *their* kind of car; the Capri would become to Europeans what the Mustang had been to Americans.

And all the while, the international marketplace was more than living up to the early expectations of Henry Ford II. In 1950, North American manufacturers had dominated the world market with a share of eighty-five percent. By the close of 1970, the share score was dramatically different: North American automakers, forty-one percent; other automakers of the world, fifty-nine percent.

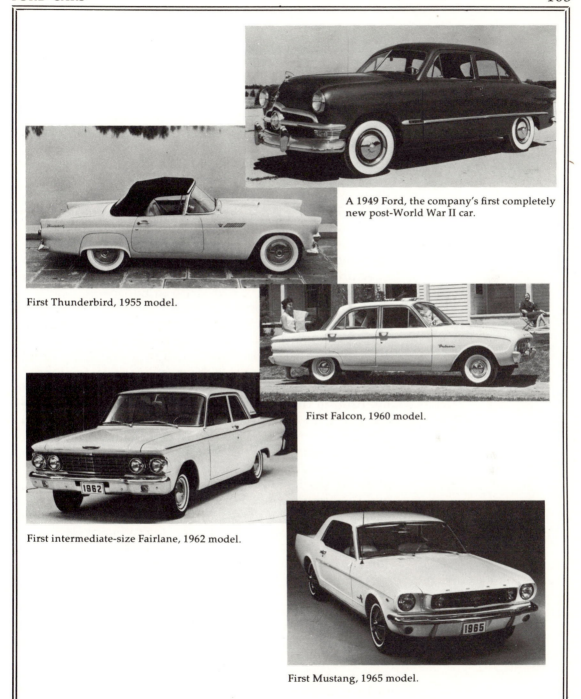

A 1949 Ford, the company's first completely new post-World War II car.

First Thunderbird, 1955 model.

First Falcon, 1960 model.

First intermediate-size Fairlane, 1962 model.

First Mustang, 1965 model.

For the entire U.S. automotive industry, the 1970's would become the decade of downsizing, and Ford would do its share of it, along with launching a major additional compact line, the Fairmont. Under new regulations from the U.S. Environmental Protection Agency, created in December 1970 to clean up the environment, automobile manufacturers would be required, by 1985, to build cars averaging 27.5 miles per gallon. The specific timetable for progress in that direction: 1978, 18 m.p.g.; 1979, 19 m.p.g.; 1980, 20 m.p.g. To the U.S. auto industry, still agonized by the EPA's earlier emissions control requirements, the fuel economy decree was nothing less than catastrophic. For Ford, the decree was much less shocking; it was comparable in many ways to what Ford already had learned to cope with in Europe.

The European Economic Community or Common Market (Germany, France, Italy, Belgium, the Netherlands, and Luxembourg) had come into being on January 1, 1958, with tariff restrictions to follow a year later. Great Britain, Sweden, Denmark, Norway, Austria, Switzerland, and Portugal—the "Outer Seven"—had responded by forming the European Free Trade Area. To Ford, operating in both the Common Market and the EFTA would ultimately force the company to meet some eight hundred separate national requirements.

As the EEC and EFTA attained solid form, Ford ranked as one of the leaders in Great Britain, Germany, Belgium and the Netherlands, but was still a virtual unknown in France and Italy, where fiscal regulations favored mini-sized economy cars. If Ford intended to maintain and strengthen its position in Europe, it would have to become one of the leaders in France and Italy—and also move into Spain, where imports from any other country were totally banned.

The only realistic answer to the problem, Ford concluded, was to build a "world" car. Ford had been tussling with the "world" car idea since the early 1960's. Numerous studies had been made, and all met the same management decision: not economically feasible. Then, in 1970, the Ford design center at Dunton, England, had come up with an intriguing new mini-car proposal, and a

Ford's first "world" car, the Fiesta, introduced in 1976.

Dearborn feasibility study of it confirmed that Dunton was on the right track—even though the cost projections were staggering.

The Dunton team was promptly given task-force support, not only from Dearborn, but from Dunton's opposite number in Merkenich, Germany, because creating a proper small car is not just a matter of scaling down a large one. It begins with a clean slate and no preconceived notions, then proceeds with in-depth studies of economics, aerodynamics, aesthetics—and ergonomics, the aspects of technology relating to the mutual adjustment of man and the machine. The job of the mini-car design-concept teams—comprised of research engineers, production engineers, cost analysts, and (later) stylists— was to begin with ergonomic considerations and develop the functional portion of a car (with in-built aerodynamic qualities), then apply a sound aesthetic concept to the functional package.

To be systematic in developing a new car concept, under Ford guidelines, meant agreeing on basic specifications, then breaking the overall job into some fourteen subsystems, such as engine, suspension, transmission, brakes, steering, and bodywork. The subsystems, in turn, would be worked on by specialist teams who would begin by reducing a subsystem to its individual components. Being systematic, in the case of the new Ford mini-car, also meant buying thirty competitive subcompacts and stripping them down to their last bolt and nut for analysis of weights, strengths, and costs.

On December 3, 1973, the combined results of all the English, German and U.S. development work were brought to the Ford board of directors for an awesome decision: the board was asked to invest over one billion dollars—the largest one-car outlay in automotive history—to produce the smallest car the company had ever made. Ford directors, satisfied that almost a decade of searching, in-depth questions had all been answered, gave their approval.

The project called for a "world" car, Ford's first truly universal car since the Model T, which could be sold— and perhaps produced—in any country, including those of the Third World. The car would be less than twelve feet long and not over fifteen hundred pounds, but it would carry four adults and a reasonable amount of luggage, have a maximum speed of 55–60 m.p.h., and a price tag no higher than sixty percent of Ford's successful Escort. Production was projected at 250,000 per year and called for assembly in Germany, England, and in a new plant yet to be built in Spain, with components coming from those plants and from others in France and Ireland.

By the end of 1973, Ford had become the strongest of the American automakers in Europe—and the new "world" mini-car was scheduled for introduction in 1976.

The new Ford mini-car concept was now plunged into a massive program of consumer opinion research—a series of "clinics" in which motorists, carefully qualified as potential mini-car buyers by door-to-door interviewing, would be given a chance to see Ford concept cars alongside typical competitive cars, make their own comparisons, and express their opinions. Plans were drawn for clinics in each of five countries—Germany, France, Italy, England, and Spain—then abruptly changed because it would take too much time to trundle the cars around Europe. Instead, it was decided to exhibit the cars in one central location and fly the "judges" there, all expenses paid.

Lausanne, Switzerland, was chosen as the best central location. To Lausanne's Palais de Beaulieu, during the first two weekends of December 1972, Ford brought seven hundred consumer judges from the five countries to examine, compare and express their conclusions about seven cars, all painted white to remove color bias, and all stripped of nameplate identification. Three of the cars were Ford concepts—one styled by Ford's think-tank Ghia studio in Turin, Italy, and two from the styling studio in Dearborn (one with front-wheel drive, the other with conventional rear-wheel drive). The competitive cars were Fiat 127, Renault 5, Peugeot 104, and Honda Civic.

On the basis of detailed ratings by the consumer judges on appearance, comfort, efficiency, and safety, the Ford concept cars out-scored all the others. Within the Ford trio, the Turin design was favored for its front end; the Dearborn front-wheel drive design was favored for its sides and rear; and the front-wheel drive was unanimously favored over the conventional rear-wheel drive. Ford moved immediately into follow-up clinics at San Mateo, California and São Paolo, Brazil (to which Argentines also were invited), and drew the same basic reactions.

All this while, marketing research of another kind was being conducted to determine more precisely what the market potential would be, and what percentage of it would be new, added, "conquest" business, i.e., taken from the competition and not just diverted from the Escort and other Fords.

Ford's new "world" car now had everything but a name. Lists of name suggestions had been prepared and finalist names had been selected; but the final choice, by his order, would be made by Henry Ford II. "The last time I left it to a committee," he said, "they chose the wrong name for a new car."

He studied the five finalist names—Bravo, Fiesta, Amigo, Stada, and Pony—reflecting on how well they would be understood in a wide range of countries, and speaking them aloud to get a feel for their sounds. The first two had tied for first place in opinion research tests; but Fiesta had a legal complication: it had once been used by Oldsmobile and was still that company's property. Henry Ford II promptly phoned Thomas A. Murphy, chairman and chief executive of General Motors. The conversation was both pleasant and decisive. "You want Fiesta?" said Murphy. "It's yours."

Exactly on schedule, at the end of May 1976, the first production Fiesta rolled off the assembly line at Saarlouis, Germany. In September, the Fiesta was on display throughout Europe. By the following fall, more than five hundred thousand Fiestas had been built and sold to make it the most successful new car in European motor history. And Philip Caldwell, who had been playing a key strategist's role in the Fiesta program and other Ford international efforts, would soon be in line for even more responsibility.

Philip Caldwell

Back in Dearborn, as Ford Motor Company entered the 1980's, it had grown to be one of the top multinational companies, with manufacturing, assembly and sales operations in thirty countries; with sales of about one billion dollars in every ten-day period; and with approximately half a million employees. Dealers, worldwide, numbered about 11,600. Ford stock, first made available to the public in 1956, was now owned by more than three hundred thousand shareholders.

The company had greatly expanded the iron and steel operations founder Henry Ford had started back when he dreamed of making every component of a Ford car, and had gone on to become a major force in glass, vinyl, and paint as well. The company also had become one of the leaders in aerospace, a sequel to the time when Edsel Ford took the company into its Ford Tri-Motor and other early aviation activities. Among numerous other Ford ventures: a Ford land-development company whose first project was Detroit's spectacular Renaissance Center, founded by Henry Ford II as one way to help revitalize his home town. It became the largest privately-financed development in the world.

But the company's backbone activity continues to be cars and trucks—and, of course, tractors, something the original Henry Ford was experimenting with long before he turned to automobiles. Grandson Henry II had continued the tradition from 1945 until he turned his chief executive duties over to Philip Caldwell in the fall of

Detroit skyline, with the new Renaissance Center, the first project of a Ford land-development company, at right.

1979; and he expects to look out from his position on the board of directors and see the tradition extend far into the future.

"By the year 2000," he says, "we expect to be building three types of cars: small, two-and-three passenger cars for urban use; five-and six-passenger freeway cars, smaller than the ones of today; and functional and recreational vehicles. There will be some small electrical vehicles for urban use; but the basic power plant will be the familiar internal combustion engine for at least twenty-five years.

"You can never progress too far in this business. Somewhere along the line, there's always something more. Our job is to find it, refine it, and get the public accustomed to it."

MARKETING INSIGHTS

At the time Henry Ford II was elected its president, Ford Motor Company was on the brink of becoming the greatest ruin in all industrial history. Its plants were obsolete; it had no adequate new-model plans; it was losing ten million dollars a month; and, worst of all, its management team had faded away. The company's return to successful operations within four years thus ranks as industrial history's most remarkable comeback.

As his first step in the turnaround, Henry II heeded the

advice to "GM-ize" his company: apply the organization and operating principles that had made General Motors so successful, and recruit GM management talent.

This "me-too" follower approach put Ford Motor back in a stronger, more competitive position; but the company continued to be severely penalized by its small-car image and its limited representation in the then prosperous, medium-priced field. The effort to establish a new brand (Edsel) in the medium-priced field was a bitter disappointment. Meanwhile, however, the company had broken down some old, conventional price class barriers with its introduction of two "lifestyle cars," the two-passenger and four-passenger Thunderbirds of 1955 and 1958, which together created a new "personal car" market for Ford.

Ford scored another victory for its lifestyle cars in the mid-1960's with its Mustang. It buttressed its total company leadership stance during the same decade with racing successes and with the introduction of the compact Falcon, the intermediate Fairlane and the subcompact Pinto. During a time when imports were undermining the traditional U.S. medium-priced field, Ford thus was establishing three new price classes below its standard-size Ford car.

In the same era, Ford Motor was looking beyond the U.S. market and beginning to plan a "world" car. In the burgeoning European market—where a small-car image was a major advantage, and where Ford had better name recognition than other U.S.-based auto makers—Ford Motor moved ahead of GM in the mid-1960's and then proceeded to strengthen its position as an international company with the 1976 introduction of its "world" car, the Ford Fiesta.

As a marketer, at the time Henry Ford II arrived, Ford Motor Company had long been stereotyped by founder Henry Ford's often-quoted remark, "They can have any color they want, as long as it's black." The senior Ford's single-minded purpose was to build a reliable car at the lowest possible price for "the average man," and he frankly admitted he had no interest in consumer opinions about style and color. He believed a car should publicize itself with its performance, and regarded advertising as a necessary evil.

Under Henry Ford II, the company's attitude toward marketing made an abrupt turnabout. The planning of the Mustang, for example, involved a broad variety of attitude studies covering design, size, performance characteristics, interior arrangement, and price. Design clinics were held to recheck design decisions. The Mustang markets were delineated as "young people, young marrieds, sophisticates, older groups still 'young at heart,' and families with two or more cars." A marketing program was planned for each of these market segments.

To maintain its feel of consumer opinion on a continuing basis, Ford Motor Company conducts phone and mail surveys, shopping mall "intercepts" where selected types of prospects are questioned, group discussions, and design clinics where consumers are invited to evaluate actual prototype vehicles. Supplementary attitude research includes a National New Car Buyer Study, conducted a few months into each model year, covering demographic details on car buyers and their patterns of switching to or from Ford Motor Company products.

When the new models are introduced, the company's advertising campaigns are augmented by extensive "visibility" programs; the cars are displayed at shopping malls, airport terminals, and other high-traffic locations; cars are provided for test drives and reviews by top automotive magazine writers, and offered as prizes for contests and sports events; still other cars are made available to motion picture and television production companies for use in movies and TV programs.

With the coming of Ford's "world" car, the Fiesta, all consumer studies are now being conducted on a global scale.

GERBER BABY FOODS

"We had to be expert about babies as well as baby foods."

Daniel F. Gerber, who gave his wife a helping hand and soon found himself in the baby foods business. (At Dorothy Gerber's request, no photos of her are available for publication.)

13 Dan Gerber surveyed the suppertime scene in his kitchen and glanced nervously at the clock on the wall. He and Dorothy were due at a social engagement, and here she was, arms and apron speckled with green, patiently preparing a serving of strained peas for seven-month-old daughter Sally. Dan cleared his throat, a bit noisily. Dorothy looked up, read his expression and smiled. "Here," she said, "if you'll just finish this, I'll go get dressed." Twenty minutes later, Daniel F. Gerber, professional canner of vegetables and fruits, grumbled softly to himself that the straining of peas was a uniquely frustrating chore. It was 1927, and Dorothy's pediatrician had said the time had come for a basic change in baby feeding: from a liquid diet during most of the first year to the feeding of solid foods—all strained, of course—within the first six months.

The next morning, in the cutting room of the family-owned Fremont (Michigan) Canning Company, Dan gathered a formidable assortment of straining utensils, opened a can of Fremont's most tender peas—and once again became a study in instant frustration. By week's end, he was asking his father, Frank, if he thought mothers around the country would welcome a line of commercially-prepared baby foods.

Frank Gerber frowned. The company was working at peak capacity. But Frank was a man who often reminded himself that his family had started with a tanning business when Fremont was surrounded by forests. When the forests gave way to farming, the Gerbers had the flexibility to make a fresh start in the food business. So Dan got the go-ahead he expected, and the Gerber production men were soon putting together some sample batches of strained vegetables and fruits.

Sally Gerber would be the first tester. (The Gerber's other daughter, Scotti, at three years of age, was judged a

Left: Flavor conference. What these professionals decide will not become final until panels of babies agree. **Right:** Gerber flavor tester at work.

bit "sophisticated" for objective testing.) Sally would soon be joined on the "panel" by the babies of other Fremont Canning Company families, and their lip-smacking reactions would be translated as "Better than home-prepared." The reasons for the definite preference, Dan Gerber concluded, were that his plant could obtain fresher produce than was available at stores, and that fast commercial straining and cooking excluded enough air to make a noticeable difference in flavor.

In a town of two thousand people, this supposedly confidential experiment was soon bringing requests for samples, and the samples were bringing questions of "Where can we buy more?" Frank and Dan Gerber soon had a decision to make.

Cautiously, in the summer of 1928, Dan Gerber packaged a sample line of the new strained foods and took it to the family pediatrician. The pediatrician listened carefully to Dan's report on new processing techniques and sales predictions. The doctor then stated flatly that Dan was badly underestimating the potential for this product. In subsequent talks with home economists, Dan Gerber heard the same favorable comments.

But some wise business friends were saying, at the same time, that the baby foods would be a dangerous move. "You have a fine reputation with the trade and with consumers," they said. "One bad mistake, in something as sensitive as baby foods, could break your company." And Dan soon found that he was not the first person with the concept of commercially-prepared baby foods. They were already on the shelves of some eastern drug stores at thirty-five cents a container.

Nevertheless, Dan decided to go ahead with a national survey; and, even as the results trickled in, he was readying a line of five varieties: peas, prunes, carrots, and spinach, to sell in 4.5-ounce cans for fifteen cents each, and a 10.5-ounce can of vegetable soup with beef to sell for twenty-five cents. He planned to market through grocery channels, not just because the Fremont Canning Company was established there, but because food wholesalers and retailers could be expected to operate at low profit margins and hold the prices down.

The survey results confirmed his hunch that mothers would indeed like prepared baby foods—*if* they were reasonably priced and could be bought during a regular grocery-shopping trip. But the survey, to many food brokers, was far from convincing. "How many mothers," they asked, "would pay fifteen cents for a 4.5-ounce can of strained peas when an 18-ounce can of regular peas is selling for a dime?" Only a few brokers were genuinely enthusiastic about the prospects.

Dan promptly hired one of the enthusiasts as Gerber's new baby foods sales manager, and allocated funds for a three-month national advertising campaign to start in late 1928.

Because the advertising budget was severely limited, the advertisements would have to be small—and that was an extra reason, Dan decided, for including an illustration of a healthy, happy baby as a quick attention-getter. A variety of such illustrations was collected for review— all of them colorful, life-size oil paintings, meticulously finished to the last brush stroke. Then, at the last moment, artist Dorothy Hope Smith submitted a small, unfinished charcoal sketch of a baby's head. "If this baby's age is about right," she told the Gerbers, "I'll go ahead with the painting."

When the judges saw the little sketch amid the lavish display of oils, they agreed unanimously that it should not be touched in any way. Ultimately, it would be established as an official trademark, reprints of it would be in continuing demand, and surveys would indicate that it was "America's best-known baby."

Along with the baby picture, the little advertisements displayed a coupon offer of six cans of Gerber Strained Vegetables for one dollar. The coupon asked for the name and address of the mother's grocer as well as her own. Returns were good. Food brokers called on grocery wholesalers with coupons in hand, and orders began to materialize. Within sixty days after the advertisements appeared, Gerber could see the beginnings of national distribution; within six months, the product was on grocery shelves in most major areas. By the end of the first selling year, in October of 1929, Gerber stepped up its production schedules and expanded its advertising—just days before the stock market collapsed and the country began to slide into the Great Depression.

The Fremont Canning Company faced a critical decision: should it suspend the new, relatively high-priced baby food line in order to maintain strong promotion behind its mainstay adult food line? Frank and Dan Gerber decided to gamble. They accelerated their promotion of the baby food line, installed an experimental kitchen, and set up a fully-equipped research laboratory. As soon as sales were moving steadily upward, they added still another program: agricultural technicians were hired to work with growers, experimental stations, and agricultural colleges to improve the crops for Gerber and add to the variety of the line. By 1932, the original five varieties had been expanded with tomatoes, green beans, beets, and canned cereal for a total of nine.

At about the same time, Gerber's success brought some aggressive competition into the baby food business. After the initial shock, Dan Gerber watched the effects of the competition and decided it was a boon. Later he would report: "To sell our product in volume, we had to educate

This unfinished charcoal sketch, submitted on speculation by artist Dorothy Hope Smith, became "America's best-known baby."

consumers about the convenience and nutritional advantages of commercially-prepared baby foods. Our competitors helped to carry a part of that responsibility. With competition, our share of the baby foods industry reached much greater volume than we could have attained had we been operating alone."

But there was still another and more important lesson to be learned from that early competitive period: "If we were going to maintain leadership against the food giants entering the field," Gerber concluded, "we had to be expert about babies as well as baby foods." Gerber expanded its close relationship with the medical and dietetic professions; provided them with a series of noncommercial infant care booklets for distribution in doctors' offices, hospitals, and clinics; and ultimately set up a fully-staffed Professional Services Department. The early infant care educational program was extended with noncommercial publications for dieticians and home economics teachers and students in high schools and colleges; and tens of thousands of mothers were invited to participate, with their babies, in Gerber flavor and variety research panels.

In the early years, it was Dorothy Gerber who answered all consumer questions. Examples included: "How can milk stains be removed from a bib?" . . . "What toys would you suggest for a four-month-old baby?" . . . "How do you teach a baby to take regular naps?" In time, the incoming personal mail would reach a level of twenty thousand letters a month. Many were classic testimonials; but never were these mothers' letters used in Gerber advertising. To Dorothy Gerber, the correspondence was "personal," between two mothers.

By 1941, the volume of baby foods overtook the adult canned foods and the Fremont Canning Company changed its name to the Gerber Products Company. Two years later, the company discontinued its adult food line in favor of promoting baby foods exclusively—complete with a new slogan: "Babies are our business—our only business."

At about the same time, acquisition of a plant in Oakland, California, provided the Gerbers with a West Coast

Left: Hydrostatic cookers call for a sixty-foot tower; but each cooker can handle one hundred thousand jars of baby food at a time. **Right:** To enhance its expertise, Gerber opened the world's first research center devoted exclusively to baby foods and baby needs.

Gerber agricultural research extends from planting to harvesting, and has helped to develop new strains of fruits and vegetables.

production and research facility. Subsequently, food processing plants were added in Rochester, New York; Asheville, North Carolina; and Ft. Smith, Arkansas.

The baby boom of World War II was about to carry Gerber to new volume levels it had never thought attainable. Dan Gerber initiated plans for new acreage and additional plants. The post-war surge continued into and through the 1950's. In the early 1960's, Gerber would enter into an agreement with Corn Products Company, a leading food producer with extensive international operations, to produce Gerber baby foods in Europe—where the market, to Dan Gerber, seemed to be in about the same pioneering stage as the U.S. market of 1928.

Also on the international scene, Gerber subsidiaries were established in Canada, Mexico, Costa Rica, and Venezuela, as well as licensees in Australia, the Philippines, and South Africa, and a joint venture in Brazil.

The baby boom was spectacular; but, to Gerber marketing planners, it was a source of apprehension as well as joy. Sociologists were viewing the boom as part of the wartime philosophy of "make love while you can, for tomorrow we may die." It could be a short-lived phenomenon.

Back in the depths of the Depression, Dan Gerber had said: "If we were going to maintain leadership against the food giants entering the field, we had to be expert about babies as well as baby foods." By applying that conviction, year after year, his company had won an enviable level of trust among America's mothers. Long before Dan Gerber's death, in 1974, he and his marketing planners—looking ahead to the time when the birth rate would flatten out, or even decline—could see a broad choice of future growth plans, including: (1) they could sell more baby items to their present customers by adding nonfood as well as food products to the line; (2) they could expand their distribution of baby items beyond grocery channels into drug, infant specialty and department stores; and (3) they could resume the marketing of adult foods.

Gerber's first move toward diversification was made in 1957, with the addition of vinyl bibs and pants to the product line. The program would continue with introductions of nursers, baby stretchwear, outer garments and sleepwear, vaporizers, humidifiers, baby shampoo and powder, stuffed toy animals, and even life insurance, sold by mail to the families on Gerber's extensive mailing lists. Gerber took still another new step with the opening of Gerber Child Care Centers in major cities, offering not just baby-sitting services, but nursery school training. By the end of the 1970's, Gerber was doing about four hundred million dollars in sales and had some eight thousand employees.

Early in its career, Gerber began indoctrinating its employees with the basic guideline: "Babies are the most important people." What was not known in 1928 was the extent to which babies also qualify as the "smartest" people. Many years later, child psychologists would find that the "sensitive periods" when children could best learn specific skills came as early as age one and a half for development of oral language, and as early as age two for concern with its daily routines.

Obviously, as those wise young creatures grew to full consumer status, their goodwill and purchasing power would be sought by a multitude of brands. And in a spectacular number of cases, it would turn out that Gerber had been the first to earn their favor.

MARKETING INSIGHTS

Gerber Baby Foods offered mothers a work-saving way to feed their babies better; but the price of the product was relatively high, and most mothers were not vitally concerned about nutrition. To help establish baby food as an "everyday" rather than a "specialty" product—and to hold the retail price down—Gerber moved into grocery stores instead of drug stores. Later, the growing number of competitors helped Gerber with the educational job and thus expanded the market for everybody in the pioneering baby food industry.

Gerber maintained leadership in the field not only by offering a greater variety of products, but by building a reputation for being "the company that knows and cares the most about your baby's needs." Winning customer trust called for educational aids for teachers, consumer advisory panels, and extensive individual correspondence with mothers.

Social change played a dynamic part in the Gerber story: the baby boom following World War II was a giant bonus; but then came the years of declining birth rates. Fortunately for Gerber, the loyalty it had built among mothers enabled the company to diversify successfully into nonfood baby products and even into the operation of child care centers.

GILLETTE RAZORS

"I was a dreamer . . . I didn't know enough to quit."

King Gillette, as he was pictured on more than one hundred billion blade wrappers.

14 To a behavioral scientist, the clean-shaven face is a kind of "cosmetic mutilation," somewhat akin to tattooing, whereas the beard since ancient times has represented the "noble" qualities of manhood and strength. Nevertheless, man began fashioning razors of bronze and volcanic glass as early as 3500 B.C., and the practice of shaving—always subject to changing fashions throughout the world—would become a solidly-established custom with the restoration of the dandified King Charles II to England's throne in 1660.

None of this history, however, had any influence on King Camp Gillette, who was destined to do more than any other individual to popularize and perpetuate the clean-shaven face. When King Gillette invented the safety razor, in 1895, he was simply following the hard-headed business advice of William Painter, inventor of the bottle cap. Painter had hired Gillette as a traveling salesman for his company, only to find that Gillette, despite his successful record as a salesman, had spent most of his thirty-nine years trying to become an inventor instead. Somewhat testily, after one long evening discussion of the problems of the would-be inventor, Painter had urged, "Why don't you think of something like the Crown Cork (bottle cap)? When once used, it is thrown away, and the customer keeps coming back for more."

Gillette protested, "It's easy to give that kind of advice, Mr. Painter, but how many things are there like corks, pins and needles?" "You don't know," Mr. Painter persisted, "but it won't do any harm to think about it."

Gillette did more than think about it. From that moment, Gillette later recalled, he became "obsessed" with the idea of inventing something that would be used and then thrown away, and he applied the thought to nearly every material need. But not until four years later did he have the experience he described in these terms: "On one particular morning, when I started to shave, I found my razor dull; and it was not only dull, but it was beyond the point of successful stropping. . . . As I stood there with the razor in my hand, my eyes resting on it as lightly as a bird settling down on its nest, the Gillette razor was born. I saw it all in a moment . . . and it has never changed in form or principle involved—only in refinements."

In that inspired moment of invention, in 1895, King Gillette visualized a razor as a blade, sharpened on its two opposite edges (to double the service), held by "clamping plates" to which a handle would be attached. That was the concept. But then it took eight years—and the technical help of William E. Nickerson, a graduate of M.I.T.—to perfect the safety razor and bring it to market. Of this long time of testing, Gillette later wrote: "If I had been technically trained, I would have quit. But I was a dreamer . . . I didn't know enough to quit."

During its first year of marketing (1903), the Gillette Safety Razor Company sold 51 razors and 168 blades. During its second year, it sold 90,884 razors and 123,648 blades, and was awarded a U.S. patent on the razor.

During its third year, while razor sales were rising four hundred percent and blade sales were soaring a thousand percent, the Company opened its first overseas branch in London, and decided it should have a trademark with worldwide identification. What was needed, management agreed, was a mark or label as internationally recognizable as a U.S. one-dollar bill with its portrait of George Washington. Handsome King Gillette, with his wavy black hair and smartly-turned mustache, was promptly and willingly chosen as the razor world's version of the dollar bill's George Washington.

By 1918, annual razor sales had passed the 1-million mark, blade sales had topped the 120-million mark—and then came the biggest single boost in company history: the United States Government decided that the equipment of every soldier and sailor should include a safety razor. By the end of World War I, the nation's young trendmaker's had acquired the habit of self-shaving and Gillette razors—at five dollars and up—were soon selling at more than double the pre-war rate.

William E. Nickerson (shown in later years as a Gillette director) turned King Gillette's idea for a safety razor into a practical reality.

We Offer a New Razor

This is a new kind of razor. The piece of steel that does the work is two edged and is about as thin as this piece of paper. This steel is held so tight that it could not possibly cut you—arranged so ingeniously that it can be cleaned by merely holding it under the faucet or dipping it in the bowl an instant.

The main idea involved is the new process of so tempering and sharpening such thin steel as this that it will hold its edge during twenty or thirty shaves. But, even in the holder, there are hitherto unthought of improvements. You will have to see it to appreciate it.

There are no adjustments, no nuisances. You do not even need to be particular about washing your razor. It is made of silver and will not rust.

You can shave yourself with this razor, if you never could with another. No matter how expert you are with any other razor you can save time and trouble and money by using it.

Do not confuse this razor with any other you have ever seen or heard of. Its every detail is brand new. (Agents wanted.)

We have a booklet describing the razor, which will be gladly sent without cost. But the razor itself is so convincing—so astounding—that we wish you would send for it on trial. The price is $5.00 for the silver razor, with 20 blades—two years' supply—in a neat box. The gold razor will be $12.00. Send no cash—simply ask. Write a letter or use the coupon.

TOWNSEND AND HUNT
1602 Marquette Building, Chicago

Send me, express prepaid, one silver Gillette Safety Razor, for which I agree to pay $5.00, if, at the end of 30 days, however, I am not satisfied, I will return the razor, at your expense, and upon my mere statement of dissatisfaction, you are to send me back my $5.00.

Name ....

Address ....

Gillette's first advertisement, in the October 1903 issue of *System Magazine*, carried the name of its Chicago sales agent and only one mention (in the coupon) of Gillette. The first year's effort sold 51 razors and 168 blades.

And all this while, Gillette patents kept razor and blade imitators out of the market.

The basic patents would expire on November 15, 1921. In a bonded warehouse in Chicago, tens of thousands of Japanese-made razors awaited that November go-date. But Gillette moved earlier—coming to market six months ahead of the deadline with a choice of new models, including one priced at a dollar. In the year following the expiration of its patents, the company made more money than in any previous year.

The new dollar razor—like the GI razors of World War I—soon proved to be an effective way of getting the public to sample Gillette shaving, paving the way for a related boom in blades. Gillette marketing people promptly pursued the sampling strategy so vigorously that the razor became a break-even product, sold at cost. Gillette made it worthwhile for grocery stores to give away razors free with the purchase of coffee, spices, beverages, and canned goods. Wrigley bought a million Gillette razors for use as chewing gum premiums, and a maker of overalls slipped a bonus Gillette razor into a pocket of every pair.

Then the happy, headlong sampling of what Gillette later called "the give-away twenties" bumped abruptly into the depression decade of the thirties. Gillette pondered the short and long-term advantages of cutting price versus adding value. The decision: Gillette responded in 1930 with its new "strip sharpening" method of producing better blades, followed in 1932 with the long-lasting Gillette Blue Blade, and in 1934 with the handy, one-piece razor. Not until 1938 did Gillette meet cut-price competition head-on with its "Thin" blade.

During the same austere period, Gillette broadened its line with an electric shaver and a Gillette shaving cream. The electric shaver, introduced in 1938, failed to meet Gillette's sales expectations and was withdrawn from the market by 1940; but the brushless shaving cream of 1936 led the way to a companion lather cream in 1940.

Gillette was then about to receive a second major boost from a second war. The Gillette razor, in the GI kit of World War I, had launched the *self*-shave habit on a na-

Saving Shaving—

You not only save money by shaving-yourself
with the always ready and smooth working

Gillette Safety Razor

But you save no end of annoyance and bother. No stropping, no honing, no danger of cuts—no lost time or health risks in barber shops. Each razor has 20 double-edged blades—is good for 400 shaves. We rehone the twenty for 50 cents. If not satisfied after trial, money refunded. If not at your dealer's write for booklet. Correspondence solicited from dealers. Exclusive territory will be given.

GILLETTE SALES CO., 1206 Manhattan Building, CHICAGO

By its second year of marketing, 1904, Gillette was telling its story in *The Saturday Evening Post.* The promise was highly practical.

tional scale; the Gillette of World War II helped convert a nation to the *daily*-shave habit.

In 1948, Gillette added to its post-war surge by buying a uniquely compatible company, in the woman's field, that was promoting self-permanents as vigorously as Gillette had promoted self-shaving: the Toni Company. For an extra measure of profitable compatibility, Gillette and Toni products moved through virtually the same distribution channels.

Gillette was now marketing to all adults, not just men, and was steadily expanding the line of products it could sell to each customer. During the next two decades, the long, diversifying series of introductions was destined to include White Rain Shampoo, Gillette Foamy aerosol lather, the Gillette Adjustable Safety Razor, Adorn Hair Spray, Right Guard deodorant, Gillette Stainless Steel Blades, the Lady Gillette Razor, Heads Up hair grooming aids, the Gillette Techmatic Razor with a band instead of a blade, Casual Hair Color, Gillette's The Hot One self-heating shaving cream—plus Paper Mate pens and Cricket disposable butane lighters. By the end of the 1960's, The Gillette Company was marketing its wide-ranging line in more than one hundred fifty countries and territories throughout the world.

In 1971, Gillette introduced what its industry conceded was another "revolutionary" razor: the tandem-blade "Trac II." And this time—in vivid contrast to the eight-

How Gillette sharpens its blades, with Gillette-developed machines, involves so many closely guarded secrets that photographers are never permitted closer than this.

year development period of the original Gillette Safety Razor—nearly the entire effort was carried out in a crash program with an elapsed time of nine months. The Trac II was not intended to move to market in such rapid fashion; it was not scheduled to arrive until 1973. But some unexpected developments exploded the original schedule.

As the Gillette research and development people approached 1970, they were working on their "usual three or four" new shaving systems, one of which was a twin-blade approach in two different versions. In the first version, the two blades faced each other and called for an up and down scrubbing motion. In the second version, the two blades were in tandem.

The first version, with facing blades, was farther along in development than the second, had scored well in consumer-use tests in Australia, and seemed well on its way to a fall 1971 introduction. The second version, meanwhile, was encountering clogging problems around its closely-spaced tandem blades. To eliminate the clogging, R&D people had even tested a harp-like device that used sharpened wires instead of blades; but the wires could not be held rigid enough to deliver a good shave.

Then, in a sudden rush, three things happened: the facing-blade razor ran into production-development problems that killed any prospects for an early introduction; the tandem-blade razor's clogging problems were solved by an ingenious new slotted-blade design; and a Gillette researcher, studying slow motion close-up films of shaving, made a surprising discovery about tandem-blade shaving. He called it "hysteresis."

As applied to shaving, "hysteresis" meant that, as a whisker is being cut by a blade, it is also being lifted out slightly from the hair follicle—and does not recede back into the follicle until a fraction of a second after it is cut. The researcher's obvious conclusion was that a second blade, following in tandem after a first one, could cut a whisker a second time—and closer to its base—before it retracted into the follicle. Subsequent laboratory tests confirmed his theory.

All this was happening in early 1971—with the Gillette

marketing people still hoping for a major new product introduction during their fall World Series telecasts. The decision was made to firm up the fall date and organize a crash program to meet it.

One immediate need was for a unique name that could be protected by a registered trademark. The word "Tandem" was favored; but it could not be registered. Other names were compiled and tested. The winner: Trac II.

Concurrently, with small consumer panels, Gillette was getting reactions to new package designs, and to various combinations of weight, color, and surface texture for the razor itself.

By April, enough of the new tandem-blade razors were available for consumer-use tests—using five panels of one hundred sixty people each—to get consumer reactions to the new Gillette product, compared with the competitive razors they were using.

At about the same time, a variety of rough "concept" advertisements was being exposed in a series of focus-group interviews in which eight to ten people met with a trained researcher and expressed their reactions to the advertisements. The best-liked concepts of the print advertisements were then translated into rough television commercials for separate testing. By May, test results were in hand and the production of finished advertisements and commercials was underway—together with a variety of counter displays and other materials for the retailers. In the interest of thoroughness, Gillette also developed a one dollar refund deal to stimulate early purchases of the new Trac II: the consumer could simply send proof of his purchase to Gillette and receive a check for one dollar.

In early October, the Trac II was introduced during Gillette's World Series telecasts and, almost overnight, Gillette was obliged to allocate quantities of the Trac II to various regions of the country. By the end of October, Gillette had shipped more than 1.7 million razors and more than 5 million dual-blade cartridges.

During the advertising concept tests, men viewers had been described as being "not just interested but fascinated" by the mechanical working of the tandem blades—and men were the first targets of the Trac II advertising. But Gillette soon developed separate advertising to establish Trac II in the women's market, and then—following a tradition that could be traced back to World War I—the Gillette marketers launched the most ambitious sampling program in Gillette history.

Nor did they forget the earliest of all Gillette marketing concepts: disposability. Five years after the introduction of the Trac II, Gillette went to market with "Good News," a disposable version of the Trac II, priced at a quarter. It did a creditable job of paying its own way and adding to the company profits—and, most important of all, it performed an effective sampling service in behalf of the Trac II.

Another evolutionary product appeared in 1977: ATRA (from Automatic Tracking Razor Action), a twin blade razor with spring that lets the blade cartridge adjust to facial contours during shaving.

King Gillette retired from active participation in the company in 1918 and moved to California, but retained the title of President until 1931, one year before his death. The company he founded would grow to about $1.5 billion in annual sales, with over thirty-five thousand employees.

The blunt advice of William Painter—to invent something that could be thrown away—had started Gillette on his way to a fortune. Then King C. Gillette, the professional salesman, had gone two big steps beyond his teacher: he not only made his name as familiar as his invention; he also made millions of people familiar with his face. His picture, used on blade wrappers, was reproduced more than one hundred billion times—the broadest personal publicity ever given to a businessman in the entire history of world commerce.

MARKETING INSIGHTS

In his quest for a disposable product with a high repurchase rate, King Gillette decided a razor blade would be ideal; but first he needed to make a razor to hold it. Developing steadily better razors—and selling them at low prices, or even at cost—he built a steadily bigger market

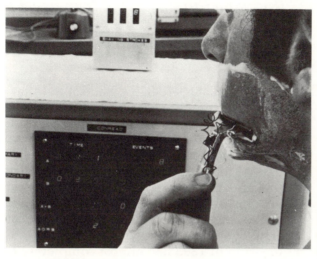

for blades. In recent times, one of The Gillette Company's best sampling ideas was a disposable Gillette razor ("Good News"), with a built-in tandem blade. Sold at a low price, this sampler paid its own way and served as an introduction to both the new Trac II razor and the Trac II blade.

To maintain its reputation for having the *best* razors and blades, Gillette introduced a long series of product improvements. When the Depression brought a pinch to blade sales, Gillette elected to hold its price and offer a *better* blade rather than cut its price and offer a lesser blade.

Selling razors and blades would lead naturally to the selling of related products—shaving cream, then other toiletries. Similarly, selling Gillette products through drug channels would lead naturally to acquiring the Toni Company, which sold toiletries to women through the same channels.

And two World Wars gave Gillette a big assist. In WW I, America's GI's were introduced to *self*-shaving; in WW II, they learned *daily* shaving. Not even Gillette, the outstanding sampler, had ever envisioned what a massive sampling force those wars would be.

Left: Testing the ATRA razor in Gillette's Research and Development Department. The test razor is wired to a Gillette electronic device that measures the percentage of shaving time that each of ATRA's twin blades is in contact with the skin during shaving. The device also counts the number of strokes the shaver makes and measures the pressure of the cartridge against the face during each shaving stroke. **Right:** In its concept tests, Gillette found high interest among men in the mechanical workings of its ATRA razor with pivoting head. Gillette promotion people promptly developed action drawings like this one.

GOODYEAR TIRES

"It is harder to stay ahead than to get ahead."

Frank A. Seiberling

Charles W. Seiberling

15 Frank A. Seiberling had set out that week to improve his temporarily bad cash position by liquidating some of his family's accumulation of industrial property; then, purely by chance, he had run into a man who was offering a vacant strawboard factory on seven acres in East Akron, Ohio, at a price so attractive that Seiberling promptly borrowed thirty-five hundred dollars from his brother-in-law to make the down payment. Only then did he reflect seriously on the best use for the new property. That was no problem. It was 1898; the traumatic depression of 1893 had almost completely faded; and his flour mill, recently converted to the making and packaging of "Mother's Oats" in order to profit from the new boom in breakfast cereals, had become a stepping stone into any new business he elected to enter.

Frank Seiberling's father, John, had organized a farm implement manufacturing company, a saw mill and grain mill, early street railways, and some banking operations; he also was credited with some one hundred fifty inventions. Frank, who had followed in his father's footsteps, was determined to build on an even larger scale and now, at thirty-eight, had a growing conviction that the manufacturing of rubber products might be the golden field of the future.

Akron's Dr. B. F. Goodrich, Civil War surgeon turned businessman, had established a company in 1870 that now seemed to be creating some Akron millionaires with its output of fire hose, raincoats, rubber boots, and numerous other products. Ohio C. Barber, whose Diamond Match Company had made him wealthy, had started the Diamond Rubber Company in 1894. Now there was a sudden promise of even greater prospects: the bicycle boom of the 1890's seemed sure to continue, and the horseless carriage—at least to Frank Seiberling—had all the makings of an invention that could start a nationwide industrial revolution.

On August 29, 1898, Frank Seiberling organized a company that would manufacture horseshoe pads, carriage tires and bicycle tires, with plans to begin making automobile tires a year later. The firm's name, he decided, should be The Goodyear Tire & Rubber Company, after the man who had discovered vulcanization in 1839 and thus made the rubber industry a reality. Seiberling found in his consideration of names that Charles Goodyear, who died penniless in 1860, had once started a company of his own, but it had not carried his name; and after going through several changes of ownership, had been bought up, along with some small companies, by the prosperous United States Rubber Company.

Some months later, Seiberling decided the company name should be accompanied by a trademark symbol; and he had one in mind. On the newel post of his stairway at home stood a statuette of Mercury, the swift messenger of the ancient gods. To Frank Seiberling, a company concerned with transportation should have a connotation of speed.

Paul W. Litchfield

Seiberling's energetic, young Goodyear Company quickly learned how to make good rubber products; but it also learned that any new company in the industry could be straitjacketed by patents Frank Seiberling had not been fully aware of. He was soon affected by litigation in both his bicycle tire and carriage tire operations.

Most alarming of all, the big companies had organized the Clincher Manufacturers Association, a group of license holders, and were about to divide up the new market for horseless carriage tires. Under the quotas, all perfectly legal at the time, the three industry leaders—Goodrich and Diamond (which later merged) and United States Rubber—were allotted approximately equal shares totalling eighty-five percent; a few other firms, like Fisk, were given around five percent each; the relatively new Goodyear Company would be limited to less than two percent of the total industry, and the even younger Firestone Company would receive similar treatment.

George M. Stadelman

But feisty, 5' 2" Frank Seiberling was undaunted by the pressures of the giants. He had set out with the long-range goal of being an important maker of tires for the horseless carriage, and he continued his travels, looking both for talented people and investment dollars, while his brother Charles handled the company finances and did an ingenious job of maintaining the loyalty and enthusiasm of the work force. On one trip, Frank Seiberling went all the way to Boston just to look up a young man named Paul Litchfield, who had been mentioned in a trade paper article as the superintendent of a small rubber company that had built tires for the first commercial fleet user of pneumatic tires.

Paul Weeks Litchfield, who for four years had walked six miles a day to and from his Boston home and the Massachusetts Institute of Technology, had entered the rubber industry with painful reluctance after a six-month job search had failed to turn up a job anywhere else. During senior year field trips, he and other members of M.I.T.'s first class in chemical engineering had visited every kind of industry in New England, and Litchfield had put rubber at the very bottom of his list. But in the hard times that surrounded his 1896 graduation, young Litchfield found himself commuting home on weekends from his first job in a Reading rubber factory, smelling so offensively of the natural African rubber then in use that the railroad conductors made him ride on the back platform instead of in one of the cars.

When Litchfield suddenly decided that the rubber industry was the place for a career, it was for two very practical reasons. First, he concluded that the newly-invented automobile needed three elements to be successful: the internal combustion engine and abundant fuel—which already existed—and a tough new kind of pneumatic tire that had yet to be developed. His second reason was that any industry as backward as the rubber companies of that era must offer above-average opportunities for an ambitious young college graduate to show results and get ahead.

Of his visit to Goodyear in Akron, and his talks with Frank and Charles Seiberling, Litchfield admitted later that he was not impressed with either the factory or the company's financial status, but that he liked the Seiberlings—Frank, the dynamic "head" of the firm, and

Charles, two years Frank's junior, the kindly "heart" of the place—and decided that at twenty-four he could afford to "gamble a few years with them." He agreed to become superintendent at twenty-five hundred dollars a year.

Paul Litchfield, who in his nearly sixty years with Goodyear was destined to give the company a long-range direction and a unique character, began his career there in 1900 by designing the first Goodyear automobile tire, writing the compounding specifications for it, and designing the mold in which it was cured. Not until 1906 would Litchfield be able to afford an automobile of his own, and not until 1908 would the company make any profit from automobile tires.

Litchfield's next concern was the development of some new type of tire that would free the company from the dead-end, less than two percent share limitation imposed by the Clincher Manufacturers Association.

The clincher tire, direct successor to the bicycle tire, used a "bead" of tough rubber to stiffen the twin inside-diameter edges that held the tire over the rim of the wheel. This bead, on both sides of the tire, had to be pried off the rim with tire irons, then pried back on again, whenever a tire needed one of its frequent repairs. The prying was too strenuous for virtually all females and could take up to an hour for a husky male; Litchfield had concluded early in his career that the automobile could never become completely practical until it had easily detachable tires that could be locked, not pried, into place.

The solution to the problem had been eluding Paul Litchfield for years. Then Nip Scott—known first as an Ohio "character" and only secondarily as an inventor—dropped in one day for one of his occasional visits and dumped the contents of a gunny sack onto Frank Seiberling's desk. The clutter of metallic parts, Scott explained, represented a new way of braiding wire for bedsprings. It had turned out to be too expensive for that purpose, and he wondered if it had any application to tires. Seiberling called Litchfield, who took one long look and said almost in awe: "That is the missing link."

Early Goodyear straight-side tire with diamond tread design.

A braided wire bead led to a locked-on tire with straight sides and thus more air capacity and better cushioning; hence the immediate names "straight side" and "oversize." Of much greater importance, of course, was the straight-side tire's elimination of strenuous prying when tires needed changing—and of rim-cutting whenever the bulging sides of the old clincher tire were hammered upward, by road shocks, against the rim.

It was the breakthrough tire news of 1905. Seiberling and Litchfield told Goodyear salesmanager George M. Stadelman to rush the technical details to the major automobile makers on whom Goodyear had been calling.

The major producers of prestige cars—Locomobile, Pierce-Arrow, Packard, and Pope-Toledo—listened politely, then explained to Stadelman that his new straight side would mean a change in rims, and they could not afford to make the change for something from a tire company as obscure as Goodyear. Persistent Stadelman promptly turned to the makers of that era's "cheaper cars"—Buick, Reo, and Oldsmobile—all of whom agreed the new straight side was worth a try. As further support for its new tire, Goodyear persuaded famous race driver Louis Chevrolet to use straight sides on his car in the next Indianapolis 500 race.

The battle of the Goodyear straight side versus the Clincher Manufacturers Association dragged out through four years of heated claims and counterclaims—and even before it ended in victory for Goodyear, Litchfield was ready with another spectacular advance: the first true nonskid tread, announced in 1908. Until then, tires were smooth-faced, carried the molded letters "Non Skid," or had leather tread with steel studs.

For his nonskid design, Litchfield began with a simple diamond-shape tread because it offered four-way biting edges for traction, braking, and protection against side skids. What Litchfield did not anticipate was the instantaneous recognition the diamond pattern brought to a Goodyear tire. Even people who could not speak English could easily indicate what tire they wanted. As an even bigger bonus, artists drawing pictures of automobiles for newspapers and magazines could create quick and easy

tires by simply adding the cross-hatched lines of the Goodyear diamond tread pattern. Overnight, the Goodyear diamond became the national stereotype of what a tire tread should be.

In a companion development in 1908, Goodyear invented a tire-building machine that ultimately was used by fifty other tire companies. And in the same year, William C. (Billy) Durant organized General Motors, beginning with pro-Goodyear Buick and Oldsmobile (with Oakland and Cadillac to follow the next year), and Henry Ford introduced his Model T, for which he had placed a Goodyear order. Goodyear, the ambitious upstart, suddenly became a major tire company and, after eight uphill years, realized its first profits from the making of automobile tires.

Frank Seiberling promptly hired the services of Claude

By 1910, Goodyear had gone from underdog to industry leader and was using spreads in *The Saturday Evening Post* to tell its story. The coupon at lower right enabled readers to book their orders for Goodyear tires in advance, as "a precaution against disappointment" when they were ready to replace their present tires.

C. Hopkins, who now ranked as America's top advertising writer with a reputed income of $50,000 a year, and appropriated $250,000 for a national advertising campaign.

In 1909, with sales double what they had been the year before, Goodyear paid its first stock dividend—one hundred percent—and planned a 1910 advertising program using two-page spreads. By 1910, Goodyear was building tires for nearly one-third of the output of the fifty automobile manufacturers, leaving some twenty other tire companies to divide the other two-thirds of the business.

The horseless carriage had suddenly become an industry that would grow faster than any other industry of the past—and Goodyear, with almost equal suddenness, had become its most trusted maker of tires; there never seemed to be enough time to keep up with the demand. (Litchfield, years later, would muse that it must have been his subconscious preoccupation with time that triggered his decision to erect clock towers at all Goodyear factories.)

It was a time of heady success; but the situation made sales manager Stadelman feel nervous. Conspicuously shy and quiet, Stadelman avoided crowds and never made a public speech in his entire Goodyear career; but his integrity, vision, and practical knowledge had won him industry-wide respect. Stadelman now felt that Goodyear should turn its primary attention from the auto makers to the motoring public. Nearly a million cars were in operation throughout the United States, and the cost of tires was being recognized as the single largest expense of car ownership. A set of four for a Ford cost up to $160, or about one-fourth the purchase price of the car, and tires on the rough roads of the day seldom lasted more than two or three thousand miles. In time, Stadelman predicted, Goodyear sales to individual motorists would be far higher than its sales to the auto makers, and he advised beginning with heavy emphasis on helpfulness. He proposed building a national network of independent dealers, supplemented by company-owned facilities, and said they should be called "service stations."

The term would in time become a part of the American language.

The consumer market was destined to live up to Stadelman's optimistic forecast. The auto maker or original equipment market, on the other hand, was headed for problems not even perceptive George Stadelman could have foreseen. The fifty-some auto makers of the day would steadily shrink to a "Big Three" and a handful of independents. Early sales calls by Harvey Firestone on Henry Ford would lead in time to a close personal friendship, with the Firestone tire prospering accordingly. And during the coming decade of the 1920's, DuPont interests would gain control of both General Motors and United States Rubber, with obvious, gloomy consequences for other tire makers.

All this while, back in his world of production, Paul Litchfield was feeling a responsibility to develop proper tires for two other forms of transportation. One was the motor truck, which he believed could rival the railroads as a major national transportation force—but only if it could ride on pneumatic tires at much faster speeds than the ten to fifteen miles per hour permitted by solid rubber tires. The other form of transportation that intrigued him was aviation. Almost since he attended his first air show, he had regarded aviation as the ultimate in transport for one very basic reason: it should take less power, he was convinced, to drive a vehicle through the air than over the uneven surface of the ground or through masses of water.

In 1909, Goodyear developed the first tire made especially for airplanes. Until then, the Wright brothers and other pioneers had used sled-type runners or bicycle tires for their landing gear. The Goodyear airplane tire, backed in 1910 by a full-fledged aeronautical department, was selected for the first U.S. airmail flight in 1911 and, in the same year, for the first transcontinental flight, a trip from Long Beach, California, to Long Beach, New York, lasting eighty-four days, with sixty-three landings.

For aircraft, the emphasis was on lightness. For trucks, it would be on strength, and not until 1916 would Goodyear develop a combination of cord and fabric strong

To prove that pneumatic truck tires were a key to the growth of the trucking industry, Paul Litchfield organized the first cross-country truck lines. In 1918, this "Wingfoot Express" truck, using Goodyear tires, had gone from coast to coast four times and had made the run from Los Angeles to New York in the world record time of thirteen days, five hours.

enough for truck service. To demonstrate the strength of the new tires in a newsworthy way, Litchfield launched the first cross-country truck line—the "Wingfoot Express"—from Akron to Boston. The first trip, in 1917, took twenty-four days and the cargo consisted mostly of spare tires. A year later, Litchfield organized a bus line, one of the nation's first, to demonstrate his truck tires in bus service.

The new Goodyear aeronautical department, meanwhile, had added to its fame by winning the International Balloon Race of 1913, thus becoming the logical choice to build the first "kite" observation balloons of 1914 for the British and the first U.S. Navy blimps of 1917.

And in its primary field, by 1915, Goodyear had moved ahead of all auto tire competition and would launch its long-running claim: "More people ride on Goodyear tires than on any other kind."

There had been no let-up in the pressure, and Paul Litchfield, during whose time Goodyear had been first a

The USS *Akron* entering its quarter-mile-long airdock in Akron, Ohio.

challenger, then a champion, gave his associates a strong personal conclusion: "It is harder to stay ahead than to get ahead."

Goodyear was now thinking and operating in global terms. An exporter since 1901, the company decided in 1915 to open sales branches in Argentina, Australia, and South Africa. In 1916, to obtain the long-staple cotton required for its truck tires, Goodyear checked out Egyptian sources, was told by the British that no cotton could be spared from the war effort, and wound up planting six thousand acres of Arizona land the U.S. Department of Agriculture had judged suitable for long-staple cotton. The same year, to begin protecting itself against the hiking of rubber prices by the rubber-producing nations, Goodyear acquired a twenty thousand-acre rubber plantation in Sumatra. Then came America's involvement in World War I and, for Goodyear, a new load of demands ranging from truck tires to balloons to airplanes.

After the Armistice, the tire industry eagerly turned back to civilian production and headed at increasing speed toward what promised to be the record-breaking year of 1920. To avoid materials shortages as business quickened, all companies rushed to buy rubber and cotton ahead of the surge of rising prices. By May of 1920, Goodyear had succeeded in building a six-month supply of rubber—all bought on a rising-price market so that the inventory was worth, at market prices, twenty million dollars more than the company had paid for it.

Suddenly, that fall, the boom up-ended into depression. Sales plummeted. Goodyear's six-month supply of rubber was now more than enough to last for twelve months—and the price of rubber was falling. By May of 1921, the same rubber that had shown appreciation of twenty million dollars a year earlier was now worth thirty million dollars less than the company had paid for it—a drop of fifty million dollars in value in just twelve months. Cotton and other raw materials took comparably disastrous swings.

During 1920, nearly two hundred tire companies went out of business. Goodyear survived, but was eighty million dollars in debt and in need of massive financing to close out its bank loans, pay off creditors and provide working capital. As the New York banking firm of Dillon, Read & Company moved in with a comprehensive plan for avoiding bankruptcy through the issuance of $27.5 million in debenture bonds, it became a legal necessity for the Seiberling brothers to move out.

The moment of change would come at the close of a dramatic New York City meeting that went beyond a deadline of midnight, May 12, 1921, as frantic long-distance phone calls were made to finalize the last commitments of the complex financing plan. The dawn light of May 13 was beginning to filter through the windows as Frank A. Seiberling convened the final meeting of the outgoing board of directors. He stated the purpose of the meeting in a calm, businesslike tone and asked for a motion to accept the resignations. With equal calmness, Charles Seiberling rose to his feet and said, "Mr. Chairman, I move these resignations before us be accepted."

Frank and Charles Seiberling then shook some hands and, with no trace of emotion, walked out of that room and out of the Goodyear world they had worked so hard to build. It was not in their nature, even for moments, to look like losers. Three years later, when the nation's economy was close to normal again, the unsinkable Seiberling brothers would organize another tire company, and this time would give it their own name.

Edward G. Wilmer, age thirty-eight, Milwaukee lawyer and financier, was installed as president, succeeding Frank Seiberling. Not long after, with Goodyear making a strong recovery, Wilmer was called away to head the ailing Dodge Brothers automobile company, which Dillon, Read had bought and would later sell to the four-year-old Chrysler Corporation.

George M. Stadelman, the sales manager of the pioneering years, was the next to take up the grim responsibilities of the Goodyear presidency. He took office in 1923, but died within three years.

Paul W. Litchfield, the man who had designed the first Goodyear auto tire, was now put in charge. He would serve as president, then as chairman of the board, for thirty-two years. In his auspicious first year, Goodyear's refinancing was completed and control was returned to the stockholders—and sales topped $230 million to make Goodyear the world's largest rubber company.

During the next year, something near and dear to Litchfield's heart would demand attention. Truck speeds had soared to a new, everyday level of sixty miles an hour, and cotton could no longer take the heat. Litchfield, father of the pneumatic truck tire, promptly launched a program devoted to applying man-made synthetic fibers to tires. Goodyear began with rayon, derived from cellulose. Rayon easily proved that it could take the heat; but it also showed a weakness: rubber apparently would not adhere to it. The solution to the rayon-and-rubber problem would soon arrive from another part of Goodyear, the aeronautical department, where the builders of a Navy dirigible had learned new things about the application of rubber to fabric. Rayon proved itself in truck tires, then moved into automobile tires—ultimately meeting its toughest test in Goodyear airplane tires for the bombers of World War II.

The bombers, in turn, led Goodyear into nylon, which had high heat resistance and about twice the strength of high-tenacity rayon. But nylon, when Goodyear applied it to truck tires, showed a strange weakness: under stress, at high operating temperatures, nylon fibers became larger, a serious fault in dual tires and when the standing height of the tire was of vital importance. Not until Goodyear developed a new fiber-tempering process would nylon, derived from coal, be ready for truck and automobile tires.

All this while, paralleling the quest for better fibers, an equally important program was being pursued in synthetic rubbers. In the early 1920's, Goodyear researchers began looking for a synthetic that could improve upon some of the characteristics of natural rubber—and, hopefully, reduce the company's often-bitter dependence on natural rubber. By the mid-1920's, the laboratory had perfected an emulsification process by which atoms could be polymerized (linked together) the way "Mother Nature" did it in the latex in the rubber tree. Turning then to commercial applications, the researchers developed key synthetic ingredients from such sources as petroleum, coal, and grain alcohol.

The wide-spectrum search took nearly two decades, but the finish was spectacular. In January of 1938, Goodyear produced the first American synthetic rubber tires, made of Goodyear Chemigum. By 1939, Goodyear had a pilot plant with a daily capacity of one ton of Chemigum. A year later, Litchfield offered a comprehensive national plan for rubber procurement in the event America became involved in the war in Europe.

In time, synthetic rubber was able to meet more than seventy-five percent of the industry's needs, and became a giant stabilizer of world rubber prices.

Back in 1904, itinerant inventor Nip Scott had received a cordial, thoughtful Goodyear audience when he walked in with a gunny sack bulging with his wirebraiding device. In 1928, an almost equally curious creation was brought to Goodyear by A. J. Musselman, inventor of the bicycle coaster brake. It was an idea for an airplane "air" wheel, consisting of a tire so "fat" that the wheel on

The *Mayflower*, one of the four Goodyear blimps in service at the beginning of the 1980's, carries night lights that are readable for at least a mile, but has only one-tenth the volume of the largest blimp built by Goodyear (the U.S. Navy's ZPG-3W). (The word "blimp" was born in 1915 in England when a young Royal Navy Air Service Lieutenant, A. D. Cunningham, playfully flipped his thumb against the taut fabric of a nonrigid airship he was inspecting. He smiled, then orally imitated the odd sound his thumb had made: "BLIMP." Bystanders picked up the word, and it soon had a place in history.)

which it was mounted was barely a hub. Litchfield and his engineers were intrigued. Work was started immediately on the design of a wheel—and a brake—to make the Airwheel practical.

At that time, in 1928, Litchfield was deeply involved in the introduction of the first Double Eagle tire for passenger cars, a tire that far exceeded original equipment specifications and reaffirmed Goodyear's determination to be the maker not only of the most tires, but of the finest quality tires. The Airwheel, meanwhile, started making a success of itself in the aviation market. The innovative, low-pressure design then prompted the auto tire division to give it a try—with the result that the Airwheel appeared on the new Ford and Chevrolet models of 1930. At about the same time, in a Florida orange grove, a Goodyear representative was trying a pair of airplane-size Airwheels on a farm tractor that had been floundering in sand. The orange grove experiment soon led to a new kind of Goodyear low-pressure, high-flotation tire for farm tractors—and then to the first giant tires for earthmoving equipment. From their work with tread designs for farm tractors, Goodyear engineers were led in turn to the development of a new mud-and-snow tire for passenger cars.

Under Litchfield, who had masterminded Goodyear production since 1900, the development of better tires for cars, trucks, tractors, earthmovers, and airplanes moved steadily and irresistibly ahead. But there were two other areas where his best intentions seemed doomed.

As a close ally of his friend Stadelman, Litchfield had been a strong supporter of the independent dealer concept from pioneer days right up to the time he became president in 1926, and could have almost any kind of dealer organization he wanted. Ironically, at that point, two giant mail-order merchandisers—Sears, Roebuck and Montgomery Ward—began to set up retail stores, with tires among their top-featured items. In 1929, oil companies began to sell and service tires at their numerous stations. By 1930, price wars among tire dealers had reached epidemic proportions, and one major tire company, Firestone, began building a national network of company-owned stores. In time, retail outlets for tires far outnumbered the combined outlets for two of the nation's basic necessities: groceries and drugs.

Other disappointments were about to come in from the department Litchfield had started in 1910 to assure the company of leadership in the "ultimate" field of air transport. In 1925, he had decided it was time to develop a dirigible fleet and establish passenger service over the Atlantic and Pacific. The U.S. Government liked the idea; it had suggested a year earlier that Goodyear pick up the zeppelin patents from Germany and keep the art alive after watching Goodyear's contributions to America's first rigid airship, the *Shenandoah*, launched in 1923.

As a relatively modest opening project, Goodyear in 1925 had built the blimp *Pilgrim*, the first commercial nonrigid to use helium. A mammoth airdock was then constructed—a hangar-like building more than two hundred feet high and nearly a quarter-mile long—and work was begun on the first of two giant dirigibles for the Navy. The USS *Akron* was launched in 1931, the USS *Macon* in 1933. Litchfield's loftiest ambition now came

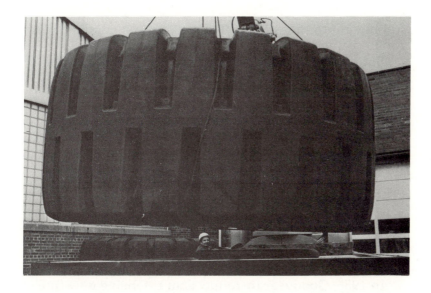

Giant earthmover tire, being loaded here for shipment, measures 11½ feet high by 5½ feet wide, weighs 12,500 pounds, and has a commercial price of more than fifty thousand dollars.

close to becoming a reality—close, but not close enough. By 1936, the *Shenandoah*, the *Akron*, and the *Macon* had all been lost in storms with a total loss of eighty-nine lives. The next year, the visiting German zeppelin *Hindenburg* met a catastrophic end, and the dirigible appeared to face certain doom.

Ironically, the spectacularly traumatic end of the rigid frame dirigibles obscured the safety record of their nonrigid brother blimps, which went on to carry more than a million passengers without a single fatality or even a serious injury. Even the remarkable blimp record during World War II—when not one of the 89,000 ships escorted by blimps was lost to attacking submarines—was often overlooked or just taken for granted.

As Goodyear moved through its extensive World War II tire and aircraft commitments and into civilian production, it was ready with a new, extremely low pressure (24 psi) "Super Cushion" original equipment tire, its first nylon auto tires, and some experimental tires using wire cord. Moreover, there would soon be a new line of tubeless tires, a development of special interest to Paul Litchfield, who had been awarded a patent for the first tubeless auto tire in 1903. The product development program seemed to be outstanding.

But there was one area in which Goodyear prestige seemed to be nonexistent. At the Indianapolis Speedway—where Louis Chevrolet had once helped to turn the original Goodyear straight side into an industry breakthrough, but from which the company had withdrawn in 1922—the winners, year after year, were riding to victory on Firestone tires. It was an eloquent tribute to the high-performance capabilities of Goodyear's archrival. The Firestone feats at Indianapolis became more than a competitive challenge to prideful Goodyear; they became an embarrassment, then a humiliation. Very systematically, in the feisty tradition of Frank Seiberling, Goodyear mapped a program for setting the performance record straight.

In 1956, Goodyear introduced an extensive new line of stock car racing tires and began to involve itself with some custom work for aspiring contenders for new land speed records. Working closely with the record-breakers would soon lead naturally to major participation in the Indianapolis 500.

It took three years for anything spectacular to happen. Then, Mickey Thompson began setting some new speed records at Bonneville Salt Flats and a year later, in 1960, broke the 400 m.p.h. barrier for the measured mile with a speed of 406.6 m.p.h. By the end of 1962, Goodyear racing tires were being used on more winning stock and sports cars than any other brand. In 1965, Craig Breedlove's jet-powered, Goodyear-tired racer jumped the world land speed record to 600.6 m.p.h.—a mark later moved by Gary Gabelich to 622.4 m.p.h.

Not until 1967 would Goodyear have its first Indianapolis 500 winner (A. J. Foyt) since the Howard Wilcox victory of 1919; but the 1967 race would be the beginning of a spectacular series. Bobby Unser won on Goodyears in 1968, and Mark Donohue did it in 1972—followed by a sweep in 1973, when twenty-six of the thirty-three Indy cars, including that of the winner, Gordon Johncock, rode on Goodyears. In 1975, for the first time in thirteen years, all Indy contenders used tires from one supplier,

Craig Breedlove set a world land speed record in 1965 driving this jet-powered racer equipped with Goodyear tires.

A. J. Foyt, after winning his fourth Indianapolis 500 in 1977.

Goodyear, with Bobby Unser capturing his second Indy victory.

In the midst of all the racing, there was still another historical event that would have brought special pride to air-minded Paul Litchfield. In 1970, when the crew of Apollo 14 did the first motoring on the moon, they rolled on Goodyear tires.

On its way to the 1980's, Goodyear was competing world-wide for both original equipment and replacement business in almost every major field of transportation—including conveyor belts. In its primary field of auto tires, Goodyear had set new sales records with its Tiempo, an all-weather, all-surface radial tire, introduced in 1977, and was developing new fuel-saving elliptic tire designs. Employment had grown to approximately 155,000, and sales had passed the six billion dollar mark.

Goodyear's wide-ranging involvement in transportation led to such diverse activities as the development of STARAN, "the world's fastest computer," for air traffic control, and of Speedwalk/Speedramp conveyor systems for airline passengers. Concern for raw materials led, through rubber tree research, to the increasing of latex production by as much as one thousand percent—and to the development of a process for turning scrap tires back into oil, steel, and carbon black. Other research generated such new products as resin for shatterproof, polyester plastic containers and Pliogrip adhesive for bonding automobile components. But none of the company's broad spectrum of activities would ever take the spotlight away from its "aerial ambassador" blimps.

By the beginning of the 1970's, Goodyear was sending the *Columbia*, the *America* and the *Mayflower* on spring and summer U.S. tours, while a fourth blimp, the *Europa*, was playing to audiences overseas. With a lazy cruising speed of about thirty-five miles an hour, the graceful blimps create unique spectaculars in the sky—up to two hundred feet long and sixty feet in girth—with the biggest ones carrying sign areas nearly twenty-five feet high and with nearly four thousand night-message lights on each side, all highly readable for at least a mile during periods of darkness. So sought after are the airborne night messages, by charities, civic organizations, and other public service groups, that Goodyear limits itself to only about twenty-five percent of the night-message time.

But that twenty-five percent is more than enough. When the computerized "Super Skytacular" opens up, beaming out anything from an animation of Santa's sleigh and reindeer to a giant Fourth of July firecracker that explodes to form an American flag, the effect is

To get a road's-eye view of a tire, Goodyear has a laboratory under a test road at its proving ground in San Angelo, Texas. A car can be driven over the water-covered glass at speeds of more than 100 m.p.h. as high-speed cameras record the effect of the speed, the weight of the car, and the water on the tire tread. The apparatus is being used here to take a still photo of a new radial tire tread.

The first tire marks on the moon were made by Goodyear tires mounted on this Modular Equipment Transporter (MET), shown here during an astronaut training session in Sonora, Mexico. The MET, used on the Apollo 14 moon mission in 1971, served as a portable workbench and equipment carrier.

enough to make a competitive advertiser blanch. And as for exclusiveness, almost every tire company can afford to promote itself in any advertising medium, but who else in the world but Goodyear has been doing it with blimps?

MARKETING INSIGHTS
Under gifted entrepreneur Frank Seiberling, young engineer Paul Litchfield saw the demonstrated results of the strong, continuing promotion of simple, clearcut elements: a distinctive, easily-spoken name (GOODYEAR); a familiar, meaningful trademark symbol (the wingfoot); and the highly relevant diamond symbol that grew out of Litchfield's own design for a nonskid tire tread. In combination, those simple elements—all designed to reflect a look of solid importance—were pridefully applied to a product that always seemed eager to prove its superiority over all challengers.

Although Litchfield's first love was product development and manufacturing, he was a thoughtful student of

marketing and became a highly successful marketing practitioner. Characteristically, his philosophy of marketing went directly to the point and can be summed up in these simple terms:

A company must offer its customers equal quality at a lower price, or higher quality at the same price—and the second approach is better, because quality will be remembered long after price is forgotten.

A company must always deliver value, and value means two things: goods that are useful, and a price people can pay.

The automobile tire is one of the most unappreciated of all complex, hard-to-make products. An automobile depends on tires for much of its comfort, handling ease, and safety; every original-equipment tire must meet exacting standards of quietness, smoothness of ride, traction and cornering on both dry and wet pavement, high-speed handling, puncture resistance, sidewall scuff resistance, fuel economy, and long mileage. But these fine points are often overshadowed by the demeaning effects of over-distribution in the replacement-tire market. Auto tires are available, in a hodge-podge mix of names, at virtually all gasoline stations, and at Sears and other major department stores, as well as at the company-owned stores and independent dealers of the tire manufacturers. Tire outlets thus outnumber the nation's grocery and drug outlets combined; and tires, frequently, are not merchandised, but "dumped."

Throughout its history, Goodyear has been obliged to compete not only against other tire companies, but against the image-eroding effects of industry over-distribution. Prideful Paul Litchfield's tires were built to thrive on performance showdowns; and his primary products for automobiles were the beneficiaries of his persistent search for excellence in the related fields of truck and aircraft tires. Ultimately, Goodyear's enthusiasm for proving its merits in performance events became an outstanding example of industrial showmanship—all capped (literally) by the uniquely relevant, spectacularly exclusive Goodyear blimps.

HALLMARK CARDS

"Good taste is good business."

16 The printed Christmas card is a British invention; the year-round greeting card is American. The British card was born when a Londoner waited too long to write his Christmas notes and turned in desperation to a printer. The concept of the American greeting card was born when a young book store clerk in Norfolk, Nebraska, studied the mundane picture postcards then in vogue and decided the public was in need of "a refined form of communication that was both inexpensive and efficient."

Most people, young J. C. Hall concluded, either lack the words or the confidence to express their emotional feelings to someone else. He saw it as a dual need: the right words, plus the assurance that the sentiments expressed were in good taste.

Today, greeting cards account for half of all U.S. personal mail. Americans send them at the annual rate of thirty cards for every man, woman and child in the nation, and every fourth greeting card is a Hallmark card. All this—plus Hallmark's international activities—makes work for more than eleven thousand Hallmark employees and pushes sales above the seven hundred million dollar mark.

"I didn't go into business with the idea of making money," lanky, plain-spoken J. C. Hall explained not long ago. "The opportunity for furnishing a service is more important than money as a motivating force for man. If you put service and quality first, the money will take care of itself."

J. C. Hall had been a self-reliant young man for at least two reasons. First, his mother had named him after a church notable, Methodist-Episcopal Bishop Joyce, and any small boy named Joyce has to assert his masculinity. Second, Joyce Hall's father, an itinerant preacher, abandoned the family when the boy was nine. "My father," Mr. Hall recalled later "used to tell my mother not to worry—the Lord would provide. But I soon learned that

Joyce D. Hall, founder of Hallmark Cards and originator of the "social expression" industry, talks new card ideas with top designer Alice Ann Biggerstaff.

it was a good idea to give the Lord a little help." Young Hall sold lemonade to circus-goers, sandwiches to passengers on railroad coaches, and cosmetics door-to-door, before his book store job started him thinking about greeting cards.

At eighteen, he decided he had enough experience to go to Kansas City, Missouri, and become a wholesaler of postcards, Christmas cards, and valentines. It was 1910. During the next five years, he added some postcards of his own, with famous quotations he had been collecting, and became busy enough to bring his brother Rollie into what now became the Hall Brothers Company. Then, one cold January dawn, he was awakened by a phone caller who reported: "Hall, your place is on fire. But don't hurry. It's all burned up."

His entire inventory was gone. "We weren't just starting from scratch again," he said later, "we were starting from seventeen thousand dollars *behind* scratch." But a banker was impressed by the sincerity of the Hall brothers. With his help, Joyce and Rollie not only rebuilt the

The all-time best seller: Hallmark's homespun "Pansies for Thought" card, introduced in 1941, is still in the line and has sold more than seventeen million copies.

original business, but acquired an engraving plant and, by year-end, were ready to market the first two Hall Brothers greeting cards. They were unfolded, a little smaller than a postcard, with handpainted decorative elements.

During the next year, 1916, the Halls published their first sentimental message, a line by Edgar A. Guest which stated simply: "I'd like to be the kind of a friend you've been to me." It sold so well, they used it on various other cards for the next fifty-five years. With that card, America's "social expression industry" was officially launched.

The company's all-time best seller, introduced in 1941, was equally homespun in character. Designed for any occasion, it showed a cart of bright purple pansies topped by the cover note: "To let you know I'm thinking of you." The message inside continued:

"Pansies always stand for thoughts—
at least that's what folks say.
So this just comes to show *my* thoughts
Are there with you today."

The "Pansies for Thought" card is still in the line and has sold more than seventeen million copies.

Because of his preoccupation with quality, it was inevitable that Joyce Hall would look one day at the "Hall Brothers" signature on the backs of his cards and decide to add three words: "a Hallmark Card." By 1923, "Hallmark" had become the only signature and, in 1954, it became the name of the company.

It also was inevitable that Joyce Hall would react favorably, instinctively, to a new slogan idea suggested in the early 1940's by his then sales and advertising manager, Ed Goodman: "When you care enough to send the very best." Mr. Hall liked the quality ring of it. Then his practical side took over and he concluded, "No. It's too long for a slogan." The slogan went back into the file, but it never quite left Mr. Hall's memory. Months later, he called Goodman: "About that slogan, Ed. Let's try it anyway." Accordingly, in late 1944, a few of Hallmark's radio commercials concluded with: "When you care enough to send the very best." The response was later described as "fantastic," and the slogan became an official part of all Hallmark advertising.

It was Joyce Hall's kind of slogan, and he made sure his cards lived up to it. Every new Hallmark design on its way to production had to win the approval of more than forty experts in a variety of fields, including a special "judge of good taste," before it could qualify for the final "O.K. J.C."

"Good taste is good business" was probably Joyce Hall's favorite piece of advice, and his company studied the public's tastes in elaborate detail.

To the surprise of some researchers, the company found, at the very outset, that plain, unsophisticated Kansas City was an ideal test laboratory for new concepts. What sold well in Kansas City would sell well anywhere in the United States and the world.

They also found that public taste tended to divide itself into three levels, designated by Hallmark as "A," "B," and "C." "A" is attached to people who regard themselves as "intellectuals," a group dominated by affluent professionals and other college graduates. "C" is attached

Left: Kansas City's new Crown Center. Hallmark headquarters is at center rear. V-shaped building in foreground is Crown Center Hotel. **Right:** Hallmark artist at work in what probably ranks as the world's largest art department.

to the so-called "John Q. Public," with some high school education. "B" is attached to the middle group which stands between—and also draws from—the other two. "We aim for a 'C+' and 'B,' " says Hallmark. "They sell best. 'A' cards don't sell well, so we make very few."

Another point that is abundantly clear to Hallmark is that people like to send cards that will make other people feel good. In a typical recent year, out of seven thousand new designs, only two were "downers." Both were valentine "gag" cards with a friendly insult for the recipient.

As for occasions, the rankings remain fairly constant, year after year: Christmas, Valentine's Day, Easter, Mother's Day, Father's Day. Birthdays are the most popular nonseason card-sending occasion and rank next to Christmas in overall sales. And about eighty percent of all card buyers are women.

To please this vast audience, Hallmark has developed what is probably the world's largest art department— more than three hundred fifty artists—and finds that the best public-pleasers are artists from mid-America. Hallmark's total active line now comprises more than twenty-two thousand different designs, with a daily production

Donald J. Hall, president
since 1966 of Hallmark Cards,
Inc.

of ten million cards and three million related, noncard
items—and Hallmark, long ago, developed retail display
systems and retail inventory control techniques to keep
the company fully informed at all times as to which items
are moving and which ones are not.

Hallmark says simply, "Greeting cards are emotions
put to pictures and words. We see ourselves as a vehicle
for one person to say to another: 'I'm thinking of you.'"
But that modest statement of purpose is global in its application. Hallmark publishes in twenty languages and
distributes in some one hundred countries. Hallmark
writers in Paris, Frankfurt and other international capi-
tals see to it that Hallmark catches all internal translation
bloopers—such as one in which a sentiment began as
"Hope this finds you feeling better" and ended up, in another language, as "Hope this finds you sitting down."

In 1951, the coming of network television gave Joyce
Hall an historic opportunity to demonstrate his conviction that "good taste is good business." He had watched
television's earlier, local efforts, and had decided they
were not his idea of quality and good taste. In his own
newly-launched "Hallmark Hall of Fame" series, he
would try to do something about those standards.

Joyce Hall, the practical man, asked about the myste-
rious "ratings" which determine the kind of fare the television networks will offer the viewing public. He found
that "ratings" were collected from a research sample of a
little more than a thousand sets in homes which, statisti-
cally, represented a demographic cross section of the
American public. Each of those research sample sets,
equipped with a mechanical device to record the turnings
of its dial, thus helped to determine what tens of thousands of other sets should be receiving.

Hallmark's computerized inventory control system
could tell what the public was reaching for, with money
in hand, in some twenty thousand retail stores every day.
Therefore, to Joyce Hall, the television approach to measuring—and programming for—public taste was primi-
tive. "Nonsense!" he concluded. "I'd rather make eight
million good impressions than twenty-eight million bad
ones."

Danny Kaye as Captain Hook and Mia Farrow as Peter Pan in a "Hallmark Hall of Fame" production of Sir James M. Barrie's *Peter Pan.*

He then proceeded to plan what many TV industry executives predicted would be a catastrophe. For his first major "Hallmark Hall of Fame" effort, he would sponsor an original opera, one hour long, to be shown on Christmas Eve.

TV programmers were aghast. The show was too "highbrow" for television. It was too expensive. And it would come too late in the season to sell any Christmas cards. But Joyce Hall went right ahead and produced Gian Carlo Menotti's *Amahl and the Night Visitors.* The response was so overwhelmingly good that Hallmark, to meet popular demand, repeated the show at Easter and on four subsequent Christmases.

In 1953, Joyce Hall took another bold step. He sponsored a full *two*-hour production of Maurice Evans' famous *Hamlet.* On that Sunday afternoon, more people saw *Hamlet* than had seen it in the three hundred fifty years since William Shakespeare had written it.

More than one hundred additional "Hall of Fame" shows would follow, and Joyce Hall's conviction that "good taste is good business" would be confirmed in a very tangible way. During the first decade of his new approach to television programing, Hallmark sales more than tripled.

And there was still another bonus, less easy to measure in dollars. Joyce Hall had been wishing, at the time, for some Winston Churchill paintings for his greeting cards. He contacted Sir Winston's solicitor, and got an immediate, negative response; but at least the solicitor said he would give it a try. The solicitor called Sir Winston and said an American company wanted to publish his paintings on greeting cards. Sir Winston wanted to know *what* American company. "Hallmark," said the solicitor. "That's a good firm," said Sir Winston. "Make a deal with them."

Donald J. Hall succeeded his father, in 1966, as president and chief executive officer of Hallmark Cards; but Joyce Hall was far from finished in his lifelong crusade for better taste. For many years, in his plants, he had been intrigued with the effects of a tasteful working environment on the levels of taste among his employees. In his card shops, too, he often observed: "I like to see the effect it has on young folks when they see fine things."

Thus, it was no surprise to his friends when Joyce Hall, nearing the age of eighty, decided it was time to transform twenty-five rundown blocks of downtown Kansas City into a tasteful new place to be known as Crown Center. It would cost four hundred million dollars in private funds to get the job done. But Hallmark had the will and, as a family-owned business, it could use its resources in any way it pleased.

"Crown Center began as my dream," Joyce Hall said at the time, "but my son soon improved and expanded the original concept. Where I had seen a great commercial and entertainment complex, Donald saw a city."

Throughout all the changes in plans, however, one basic characteristic of Crown Center remained untouched. Nothing and nobody was allowed to tamper with Joyce Hall's concept of good taste.

MARKETING INSIGHTS

Young J. C. Hall was perceptive enough to believe there was a market for "a refined form of expressing our emotional feelings to someone else." He launched the new "social expression" industry with the homely Edgar A. Guest line: "I'd like to be the kind of a friend you've been to me." Greeting cards now account for about one-half of all U.S. personal mail.

Hall found that his best market for greeting cards was the person with a "middle" amount of education—higher than those with only some high schooling, but not high enough to qualify as an "intellectual." He also found that about eighty percent of all greeting card buyers are women.

His preoccupation with quality led naturally to changing "Hall Brothers" to "Hallmark," and to adding the slogan: "When you care enough to send the very best." Because a greeting card is a gift as well as a means of self-expression—and because gift buyers generally avoid looking cheap—Hall's "very best" approach was highly practical marketing policy.

When Joyce Hall turned his back on television ratings and invested large advertising sums in such uplifting shows as operas and Shakespearean plays, he was guided solely by his personal conviction that "good taste is good business." But his conviction was a good one. The public agreed with him, and they showed it in a very tangible way. Within the first decade of the "good taste" spectaculars on television, the sales of Hallmark Cards soared three hundred percent.

HART SCHAFFNER & MARX SUITS

"The clothes a man wears are to some extent a true index of his character and tastes; but they are also an influence upon his character and tastes."

Harry Hart

Max Hart

17 On the morning of October 9, 1871, when Chicago's great fire had finally been checked, a group of famous State Street merchants met amid the still-smoking ruins of their stores to exchange views about their future in a city that was now two-thirds destroyed. Only one of them, Marshall Field, decided he would rebuild on the same spot; the others agreed it was wiser to move away.

Six months later, to State Street, came another store unknown to any of the great merchants: Harry Hart & Brother, specializing in suits for men. With twenty-seven hundred dollars their father had saved from their delivery boy earnings, Harry Hart, age twenty-one, and brother Max, age eighteen, had decided that, in a city with nearly one hundred thousand homeless people, there was a desperate need for clothing of all kinds. Customer credit, they admitted, was something they would have to work out in "one way or another."

Max was the acknowledged "expert." As a delivery boy for Mandel Brothers, he also had been responsible for affixing the labels that gave each package a look of regal quality. If they became known for quality, the brothers agreed, they could then strive for volume. So successful was their approach that, within three years, they not only had opened a second store, but were manufacturing men's clothes to meet their own needs. Within seven years, they needed more management help and brought two brothers-in-law, Levi Abt and Marcus Marx, into the firm. From "Harry Hart & Brother," the signs were changed to "Hart Abt & Marx."

But it was not until 1887, when Joseph Schaffner stopped in, shyly asking for job advice, that the organization found its proper combination of talents.

Joseph Schaffner was a good friend and distant cousin of the Harts, but the thought of working with them had never crossed his mind. As he recalled later, in a letter to a friend: "I had been in one position for seventeen years and had gone through a daily grind of bookkeeping and credit-making. After many years of service, I felt that I must resign, although it was with fear and trembling. I had no idea how I would be able to make a living, but believed I should go to St. Paul and start in the mortgage business. A few days later, I met Harry and Max Hart and asked them what they thought of the step I was taking. They said they had not made up their minds that they were going to let me go. I knew what that meant. I said, 'If you want me to stay, I will stay.' " Levi Abt already had announced his plans to leave, and the firm now became Hart Schaffner & Marx.

Joseph Schaffner

Shy Joseph Schaffner had a long mercantile background, but his principal interest was literature. A friend would later write of him: "He counted among his friends the greatest souls of history; he communed with them daily in his library and drew from them inspiration and serenity; and he carried their aroma into the counting room and spiritualized that usually arid atmosphere. No doubt the spirits of Matthew Arnold, John Ruskin, Ralph Waldo Emerson and the other great souls of literature had through him their part in humanizing modern business." In his quotations from the immortals, Schaffner stressed morals and courage, as well as common sense. Quoting Marcus Aurelius, Schaffner often reminded his associates: "Fear nothing but disgrace."

When a major customer canceled a large order without any notice of explanation, Schaffner promptly wrote him a curt letter advising him never to come back to Hart Schaffner & Marx. To those in the office who protested that sudden cancellations were an accepted part of doing business, Schaffner said softly, "I know I'm right about this and he's wrong. Don't worry about the effect on the business. When you're sure you're right, go ahead." Soon

Marcus Marx

after the delivery of that Schaffner letter, the customer called to ask that his original order be reinstated.

Hart Schaffner & Marx was now being asked to manufacture for other retailers, not just for its own stores. The inquiries were flattering, but they conjured up logistics that were frightening. Traditionally, the salesman for a clothing firm was spectacularly attired, complete with silk topper, spats and a walking stick, and always traveled with as many as twenty wardrobe trunks bulging with samples.

HS&M began by complying with tradition, but soon tried an experiment: instead of equipping their man with wardrobe trunks, they gave him a case of fabric swatches. After a period of shock, the new fabric swatch approach became industry-wide procedure.

With a similar disregard for tradition, HS&M decided the time had come to establish standard pricing in the clothing industry, to replace the age-old practice of giving special discounts to large customers. HS&M went to the trade with a new slogan, "One just price . . . and just one price." The industry soon followed.

Joseph Schaffner brought a special touch to the company's letters and coached the office staff on their full range of correspondence. To his great delight, a prestigious New England house would in time publish a book entitled *Selected English Letters,* featuring the works of Jonathan Swift, Charles Lamb, Thomas Carlyle and other English literary greats; Abraham Lincoln, James Russell Lowell, Thomas Bailey Aldrich and other famous Americans—and a letter written by a staff member of Hart Schaffner & Marx to one of its customers.

Inevitably, Schaffner came to be intrigued by the potential of advertising and, in 1897, Hart Schaffner & Marx published the clothing industry's first national magazine advertisement. The industry was unimpressed. A business writer of the time would later recall: "Mr. Schaffner was the object of much curiosity and some sympathy when he began advertising. One of his competitors told him that if a man wanted to throw money in the lake, it was a fine way to go about it."

The writer continued: "After a few more years, mem-

Along with smart fashion for the 1897 business executive, Hart Schaffner & Marx offered this leisure-time attire.

bers of the trade began to show anxiety about the matter. The advertising expenditure had increased year after year, and it was beginning to dawn on the industry that a new force was at work. There were unmistakable signs of a new leadership."

Despite Schaffner's personal interest in writing, he favored advertisements that were mostly illustration, and he engaged J. C. Leyendecker and other *Saturday Evening Post* cover illustrators to "draw people and clothes the way they really are—not smooth and unwrinkled, the way they appear in the style charts of tailors." But he was soon applying long, polished prose in booklets and other forms of "advertising which does not advertise," all mailed to the stores that carred HS&M suits.

In preparing inspirational booklets on "Courage," "Enthusiasm," "Co-operation," and similar subjects, Schaffner would often chide his advertising writers: "Don't always try to sell clothes. Let this go through without any 'clothes' in it—just be helpful, if we can, in developing better business ideas." In many cases, the only reference to Hart Schaffner & Marx in a booklet was the company's imprint on the title page.

But never, in his commercial modesty, did Schaffner minimize the importance of good clothes. In one key booklet to retailers, he wrote: "The clothing merchant of the present day sustains a relation to his community of considerable importance. The clothes a man wears are to some extent a true index of his character and tastes; but they are also an influence upon his character and tastes. They affect in an unconscious and more or less indirect way his standing in the community. This being true, it is easy to see that the clothing man has a duty to his fellow citizens which ought not to be neglected or treated lightly; and a part of that duty is to lead his customers to regard clothes and clothes-buying as a matter of importance."

Men's suits, at the time Hart Schaffner & Marx was organized, were ill-fitting, sack-like garments, and a suit labeled "all wool" usually contained as much as eighty percent cotton, flax, and other fibers. In 1900, HS&M became the first to insist that an "all wool" suit be one hundred

An 1897 suit, as fashioned by Hart Schaffner & Marx. The company pioneered the classification of males into fourteen "basic body types," offering each a "proportioned fit."

Copyright 1904 by Hart Schaffner & Marx

THE Louisiana Purchase Exposition at St. Louis will interest a good many people during 1904 ; we put a bit of it on the cover of our new Style Book, because the book interests a good many people too.

Not all the men in the country will go to the Exposition ; but all of them will wear clothes. This Style Book is an acknowledged authority on what clothes to wear ; it is widely used as a guide to men's fashions.

The cover is in six colors and gold ; the book will be fully illustrated with our leading styles for Spring and Summer, drawn from life. It is not yet ready ; but if you want to be sure of a copy send your address and six cents.

Hart Schaffner & Marx Good Clothes Makers
Chicago Boston New York

In a 1904 ad in *The Saturday Evening Post,* Hart Schaffner & Marx featured this illustration from the HS & M *Style Book,* depicting a scene from the Louisiana Purchase Exposition in St. Louis, and urged its readers to send for the "acknowledged authority on what clothes to wear; it is widely used as a guide to men's fashions."

percent wool. In 1906, HS&M pioneered again by classifying the human male into fourteen "basic body types" and offering that many "proportioned fit" shapes. Ultimately, HS&M would make more than two hundred fifty specialty sizes to fit almost any build and posture.

Continuously, since the turn of the century, the trend has been to clothes designed for more comfort and greater freedom of movement. In 1917, HS&M introduced the first tropical suit, and HS&M was first, in the

1950's, with Dacron® polyester and wool, and other blends that produced lightweight clothing.

Along with the complexity of shapes, sizes and types of fabric, the suit maker faces a bewildering mass of separate manufacturing operations for each suit. The average suit contains seventy-two pieces of fabric in the coat, thirty-nine in the pants, and thirty-six in the vest. It requires approximately 7,000 square inches of outer fabric and 8,000 square inches of varied inner fabrics. On an average, it also requires sixteen buttons, 565 yards of thread of nineteen different types, and 150,000 stitches.

In the early days of Hart Schaffner & Marx, the making of men's suits was carried out on a "contract" system—in factory lofts (generally known as "sweat shops") and in the homes of the workers. In 1911, Hart Schaffner & Marx turned its back on the contract system and became the first men's clothing manufacturer to build its own factories.

A goal of volume based on quality, low markups, and a good choice of individual styles had been an early decision by brothers Harry and Max Hart. Building their own manufacturing facilities was a requisite in maintaining proper control. With Joseph Schaffner's sensitive guidance of their advertising and internal publications, the brothers got their quality/value message across to the consumer, and communicated so effectively with their employees and the trade that the complex organization functioned smoothly.

Decades later, their successors would learn a further lesson about control: in times of severe economic depression, it can be important for a fashion- and quality-oriented marketer to have substantial control of the retailing operations and thus be able to set its standards. Says Hart Schaffner & Marx: "We learned, in the early 1930's, how tough it could be to sell suits to fifteen million men out of work."

The HS&M retail stores, now totaling more than two hundred sixty in more than seventy metropolitan areas, have the mission of "providing high quality fashion apparel and personalized service." But they carry their original, local names—Wallachs in New York, Baskin's in Illinois, Hanny's in Arizona, Root's in New Jersey, etc.—and thus serve as authentic reporting points on local fashion preferences throughout the nation. "In planning new fashions," says HS&M, "you must always distinguish between the authentic and the eccentric."

HS&M today has pushed its sales volume past the half-billion-dollar mark and has a work force of about twenty thousand. But the company's marketing objective—with one basic change—continues to be the proper and comfortable suiting of the American male.

The one big change is that HS&M has gone far beyond its classifying of the male into fourteen different basic body types. HS&M is now concerned with lifestyles—providing the man with proper attire for his various roles at the office, at home, in his leisure activities (including winter as well as summer vacations), and in his sports activities. To communicate more effectively with the sports- and leisure-minded audiences, for example, HS&M's sales organization now includes such able representatives as Jack Nicklaus and Johnny Carson.

And what about the business office, the traditional home of proper male attire? Has leisure attire stolen the spotlight from the places where wage earners work? To that possible concern, Hart Schaffner & Marx has a successful response. Not only has the company continued its strong interest in the "career man," but maintains a special career wear division to provide companies with styles designed especially for their particular businesses. Career wear customers now include a dozen major airlines, leading farm implement manufacturers, rental car companies, numerous banks and other financial institutions, and many more—even including the Boy Scouts.

Professional golfer Jack Nicklaus models the blazer manufactured and marketed under his name by Hart Schaffner & Marx.

MARKETING INSIGHTS
The young Hart brothers made ready-to-wear men's suits, for sale in their own store, and they had one marketing objective: they would become known first for quality; volume would follow.

As other retailers began to ask for the suits, the company expanded its manufacturing and would later become the first in the field to move its manufacturing from contract "sweat shops" to its own modern factories. The company also pioneered, in its field sales effort among dealers, by using swatches instead of complete suit samples, and by abandoning the traditional variety of special discounts in favor of a policy of one price for all.

Hart Schaffner & Marx became the first clothing manufacturer to advertise in national magazines, and established a high standard of honesty and believability with a strict avoidance of falsification or exaggeration in either pictures or words.

To offer its customers a better fit, HS&M studied human shapes, classified the male buyer into fourteen basic body types, and ultimately offered more than two hundred fifty specialty sizes. Later, the company would apply psychographics to its marketing effort and begin aiming at varying *lifestyles* with its sports and leisure-time clothes.

In the days of the "sack suit," Hart Schaffner & Marx was the first to bring fashionable tailoring to the average man. HS&M sells appearance as well as clothing. To carry out that mission with exacting quality controls, HS&M now maintains its own network of retail outlets, complete with fashion-trained personnel.

The partnership between Johnny Carson and a Hart Schaffner & Marx subsidiary, formed in 1969, became one of the most spectacular successes in the history of the clothing industry. Within four years, Johnny Carson suits and sport coats had topped the four hundred thousand mark annually.

HERSHEY'S MILK CHOCOLATE BARS

". . . you must do things in a large way."

Milton S. Hershey holding one of "his boys" from the school he founded for orphans. The Milton Hershey School now owns approximately two-thirds of the Hershey Foods Corporation.

18 Having become suddenly wealthy, Milton Snavely Hershey knew exactly what his next move would be. He would take the fortune from the sale of the caramel candy business and plow it back into one great final venture: a whole new approach to the making and marketing of a milk chocolate product. It was 1900, he was forty-three, and he still felt a driving need to make up for his failure-plagued early years.

His wife Catherine, though apprehensive about the boldness of the plan, did not oppose it. After all, she and Milton had been married for only two years, and it had been a time of affluence. But Aunt Mattie felt no such constraint. "When you talk like that, Milton," she snorted, "you sound just like your father!"

Until his relatively recent success in the caramel business, modest Milton Hershey had seemed destined to follow in the quixotic footsteps of Henry Hershey, one-time farmer, oft-time confectioner, and occasional artist, whose peripatetic career had cut off Milton's schooling at the fourth grade, and kept Milton and his mother in never-ending poverty. None of the misery, however, would ever undercut the conviction in Henry's favorite advice to his son: "If you want to make money, you must do things in a large way."

Milton Hersey was well into his thirties before he experienced anything but failure. At age nineteen, after a haphazard apprenticeship in a confectioner's store, he had set up shop at Philadelphia's Independence Centennial of 1876, making candy by night and selling it by day; but his health soon broke down. He then followed his father on a hunt for silver in Colorado and ended up, instead, as a short-term candymaker's helper in Denver. Father and son turned later to candy-selling ventures in Chicago and New Orleans—and failed again.

The moral in all this, Henry Hershey concluded, was

that they had been too timid. They should head for the biggest market of all: New York City. Henry had developed a cough drop of his own prescription. This, they felt, together with their candy recipes, would be the ticket to success. The venture lasted, precariously, for several years before crashing in the most abject failure of all. Henry stayed for a while in New York, trying to sell some paintings; Milton returned home to Lancaster, Pennsylvania. With a loan from Aunt Mattie, he went back to making candy by night and selling it by day from a basket carried over his arm.

When success finally came to Milton Hershey, it came in a strange and sudden way. Quite by chance, an English importer sampled some of Milton's fresh milk caramels and gave him a sizable order, with a promise of still larger orders if the product maintained its quality. The caramels had a unique flavor; Milton had learned, during his brief candymaking experience in Denver, how dramatically fresh milk could improve the flavor of candy. Within a few years, he was the owner of a large, new caramel factory, and only once did the new company encounter a major problem. While Milton was away on his first real vacation, a temporary manager experimented with a cheap substitute for fresh milk. The experiment caused a loss of sixty thousand dollars worth of business. It was an experience Milton Hershey would never forget.

Inevitably, the magic of fresh milk in candy would turn Milton Hershey's attention, more and more, from caramel to milk chocolate. Caramel was simple; milk chocolate was complex. At the Chicago Exposition of 1893, he had been fascinated by some chocolate-making machinery, which he promptly bought for a series of experiments in a wing of his caramel factory.

There was nothing new about either plain or milk chocolate. Columbus had brought cocoa beans back to Spain from his first voyage to America; there had been a chocolate factory in New England in 1765; the Swiss had developed milk chocolate for use as a beverage and, in 1876, had invented a way of making milk chocolate for eating. But milk chocolate was expensive because it involved intricate manufacturing processes. Even today, a

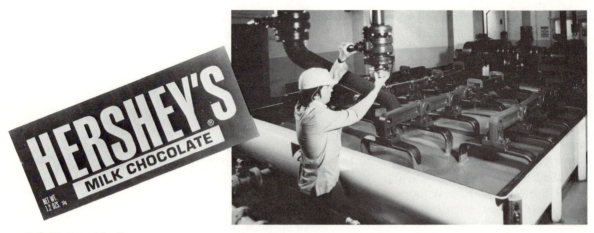

Left: Designed for "mass availability," the bluntly simple Hershey package did such an effective job of promoting itself, at the point of sale, that the company postponed its use of media advertising until 1970. **Right:** In this conching machine, milk chocolate undergoes a "kneading" action which can develop many types and degrees of flavor. Simple though it may look, a block of milk chocolate takes four or five days to make.

simple-looking block of milk chocolate takes four or five days to make, and many of the manufacturing processes can have a critical influence on the final flavor.

When Milton Hershey sold his caramel manufacturing business in 1900 to make his bold move into the milk chocolate field, he had a four-part concept in mind, and he had given careful thought to every part of it. Despite what his relatives and many associates thought, there was nothing impetuous about his big decision.

The concept began with an abundant supply of fresh milk. To Milton Hershey, this meant locating his new factory in the rolling green pasture lands of his native Dauphin County, with its great dairy herds and its clean, efficient, hex-decorated barns. Out of his Mennonite upbringing, Hershey also attached major importance to the fact that Dauphin County would deliver a bonus of honest, industrious Pennsylvania Dutch people for his work force.

The second part of the concept involved mass production, concentrated on a single product, to achieve a new low in cost. A few years later, Henry Ford would be applying the same basic approach to the making of automobiles.

The third part of the concept called for a simple product priced for everyday impulse purchasing—"a wrapped, milk chocolate bar which would be purchased with the nickel in a man's pocket." In 1900, no such product existed.

The final part of the Hershey concept was a simple but bold distribution and merchandising approach: *mass availability.*

During 1903–04, Milton Hershey built a great new factory in a cornfield near his birthplace, Derry Church. The site would soon be renamed Hershey and, unlike other "company towns," it would be a place where employees would be given financial backing in building their own homes. In time, the company would also build a community center, schools, a stadium, a major medical center, and other facilities, and would employ approximately seventy-five hundred people.

The factory was equipped to produce Milton Hershey's own exclusive formula for milk chocolate. "He worked it all out for himself," close associates recalled later. "Milton did everything the hard way. No short-cuts."

Then came the recruiting and training of a massive sales force, to which the final instructions were: "Put the Hershey Milk Chocolate Bar on every counter, shelf, stand, and rack in every retail establishment in the United States—food store, restaurant, drug store, ice cream parlor, and soda fountain."

Mass availability, a revolutionary idea at that time, resulted in mass awareness and high levels of trial. In turn, the product's consistently fine quality resulted in high levels of repeat purchasing. Year after year, Hershey's Milk Chocolate Bar would continue its gains until it accounted for several hundred million dollars in consumer sales annually—and the proponents of national advertising would be mystified by Hershey's spiraling successes with only point-of-sale display to support the sale of its products.

In time, of course, the original concept of 1900 was destined to run into the problems of change. The problems finally arrived in the form of surging price increases for the company's principal raw material: cocoa beans from Africa, South and Central America, and such Pacific islands as New Guinea, Samoa and Java. From 1971 through 1976, for example, cocoa bean prices jumped over four hundred percent.

Anticipating the problems of cocoa bean supply, the Hershey Chocolate Corporation converted itself during the 1960's from a basically one-product, one-plant firm to a multi-product, multi-plant organization, and became Hershey Foods Corporation. Today, even though chocolate bars and related items still account for about eighty-seven percent of its more than $750 million in sales, the company is marketing an expanding line of food products and, since 1970, has used national advertising to pre-sell its products well in advance of the consumer's visit to the store.

Milton Hershey had seen more than his share of poverty. He frankly admitted that his greatest ambition had always been to make enough money to end the fear of poverty forever, for himself and Catherine, for his parents, and for the children he hoped would follow. And most of the dream came true—all but the final part.

His father, Henry, lived to see the caramel factory in operation; his mother Fannie and his Aunt Mattie lived to see the chocolate business become a national succcess. But Catherine Sweeney Hershey had become an invalid long before her death in 1915. Early in their marriage of seventeen years, she and Milton knew there would never be any children, and they agreed on another plan. In 1910, they gathered four orphan boys and provided them with the home and the school opportunities Milton Hershey had missed.

The school grew, over the years, to more than one hundred times its original size. As The Hershey Industrial School—later the Milton Hershey School—it would accept worthy and needy boys who had lost one or both parents. And Milton Hershey, who was too shy ever to make speeches to the boys, would be among the school's most faithful visitors. After one visit, he confided to a friend: "I would give everything I possess if I could call one of these boys my own."

Milton Hershey died in 1945 at eighty-eight; but he had donated his entire company long before—in 1918— to the school for orphan boys. Not until 1927, when addi-

tional funds for expansion of the company were needed, did the school release part of its stock for public sale. And even today, approximately two-thirds of the Hershey Foods Corporation is owned by the school Milton Hershey established to give other boys, and now girls, a better start in life than he had ever known.

MARKETING INSIGHTS

By 1900, solid milk chocolate had become a popular delicacy in the United States; but it was available only in large, one and two-pound boxes at high prices, in relatively few stores. Milton Hershey, an experienced candymaker, decided there was a definite market for milk chocolate, if mass production methods could be applied to make a quality product using fresh milk at a low price.

His product concept was completely new: individually wrapped bars that could be sold as an everyday impulse purchase "for the nickel in a man's pocket."

His marketing concept was equally new: *mass availability* of the product in high visibility locations at the point of sale and in a self-promoting package.

The bold combination of mass production, mass distribution, and point-of-sale display was highly effective. Though the Hershey Milk Chocolate Bar was not advertised in conventional media, it had its own unique, built-in promotional formula.

Left: The popularity of its plant tours persuaded Hershey to build a new visitor complex, Chocolate World. One section is devoted to gardens where cocoa bean trees, banana trees, coffee trees, and many other exotic plants grow. Another section has displays of the basic steps in manufacturing chocolate, from roasting oven to milling machine. **Right:** Highpoint, the home Milton Hershey built in 1908, is now the corporate headquarters of the Hershey Foods Corporation. It is included in the National Register of Historic Places.

IVORY SOAP
"99 44/100% pure—it floats"

Co-founder William Procter

Co-founder James Gamble

19 Three-quarters of a century later, marketing people would acclaim his work as a classic example of building "brand image." But on that morning in 1879, what Harley Procter was doing would be considered, by family standards, to be just plain sinful. Not only was he thinking business thoughts on the Sabbath, but he was doing it right in the midst of a church service.

To Harley Procter, however, it seemed reasonable that *somebody* in his family should be worrying—even in church—about the critical importance of a new soap development in a company that was deriving three-fourths of its revenue from candles and lard oil. It was Harley, age thirty-two, who bore the responsibility for Procter & Gamble sales.

His father, William Procter, co-founder of the business, had been a candlemaker; and now, at age seventy-seven, he stubbornly refused to believe that the future of the candle was being threatened by the improved kerosene lamp, the rapid spread of illuminating gas, and the experiments with electric lamps. And Uncle James Gamble, seventy-six, the other co-founder—speaking as the original soapmaker of the partnership—pointed out that the company was currently producing twenty-four different kinds of soap, which ought to be a broad enough choice for anybody.

At this point, forty-four years had passed since William Procter and James Gamble, who married Cincinnati sisters, had formed the partnership of Procter & Gamble.

Harley's oldest brother, William Alexander Procter, agreed with the co-founders; but Harley had an ally in cousin James N. Gamble, a university-trained chemist, who now supervised product development. Despite what his father had said, James N. Gamble was convinced that, if Procter & Gamble wanted *quality* leadership in the soap industry, it must market a hard white soap that would equal the expensive, imported castile soaps in both purity and performance. James N. Gamble already had perfected such a soap, and it was being shipped to customers, but without any promotion. It was designated only as "Procter & Gamble's White Soap."

In the midst of the church service, Harley Procter was suddenly aware of the voices around him. The congregation had turned to Psalms 45:8 and was reading: "All thy garments smell of myrrh, and aloes, and cassia, out of the ivory palaces whereby they have made thee glad."

Harley had a sudden urge to slip quietly out of church and rush to his family with his new name for the white soap. But he could not. It would have to wait for the family's regular Monday morning meeting. It was against the rules for the Procters and the Gambles to discuss business on the Sabbath.

On July 18, 1879, Ivory Soap made its first appearance as a trademarked product. It would be three years before the members of the firm (the co-founders and their firstborn sons) would give Harley any funds for advertising. The members of the firm had agreed that no individual would draw a salary of more than five thousand dollars, in order to re-invest more money in the business, and they already had reprimanded Harley about his expenditures, including excessive use of the telegraph in his communications. But Harley pushed ahead with his planning.

Harley Procter, son of the co-founder. He gave Ivory Soap its name and mapped its marketing strategy.

The new "Ivory" soap, he decided, would be marketed as a dual-purpose product: "the only laundry soap that successfully answers for toilet use." Further, as the basis for Ivory's versatility, he would use the element of mild *purity:* "a laundry soap good for the nursery." To dramatize the two uses, he designed a laundry-size bar with a notch on each side to make it easy to divide the bar into two toilet-size cakes—and earned a patent for his idea.

He then engaged a nationally-recognized chemical consultant to analyze four samples of soap for purity. Three were the leading brands of imported castile soap, containing expensive olive oil; the fourth was Ivory Soap, made with domestic oils. The consultant soon reported that the fourth sample (Ivory) had fewer impurities than the other three samples, and that its impurities were: car-

James N. Gamble, son of the co-founder. He developed the formula for Ivory Soap.

THE "IVORY" is a Laundry Soap, with all the fine qualities of a choice Toilet Soap, and is 99 44-100 per cent. pure.

Ladies will find this Soap especially adapted for washing laces, infants', clothing, silk hose, cleaning gloves and all articles of fine texture and delicate color, and for the varied uses about the house that daily arise, requiring the use of soap that is above the ordinary in quality.

For the Bath, Toilet, or Nursery it is preferred to most of the Soaps sold for toilet use, being purer and much more pleasant and effective and possessing all the desirable properties of the finest unadultered White Castile Soap. The Ivory Soap will "float."

The cakes are so shaped that they may be used entire for general purposes or divided with a stout thread (as illustrated) into two perfectly formed cakes, of convenient size for toilet use.

The price, compared to the quality and the size of the cakes, makes it the cheapest Soap for everybody for every want. TRY IT.

SOLD EVERYWHERE.

Ivory Soap appeared in 1879; but it would be three years before members of the firm would appropriate money for the first ad, which introduced Ivory as a dual-purpose product and showed how easily a bar could be divided (with "a stout thread") for use as a laundry soap and a toilet soap.

bonates, 0.28 percent; mineral matter, 0.17 percent; uncombined alkali, 0.11 percent.

Harley added the fractions, subtracted the total from 100, and was pleased to see the memorable result: 99 $^{44}/_{100}$ percent. Later, he would be surprised by the attention the figure commanded. At a time when many soaps were suspect, because some used flour to bind the ingredients and others used marble dust to enhance the weight—and at a time when bombastic advertising was loaded with promises of "absolutely pure"—Harley Procter's "99 $^{44}/_{100}$% pure" introduced an electrifying kind of credibility.

Then, to Harley's desk, came a strange letter from a retailer who asked P&G to ship him "more of that soap that floats." Puzzled, Harley took the letter to cousin James N. Gamble, who promptly investigated and reported back: a careless workman had apparently forgotten to shut off his crutching (stirring) machine during the lunch hour; the resulting batch of soap had been impaired so slightly that it had passed inspection, but obviously had gone out with a slight admixture of air. Precautions would be taken, James reported, to prevent such errors in the future.

Harley Procter hesitated. Customers had *liked* the idea of a floating soap. Why? The answer was obvious: when a person dropped a cake of soap in a tub of murky water, there was no need to fish around for it. This could be important in dishpans, in the wash pails used by workmen—and in the bathtubs that were appearing in more and more homes. In the late 1870's, throughout America, a surprising number of families were embracing a new custom they called "the Saturday night bath."

Harley asked cousin James to adjust the crutching machines to produce a product with uniform floating qualities. It might be worth mentioning, he said, when they started to advertise.

In 1882, with some misgivings, the members of the firm voted Harley an advertising appropriation of eleven thousand dollars. They knew that he was opposed to the conventional use of small "business card" advertisements in almanacs and religious weeklies; that he favored "important space." But they also could see that national magazines, by 1882, were beginning to accept advertisements

Left: P&G's first research and development and quality control laboratory, opened in 1887. **Below:** Early P&G sampling crew, about 1880.

and that business-card sizes were going out of style. The first consumer advertisement for Ivory Soap was promptly readied for appearance in December, 1882. It showed a pair of feminine hands using a heavy thread to divide a bar of Ivory into two cakes and was headed: "The 'Ivory' is 99 $\frac{44}{100}$% pure." The text concluded with the incidental point: "The Ivory Soap will 'float.' "

Within a year, Harley was urging his readers to buy Ivory Soap a dozen bars at a time and to keep a cake handy in every room. Later, to dramatize the mildness of Ivory, he introduced "The Ivory Baby" and provided every grocer with a life-size cardboard cutout for display. He then promoted his safe-for-babies soap for the laundering of napkins, handkerchiefs, table linen, and other fine fabrics.

To enhance the appeal of his advertising, and to extend its reach, he pioneered the use of pre-printed color inserts in the early magazines (in which color had been limited to the covers); he was the first to use outdoor posters for product advertising (they had previously been used only as theatrical and circus posters); he commissioned leading artists to paint babies and children for his advertisements, and then offered reproductions suitable for framing; and his advertisements included such offers as a free booklet on baby care written by a graduate nurse. As one who liked poetry, Harley Procter also decided there should be at least one contest with prizes for the best verses about Ivory Soap, for use in Ivory ads. It drew 27,388 entries.

In 1878, when Harley Procter was thirty-two and the first shipment of the "White Soap" was on its way to market, he had resolved to retire from business by age forty-five. He bettered that schedule by a year and moved off to Massachusetts, his wife's home state, in 1890.

Innovative, consumer-minded Harley Procter built a marketing foundation for Ivory Soap that continues, virtually unchanged, into its second century. So fundamentally sound was his concept of "purity and mildness—safe for baby's skin" that it provided a launching pad for the introductions, years later, of Ivory Snow and Ivory Liquid.

His consumer-mindedness also left its mark on a continuing series of Procter & Gamble marketing advances. When Ivory moved into the new medium of radio, a "Mrs. Reilly" delivered dissertations on baby care. But Procter & Gamble's pioneer consumer attitude researchers soon reported that "the listeners want to be entertained, not instructed," and P&G program planners developed radio's first daytime serials. Author and lecturer Hendrik Willem Van Loon referred to many of the daytime serial scripts as "the greatest folk writing in America today"—but some critics dubbed them "soap opera," and the label stuck.

P&G marketing researchers also conducted the first studies to measure the size of radio's audiences. Rating services came later.

Again, when the new medium of television arrived, Ivory Soap was among the first products advertised—dating from 1939—and P&G attitude researchers were busily finding out what the viewers did and did not like. An early finding: "viewers want a TV show to flow as smoothly as a movie." Acting on that consumer guidance, P&G became the first to go to Hollywood for the filming of an entire television show, the weekly, thirty-minute "Fireside Theater."

Other advertising innovations would follow, and Procter & Gamble would go on to become the largest advertiser in America.

But perhaps the most unusual result of Harley Procter's advertising pioneering was the influence it had on his nephew, William Cooper Procter, the son of William Alexander Procter and grandson of the co-founder.

Young William Cooper Procter was just weeks away from a Princeton graduation, in 1883, when his grandfather died. He was promptly called home to the family business, and the problems he faced were awesome. Work stoppages had suddenly become a national epidemic, and P&G was getting its share. The Federation of Organized Trades and Labor Unions, formed in 1881, was on its way to becoming the American Federation of Labor, and factories everywhere were in trouble.

Boyish-looking Cooper soon proved that he had a ma-

Scripts in hand, the cast of "The O'Neills," a 1935–42 daytime radio serial sponsored by Ivory Soap, awaits the "on-air" signal. Hendrik Willem Van Loon called early serials "some of the greatest folk writing in America today"; but listeners learned to call it "soap opera."

ture grasp of the problem and that his sympathies were on the side of the workers. One of his early recommendations was to give all employees a free Saturday afternoon, without loss of wages. It was a radical idea at the time; but the company gave it a try and decided it was a good move. Cooper's next project was an employee profit-sharing plan; and again, after strenuous discussion, he got what he wanted. By 1895, James N. Gamble and his son David were withdrawing from active management, William Alexander Procter was serving as a consultant, and William Cooper Procter was the man in charge of the company.

In 1920, after a long series of personnel moves that included putting plant workers on the Board of Directors, William Cooper Procter was ready to apply Uncle Harley's advertising theories to what Cooper had decided was the company's most important personnel need. To Richard R. Deupree, the sales director who would later become chief executive officer, Cooper pointed out that the wholesalers in the soap industry frequently bought and stockpiled goods when they anticipated price increases. The result was a succession of peaks and valleys in factory production, with periods of overtime work followed by layoffs.

The Ivory Baby, as updated in the mid-1920's by artist Dorothy Hope Smith.

Could advertising be used, William Cooper Procter wanted to know, to maintain such steady consumer demand that the company could market directly through retailers to consumers and thus eliminate the wholesaler fluctuations?

Richard Deupree analyzed the problem and concluded that advertising and his sales force could do the job. As of July 1, 1920, Procter & Gamble began marketing directly to retail stores. Just three years and one month later, on August 1, 1923, P&G was able to tell its employees that the company "hereby guarantees full pay for full-time work for not less than forty-eight weeks in each calendar year."

The New York Times was sufficiently impressed by the P&G program to refer to it editorially as "the boldest attack on uncertain tenure of jobs—and the industrial and social evils entailed thereby—that has ever been made in this country."

And there was still another great benefit from the Deupree study that would have been of special interest to product salesman Harley Procter. Having proved that advertising could maintain steady enough consumer demand to make direct factory-retailer-consumer marketing possible, Procter & Gamble was ideally prepared for the

William Cooper Procter, grandson of the co-founder. Using advertising as the foundation of his plan, he introduced America's first guaranteed annual wage for factory workers.

coming of the modern supermarket and the age of self-service. After that, it was just a matter of time before P&G would be adding a Drug Products Division, then a Food Products Division, and then a Paper Products Division, all selling to the women shoppers in the supermarkets.

In 1923, the William Cooper Procter approach, strongly influenced by his Uncle Harley's advertising expertise, had been important to some fifty-five hundred workers in three plants. By the 1980's, the William Cooper Procter approach, carried forward and expanded by successor chief executives, had become important to some fifty thousand Procter & Gamble people in over sixty plants throughout the world.

MARKETING INSIGHTS

It was probably Harley Procter who first recognized the importance of "product image," "brand promotion" and "consumer orientation"—and did something specific and positive about it all.

His company, at the time, offered twenty-four different kinds of soap, but lacked quality leadership because none of the twenty-four was regarded by consumers as the equal of the imported white castile soaps. Ironically, one of the twenty-four—"Procter & Gamble's White Soap"—was as pure as the castiles, but its virtues had never been promoted.

Harley Procter obtained proof of the white soap's purity, and promoted it as an individual brand with a new brand name connoting purity, and a specific supporting promise: "Ivory Soap—99 $\frac{44}{100}$% pure." He gave further support to his promise of purity with "the Ivory baby." The "purity and mildness" image, in turn, paved the way for such companion products as Ivory Snow and Ivory Liquid.

When an early-day production error resulted in some aeration that caused Ivory Soap to float, Procter noted that consumers liked the floating feature; he promptly made it a standard product characteristic.

Harley Procter's consumer-oriented advertising approach proved to be so effective that nephew William Cooper Procter later would be able to stabilize sales so consistently—through the systematic use of advertising—that he could offer America's first guaranteed annual wage for factory workers.

By learning how to build continuous consumer demand for its brands, Procter & Gamble was among the first companies to benefit from the coming of the supermarket and the age of self-service. The company's mastery of "selling to women through supermarkets" led naturally to P&G diversification into food, toiletries and paper products.

Procter & Gamble is now well-established as the nation's largest advertiser and serves as a comprehensive example of what is meant by such often-used terms as "marketing mix" and "promotion mix."

At P&G, "marketing mix"—all the elements in a company's marketing effort—includes: product development to serve the needs/desires of individual market segments; packaging; marketing/attitude research; pricing; selection of distribution channels; personal selling; promotion; display; physical handling; technical servicing; fact-finding and analysis.

P&G's "promotional mix" (within the overall marketing mix) includes: personal selling; advertising (television, radio, magazines, newspapers, outdoor, direct mail); and sales promotion (point-of-purchase materials, sampling, couponing, special shows and demonstrations, package offers and other "deals").

Early advertisement endeavored to make every user a *heavy* user with this promise: ". . . buy a dozen cakes at a time, take off the wrappers, and stand each cake on end in a dry place; for, unlike many other soaps, the Ivory improves by age. Test this advice, and you will find the twelve cakes will last as long as thirteen cakes bought singly."

Our advice to consumers of Ivory Soap is, buy a dozen cakes at a time, take off the wrappers, and stand each cake on end in a dry place; for, unlike many other soaps, the Ivory improves by age. Test this advice, and you will find the twelve cakes will last as long as thirteen cakes bought singly. This advice may appear to you as being given against our own interests; on the contrary, our interest and desire is, that the patrons of Ivory Soap shall find it the most desirable and economical soap they can use. Respectfully,

PROCTER & GAMBLE, Cincinnati, O.

JANTZEN SWIM SUITS

"A good organization will have a good business."

Carl Jantzen

John Zehntbauer

20 When the nice young man stopped in that morning, saying he did not want to buy anything, but would like a dozen catalogs, sales clerk Minerva Zehntbauer was almost beside herself with curiosity. But not until later did her associates in the store give the incident a moment's thought.

A more pressing matter, at the time, was finding a proper new trademark for the company. Within five years of its 1910 founding, it had outgrown its original trademark, PK, the initials of Portland Knitting Mills. Prospective customers were beginning to hear about Carl Jantzen's stretchy new rib-stitch bathing suits and were writing to the "Jantzen Company." Now the company was about to start its first advertising program and a decision had to be made.

The name "Zehntbauer" had been suggested because brothers John and Roy Zehntbauer had taken the first steps toward starting the company before inviting their friend Carl Jantzen to join them. Moreover, John Zehntbauer had been studying salesmanship and commercial correspondence at the Y.M.C.A. night school; he had the best "management" qualifications. But John Zehntbauer gently but firmly refused to consider it. "That name," he said, "is much too long and hard to pronounce. Carl's name is the one to use."

For his part, quiet Carl Jantzen was equally adamant: "I just don't like the sound of my name."

The name-suggesters tried a compromise: "Jan-Zen." Or what about "Portknit?"

Gentle John Zehntbauer did not like arguments, and he had a good reason to ask to be excused from the meeting. He had to see Joe Gerber, the printer, about the new stationery. Without mentioning it at the meeting, he already knew what he would tell Gerber to put on the stationery.

"When the new stationery arrived, with 'Jantzen' all

over it," John Zehntbauer recalled later, "Carl was surprised and chagrined. But he took it good-naturedly, and after a while he got used to it."

Now John's sister Minerva could give her report on the young man who had asked for the dozen catalogs. "He just wanted to cut out the red diving girl on the cover." She paused in embarrassment; she had not even thought to ask the young man's name. "He said he had pasted one of our red diving girls on the windshield of his car, and a lot of his friends asked him where *they* could get one. So, when he was driving in to Portland. . . ."

John Zehntbauer was delighted and said his friend Joe Gerber would be, too. Joe had picked the design from some suggestions submitted by Portland free-lance artists Florence and Frank Clark. The Clarks had recommended against showing a young woman posed realistically in a dive. Instead, they favored a female figure in a graceful, curved position, "just diving through the air." Along with her brilliant red Jantzen suit, she wore a red bathing cap and red, mid-length stockings.

Roy Zehntbauer

Here, the partners promptly agreed, was the central idea of the new advertising program. Along with the advertisements, they would produce several thousand cutouts of the red diver for store displays, and give out stickers to everybody who asked for one.

Until Carl Jantzen had started tinkering with the machinery, trying to develop his new rib-stitch idea, the Portland Knitting Mills had been content to produce a line of warm, well-made, woolen sweaters, sox, caps and mittens—and, with a little luck, sell enough to keep the little mill over the retail shop alive. The young partners, just now in their thirties, had been clinging to one big, bright hope: Portland, Oregon, whose population had just passed two hundred thousand, was too small to support its many present knitting mills in any kind of style, and was isolated from America's largest markets—but Portland, the *port*, could make the whole world their market. Prospects looked good, and Carl's invention would help in that direction.

Minerva Zehntbauer

Carl Jantzen's new rib-stitch had been aimed at making a trimmer sweater cuff with outstandingly springy stretching qualities—but it soon drew an order for something completely different: a pair of trunks for a Zehntbauer teammate at the Portland Rowing Club. So pleased was the rower with his trunks that he ordered a full suit for swimming. He returned a third time to report that the suit was the best-fitting bathing suit he had ever worn, and was warmer than any other, but that it was too heavy when wet. Could they make it in a lighter weight?

The Zehntbauer brothers, Carl Jantzen, and printer friend Joe Gerber promptly became a test team for the development of a new lightweight, rib-stitch bathing suit. Their test facilities were the Y.M.C.A. pool and the Willamette River. In short order, they developed a suit so springy that Jantzen salesman Mitch Heinemann could soon amaze The Emporium in San Francisco by barging into the Big E's merchandising office, pulling a small Jantzen bathing suit on over his street clothes.

Then came the "Red Diving Girl." The young partners abruptly turned their backs on the market for knitted jackets, and put their entire first year's (1916) advertising budget—four hundred dollars—into promoting the red Jantzen diving emblem. The Jantzen bathing suit went on to achieve national distribution by 1918, and the company changed its name to "Jantzen Knitting Mills." Not until 1938 would the company concentrate on anything but swim suits.

Buyers of the stretchy suits soon asked for a diving girl emblem they could apply. The company obliged with a fourteen-inch felt cutout, and began stitching it across the chests of all suits in production. After a little reflection, it was later decided that the fourteen-inch emblem detracted from the beauty of the garment. It was reduced to a ten-inch size and sewed to the lower part of the suit. Meanwhile, Red Diving Girl windshield stickers were persuading one observer to report: "It seems as if half the cars on the Pacific Coast now have Red Diving Girl stickers!"

Moving swiftly against the new opportunity, the company changed the designation of the product from "bathing" to "swimming" suits and adopted the slogan: "The suit that changed bathing to swimming." By 1922,

The original Jantzen "test team" of 1913 (*left to right*): Roy Zehntbauer, Sam Street, John Zehntbauer, Carl Jantzen, Joe Gerber.

The original Jantzen diving girl, as drawn by Florence and Frank Clark.

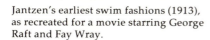

Johnny Weissmuller, who became even more famous as "Tarzan" than as a world champion swimmer, was a loyal Jantzen wearer. He is shown as a member of the 1924 Illinois Athletic Club team.

Jantzen's earliest swim fashions (1913), as recreated for a movie starring George Raft and Fay Wray.

Typical action during a 1930 Jantzen "Learn-to-Swim Week." Note the Red Diving Girl emblem on the umbrellas.

Jantzen had moved into *The Saturday Evening Post*, and no less an illustrator than McClelland Barclay was drawing the Red Diving Girl. Simultaneously, the energetic Jantzen team was launching a national "Jantzen Learn-to-Swim Week."

John Zehntbauer had come to Portland from Purdin, Missouri, as a farm lad of seventeen, and had inquired at the first "Boy Wanted" sign he saw. It was in the window of the Luke Knitting Company. He soon set a record for sock production by inventing a little cam which prevented drop stitches at high speed. He also went to night school, and later, when his family followed him to Portland, he helped his brothers and sister with their schooling. Within two years of his Portland arrival, forced to take a vacation to regain his health, he headed for the peaceful apple orchard country of Oregon's Hood River and there, by chance, met Carl Jantzen, who had been brought there by his parents from Denmark at the age of seven.

John and Roy Zehntbauer, and Carl Jantzen, were

much the same in many ways. They were quiet, unassuming, earnest young men, weak in education but strong in their willingness to work. When, in 1910, they became partners in the little knitting mill in a loft over a retail store, John Zehntbauer observed that "it was not of material things, but an expression of the ideas of individuals."

Years later, John Zehntbauer would look back at the company's beginnings and write: "It was our theory that a good organization will have a good business, and that an organization good enough will always solve its problems to the best advantage. We chose each employee first for his good character, then trained him to fit into a high-class organization dedicated to giving good service and producing high-quality merchandise."

Once it began to roll, John Zehntbauer's team was unstoppable. By 1925, the Jantzen sales force was moving into Europe and a new representative in Vienna would report: "Our method of dramatizing the elasticity of the Jantzen swim suit by putting it on over our jacket and pants, to show how this little tightly knitted suit expanded to fit a size 36, 38 or 40, etc., was revolutionary, and really the talk of the town wherever we went to introduce the garments."

From Europe, the international trail led to India, South Africa, Canada, South America, Australia. By 1928, worldwide distribution was a reality, and Jantzen salespeople were responding with alacrity to the individual wishes and customs of the different countries. When Sweden, for example, took a liking to the Jantzen "beaner," a little knitted cap, all the woolen remnants in Portland were converted to beaners. And in Taiwan, the Jantzen people learned, the proper way to introduce a new line of swim suits is with a fifty-piece brass band and fireworks.

Meanwhile, back in Portland, the production people were expanding the technology of knitting—inventing new machines, when needed, to carry out the new ideas. And the company was developing an interest in fashion design that would soon stand it in good stead. John Zehntbauer decided this kind of teamwork should be rewarded with an ownership in the business; he announced a stock purchase plan, and numerous Jantzen

"Jantzen is the original elastic-stitch swimming suit," said this 1922 advertisement in *The Saturday Evening Post.* "It fits perfectly—wet or dry—not accentuating any part of the body." The advertisement was signed: "Jantzen—The National Swimming Suit—Never binds, never sags."

The answer to
nude bathing

New Molded-Fit Jantzens that give that
thrilling sensation of swimming with no
suit on at all!

New fashion fabrics have been created
by Jantzen—marvelous fabrics of luxurious softness and almost incredible lightness—fabrics amazingly elastic in every
direction. Knitted from Jantzen Miracle
Yarn, the new Molded-Fit Jantzens fit the
body like another skin and have actual
figure-control to a surprising degree.

Never before has it been possible to
so beautifully mold the body in a swimming suit—never before has such freedom, comfort and beauty been achieved.

See the Molded-Fit Jantzens in the new
Featherwool, Sun-Tweed and Krinkle-
Knit fabrics at your favorite shop or
store. . . . $5.00 to $9.50. Standard
Jantzens $3.95.

Jantzen
MOLDED-FIT
swimming suits

Left: Along with the Depression, the early 1930's brought
a special threat to Jantzen: a
broadscale revival of interest
in nude bathing. Jantzen
promptly responded with
this advertisement for
"molded-fit" swim suits "that
give the thrilling impression
of swimming with no suit on
at all!" **Right:** Jantzen releases a new line every three
months, in both the men's
and the misses' divisions.
When new styles "take off,"
Jantzen is ready to "run"
with them.

employees became stockholders of the company.

Like all other companies, Jantzen felt the economic
pinch of the early 1930's. Then, to Jantzen, came an even
greater threat: a massive revival of interest in nude bathing. To a maker of swim suits, the possibilities were terrifying.

Jantzen met the issue head-on. A typical Jantzen advertisement of that time was headlined, "THE ANSWER TO
NUDE BATHING," and went on to say, "New molded-fit
Jantzen gives a thrilling sensation of swimming with no
suit on at all—yet assures fashionable and modest appearance."

The nude bathing threat inspired a cram course in fashion appeals and lighter fabrics, and the company made good use of its new knowledge. In 1938, Roy Zehntbauer opened Jantzen's new fashion-oriented sweater division. For two years, Jantzen management had been convinced that its expanding technology and fashion talents called for a diversification program, and sweaters were the logical first move—followed by related introductions of foundation garments and active sportswear. What if nude bathing should ever become a reality?

World War II called a temporary halt to the diversification plans, but it also provided essential experience that helped make later diversification even more successful. From fashionable sportswear, Jantzen turned to wartime production of such humdrum items as sleeping bags and gas masks—but the company learned new volume techniques, new woven as well as knitted technology, and the new science of combining natural with synthetic fibers.

When the postwar boom began in casual wear, Jantzen was ready. An extensive survey had indicated that the Red Diving Girl was solidly established as the world's leading symbol of fashionable attire for the great outdoors, and Jantzen's technology and fashion skills were overdue for a new challenge. Jantzen Knitting Mills became "Jantzen Inc." and went ahead with the finalizing of four autonomous divisions: Misses, Men's, Women's Intimate Apparel (later discontinued), and International. Along with its new fashion talents, Jantzen became the first garment manufacturer to blend synthetic and natural fiber, and would later become the pioneer of double-knit fabrics.

In the American apparel industry, with nearly twenty thousand companies competing for the consumer's favor, Jantzen, which began with Minerva Zehntbauer as its sole employee, has grown to more than four thousand employees worldwide and rolls up a sales volume of about $125 million annually.

John Zehntbauer, the founder, continued his leadership of the company until 1966 and had occasion, many times before his death in 1969, to reflect on the rightness

Jantzen designer checks the measurements of a new swim suit.

of his early belief that "a good organization will have a good business." Co-founder Carl Jantzen died in 1939, but his son, Carl Jr., continued the Jantzen tradition of innovation in the company's new fashion design operation.

Throughout all their years of working together, John Zehntbauer once observed, "there was never a cross word." And others would say of the founders: "Their greatest characteristic was humility. They had a strong belief in an individual's right to freedom and dignity—and in the right of the individual to assert his own ways of contributing to team achievement."

The early promise of "a world market from the port of Portland" had taken a sudden and surprising detour away from the markets for knitted jackets; but the promise came true just the same. And the early challenge of better ways to knit became the greater challenge of designing better appeals to the world's tastes in fashions.

"Predicting new fashion trends is one of the world's most difficult jobs," today's Jantzen management agrees, "and we're not about to tell you how we do it. But we can assure you that good fashions are evolutionary, not revolutionary."

In the apparel industry, Jantzen freely admits, "no two days are ever alike. Many months in advance, we pick colors, fabrics—and from that point on, we're committed. Then it becomes a matter of planning by style, by color, by size—followed by the task of balancing constantly to sales as they come in, and being concerned with a tremendous number of stockkeeping units, at the same time loading our factories in such a way that the tops and bottoms and colors and sizes will all arrive at the distribution point to be shipped together. Some of the styles will then 'take off'—and 'running' with them will mean getting more fabric, rearranging factory production, speeding up shipment, and so on.

"But these," the company notes, in the Zehntbauer tradition, "are not regarded as 'problems.' We think of them as opportunities to win a bigger share of the market. We release a new line every three months, in both the men's and the misses' divisions. So you can see how the opportunities keep adding up."

MARKETING INSIGHTS

One of Jantzen's early success secrets was the open-minded flexibility of its marketing effort. Carl Jantzen's newly-invented rib-stitch had been aimed at making a trimmer cuff for everyday sweaters; then, purely by chance, a friend asked for a rib-stitched bathing suit, and Jantzen obliged. Similarly, an emblem of a female diver became an overnight success; the company immediately applied the Red Diving Girl symbol everywhere.

A threatened revival of interest in nude bathing would later persuade the company to study fashion and apply its knitting technology to a dressy line of sweaters; then the move into the world of fashion would receive a giant boost from Jantzen's development of doubleknit fabrics.

Open-minded marketing flexibility—and swift production support of the marketing effort—continues to be one of the prime reasons for Jantzen success in fashion apparel as well as in swim suits. The company releases a new line every three months—for women and for men. As some of the fashions become instant hits, Jantzen promptly rearranges production schedules to "run" with them. In wave after wave of those quarterly releases, Jantzen creates opportunities for increasing its share of a market it participates in with some twenty thousand competitors.

KITCHENAID DISHWASHERS

"If nobody else is going to invent a dishwashing machine, I'll do it myself!"

Josephine Garis Cochrane, amateur inventor of the mechanical dishwasher.

21 The mechanical dishwasher was invented by a socially-prominent woman in Shelbyville, Illinois, who knew nothing about inventions, and seldom did her own dishes, but whose patience finally reached the breaking point over servants who persisted in cracking her expensive, imported china.

Josephine Garis Cochrane was the strong-minded daughter of noted civil engineer John Garis, and the staunchly loyal wife of W. A. Cochrane, an Illinois political leader of the 1880's. She had grown up in Chicago, in a home staffed with trained servants; now, in a small prairie town, she was entertaining the bluebloods of central Illinois—and every formal dinner was ending, disastrously, with a shattering of expensive porcelain. After one especially trying evening, she exploded. "If nobody else is going to invent a dishwashing machine," Josephine Garis Cochrane exclaimed in desperation, "I'll do it myself. That's all there is to it!"

In a woodshed adjoining her home, Mrs. Cochrane fashioned wire dish compartments, attached them to a wire wheel, and installed the wheel in a copper wash boiler. She then devised a way of making the wheel turn as soapy water was pumped out of the bottom of the boiler and sprayed down over the dishes. It was crude, but it worked; and she had made it herself. With forthright pride, she labeled it "the Garis-Cochrane," demonstrated it to her circle of influential friends, and was soon receiving inquiries from hotels and restaurants. She also received a U.S. Patent in December of 1886, and her machines went on to win the highest award at the Columbian Exposition in Chicago in 1893 for "the best mechanical construction, durability, and adaptation to their line of work."

With the dedicated help of her friends and business associates, Annie F. Colt and machinist George Butters, Josephine Garis Cochrane resolutely built her Garis-

Cochrane enterprise into Bromley-Merseles Manufacturing, Inc., later the Crescent Washing Machine Company, became a major supplier of dishwashing equipment for hotel, restaurant and institutional kitchens, and later supervised the development of what was considered the first successful model of a dishwasher for the home. She actively directed her company right up to the time of her death in 1913.

Meanwhile, in Ohio, an only slightly younger company had also become a major supplier of heavy-duty equipment—but of a different kind—for hotel, restaurant and institutional kitchens. The Hobart Manufacturing Company, of Troy, after starting its corporate life in 1897 as a maker of motors and dynamos, had decided early to specialize in the application of electric power to the difficult, manual tasks "in places where food was purchased, prepared and served."

Hobart began by coupling its motors with belts to the flywheel of the heaviest machine then operating in a grocery store: the coffee grinder. Hobart then improved on this arrangement by inventing the first electric coffee mill.

From the electric coffee mill, Hobart moved in logical steps to grocery store machines for grinding hamburger and peanut butter. To the line of grinders, Hobart then added mixers and slicers; and the grinders and slicers were soon followed by heavy-duty meat saws and processing equipment.

Hobart, by now, had expanded from the grocery store market into the larger and busier world of hotel, restaurant and institutional kitchens—and bakeries—and would in time become the world's largest manufacturer of heavy-duty food equipment and systems. At the same time, Hobart was developing a deep admiration for the rugged Cochrane-design dishwashing machines they observed in so many of those big, bustling kitchens.

So it was high praise for the amateur inventor of Shelbyville, Illinois, when Hobart decided that the company founded by Josephine Garis Cochrane should become part of the Hobart Corporation. The acquisition was completed in 1926, and the Hobart name became synony-

Left: One of Josephine Cochrane's early (1911) Crescent machines. **Right:** After long experience in hotel and restaurant kitchens, Hobart introduced its KitchenAid dishwasher to the home market in 1949.

mous with heavy-duty dishwashers—some of them up to sixty feet long—as well as with grinders, mixers, and slicers.

But not until 1949 would Hobart enter the home market with its KitchenAid dishwasher—using the brand name Hobart had introduced on a home mixer in 1918. What took them so long? The answer is simply: the home market was not ready.

Josephine Garis Cochrane had developed a home dishwashing machine, prior to 1914, which had many of the basic features of today's finest machines. But the average home lacked an adequate supply of heated and softened water for proper mechanical dishwashing. And, as the years rolled on, the careless-servant problem that had motivated Mrs. Cochrane began to disappear as servants disappeared.

Finally, for the makers of dishwashing machines, there was the deterrent of the homemaker herself. Too often, she did not regard dishwashing as a heavy, disagreeable chore, akin to laundering clothes. Often, in fact—according to marketing researchers—she regarded "doing the dishes" as a welcome relaxer after the tension of preparing and serving a meal. Watching dishes and glasses emerge, glistening, from the pleasantly warm, sudsy water was often perceived as a rewarding interlude in the working day. Why spoil all that with the extravagant purchase of a dishwashing machine?

Josephine Garis Cochrane, who had built the first dishwashing machine for her own home use, had never bothered to do battle with the prejudice of other homemakers. Selling to hotels was a lot easier. But an independent (non-Hobart) group of male marketing researchers in the consumer motivation field was more persistent. Many women, they discovered, would have liked to possess a mechanical dishwasher in order to ward off feelings of guilt: it made them feel guilty to look at a late-evening stack of dirty dishes and to decide, reluctantly, that they would rather go to bed and do those dishes in the morning. The guilt element was so strong that one (non-Hobart) researcher concluded, flippantly, "What the market needs is just a big, hollow dish hamper, where dirty dishes can be *hidden* overnight!"

There was, of course, an even stronger reason for mechanical dishwashing: the final sterilization of dishes and glasses, using more heat than hands could ever withstand.

So the mechanical dishwasher, long delayed, came swarming into the home market, and Hobart's KitchenAid moved into the leadership of the field. In the Hobart tradition of invention, the home dishwasher would be joined in time by KitchenAid disposers, hot water dispensers, and trash compactors, as well as by new models of KitchenAid mixers and home coffee mills.

Meanwhile, Hobart had not forgotten its original customer, the grocer. Not long after acquiring the Crescent Washing Machine Company, Hobart also acquired the Dayton Scale Company and proceeded with the development of Hobart Computing Scales that weigh, compute price, and issue a printed price ticket for the package you buy—all in one operation.

For Hobart, it all adds up to an annual sales volume of more than $540 million and makes employment for approximately thirteen thousand people. But, basically, it is all just part of following the original, single-minded Hobart goal of specializing in the application of electric power to the difficult, manual tasks, "in the places where food is purchased, prepared or served."

MARKETING INSIGHTS

Josephine Garis Cochrane invented the dishwashing machine to protect her delicate china against breakage; but her best early markets were hotels and restaurants, where the only concern was volume. By 1914, her company had developed a dishwasher for the home; but the home market would not be a profitable one for her invention until thirty-five years later.

Why the long-delayed favorable reaction to an important work saver? One answer, attitude researchers found, was that many homemakers simply did not perceive dishwashing as disagreeable "work"—it could be an almost-pleasant interlude in the day's routine. Ultimately, a major reason for buying a dishwasher had nothing to do with washing; it was the germ-killing effects of the heat cycle, using far more heat than human hands could withstand.

Once the home market was ready for the automatic dishwasher, the Hobart-built KitchenAid—the direct successor to the original Cochrane machine—became a natural leader because of its ruggedly reliable performance. Hobart, the first to apply electric power to difficult tasks "in places where food is purchased, prepared and served," had become the world's largest manufacturer of heavy-duty food equipment. In its KitchenAid dishwasher, Hobart brought the same kind of heavy-duty dependability to the home.

KLEENEX TISSUE

"Don't put a cold in your pocket."

22 At the time Kimberly-Clark's marketers introduced Kleenex tissue, their assignment was to establish a new use for a ten-year-old material made from wood pulp. And they had good reasons for avoiding what might have appeared to be the "obvious" approach, with a promise of health benefits.

Kimberly-Clark's Cellucotton brand wadding, from which Kleenex tissue was made, already had a solid health-care pedigree—but it was closely related to World War I, an experience the nation was trying to forget. The daily newspapers, having finished with the giant drama of the War, were still carrying an abundance of reports on how well the French and Belgian troops were progressing with their occupation of the Ruhr for the enforcement of reparations.

On the bright side, glamorous Hollywood was setting new box office records. Mary Pickford, continuing her reign as "America's Sweetheart," was being joined by Janet Gaynor, Helen Hayes, and other glittering stars; and Lee de Forest was exhibiting the world's first sound-on-film moving picture as just one indication that Hollywood's future was almost too magnificent for human comprehension.

The remarkably absorbent Cellucotton material had been developed in 1914, just in time to replace scarce cotton for surgical dressings in wartime hospitals and first aid stations. Near war's end, a super-absorbent version of Cellucotton was perfected for use as a gas-mask filter, and it was this material which came to market in 1924 as Kleenex tissue.

Hollywood stars were among the first to try samples of the product and proclaim it to be a great new remover of cold cream and other cosmetics—which was precisely what the marketers had planned for this new product. The package carried the descriptive phrase, "Sanitary Cold Cream Remover," and advertisements for Kleenex tissue would soon follow with endorsements from such stars as Helen Hayes, Gertrude Lawrence, Ronald Colman, Elsie Janis, and many more.

The product gained steadily for five years and the consumer mail, which Kimberly-Clark always read with care, indicated that the product was living up to all its advertised promise.

But the mail also brought the occasional blunt question: "Why don't you ever say it's good for blowing your nose?"

The question began to appear with increasing frequency, and the company's marketers decided it deserved an objective answer. They responded in early 1930, in Peoria, Illinois, with a simultaneous, split-run test of two newspaper campaigns. One campaign, reaching half the readers on an approximately alternating basis, was headlined, "We pay to prove there is no way like Kleenex to remove cold cream." The other approach was headlined, "We pay to prove Kleenex is wonderful for handkerchiefs." The "pay" was a free box of Kleenex tissue, and the ads carried coupons good for redemption at drug and department stores.

By the end of four weeks, the vote was tallied, and it was decisive: sixty-one percent of the coupon-redeemers had responded to the "handkerchief" ads.

The Kleenex tissue marketers promptly divided the current advertising effort into two principal approaches, with the handkerchief approach as the dominant one. Among the early headlines was: "Don't put a cold in your pocket." Sales soared to double the volume of the previous year—and then doubled again in the year that followed.

The credit, however, did not belong entirely to the new advertising approach. Package designers had made a spectacular contribution to the marketing mix by inventing a unique dispensing package, which they introduced in 1929, just ahead of the new "handkerchief" advertising.

To make the new "Serv-a-Tissue" box possible, packaging engineers developed a method whereby two separate rolls of tissue were mechanically interfolded. Thus, when

Evolution of the Kleenex package. Original box is in upper left.

These split-run test ads switched Kleenex from a "cold cream remover" to a "nose-blowing" marketing strategy.

Ultimately, Kleenex tissue was promoted for nose-blowing and some forty-seven additional uses.

one double sheet was pulled up through the dispenser slot in the top of the box, the next double sheet would automatically be pulled up in the slot.

With its new POP-UP® box feature, Kleenex tissue was promoted not only as a product for the home, but for the office and car as well. To its basic handkerchief function were added such other uses as cleaning out pans, draining fried foods, and wiping windshields. By the mid-1930's, package inserts listed forty-eight "typical" uses.

From its original price of 65¢, the two-hundred-tissue carton dropped to 50¢ in 1926, to 35¢ in 1932, to 18¢ in 1934, and finally, in 1937, to 13¢ or two for a quarter. Although prices have increased since then, consumers today pay about the same for the product as in 1924.

In 1948, consumer mail brought another unique package to the marketplace: the twenty-four-tissue "Pocket-Pack" with the same POP-UP® feature as the regular boxes.

Sales continued to grow. But so did the competition. Kimberly-Clark Corporation of Neenah, Wisconsin, founded in 1872 as a manufacturer of printing papers, had no monopoly on wood pulp. The success of Kleenex tissue attracted a swarm of national, regional and local brands. Ultimately, what Kleenex tissue started would become known officially as the "disposable tissue industry," with total retail sales of more than $450 million annually.

What Kleenex tissue started would also lead to a whole new generation of cellulose-based disposables: napkins, towels, diapers, bed linens, lab and shop coats, and many more, most all of which are sold worldwide under the Kleenex trademark.

With the massive help of its Cellucotton developments, Kimberly-Clark has grown to an organization of some twenty-eight thousand people, with sales of more than $1.5 billion and plants in nineteen states and twenty-one countries.

And sometimes you can not see the plants for the forests, because Kleenex tissue literally grows in trees. To make sure its disposables and other products continue their steady flow to market, Kimberly-Clark engages in cooperative and company-sponsored research programs in forest genetics, fertilization, fiber utilization and management as part of its on-going effort to improve the quality and yield of forestland. The company owns or controls nearly thirteen million acres in the United States and Canada—an area equivalent to the states of Connecticut, Delaware, Hawaii, and New Jersey combined.

MARKETING INSIGHTS

Kleenex tissue is closely related to health care; but its marketers had a logical reason for avoiding that appeal when they introduced Kleenex. Its health-care background had begun in World War I, and the nation was trying to forget the war. The marketers turned instead to the happy glamour of Hollywood and featured cold cream removal.

Consumers, however, kept suggesting that Kleenex tissue was great for nose-blowing. Open-mindedly, the company tested the nose-blowing appeal and found it was highly effective. The company also found that "Don't put a cold in your pocket" was an adroit way to communicate the message in polite good taste.

To avoid positioning the product as something to be used only during the season of colds and sneezes, its marketers reminded the public of nearly fifty additional uses.

In the success of Kleenex tissue, packaging played as important a part as advertising. Packaging engineers developed a method whereby two separate rolls of Kleenex tissue were mechanically interfolded. When the user pulled one double sheet through the dispenser slot in the top of the box, the next double sheet automatically was pulled up into the slot.

The Kleenex packaging and advertising effort had a lasting impact on our nose-blowing and many other hygienic practices. Significantly, modern motels usually have built-in compartments for tissue dispenser boxes, and so do many modern homes.

And there was much more to come. The success of Kleenex tissue paved the way for a whole new age of cellulose-based disposables: napkins, towels, bed linens, diapers, lab and shopcoats, and many more.

LANE CEDAR CHESTS

"Make a good product, and sell with an idea."

Edward Hudson Lane at the time of his company's fiftieth anniversary.

23 As Edward Hudson Lane summed it up years later: "In the month of March, 1912, my father attended a public auction and paid five hundred dollars for an old packing box plant which had gone bankrupt. In June, he suggested to me that I go over to Altavista, where the little box plant was located, and start manufacturing cedar chests. I was nearly twenty-one years old at the time. I had no manufacturing experience, and I had never heard of a cedar chest."

To young Edward Hudson Lane, it did not seem much different from the other assignments he was accustomed to receiving from his father, John Edward Lane, from running the family farms, to betting on race horses, to setting up sawmills. The elder Lane, left fatherless at six by the Battle of Gettysburg, was active in the heavy contracting business while still in his teens, and had become one of the leading rebuilders of the war-torn South's dams, bridges, water works, power plants, and railroads. It was in the course of building a railroad that he had founded the town of Altavista, Virginia in 1907. John Edward Lane was a doer. He was also a stern man. Even after bearing him five children, his wife, whether in public or private, never addressed him as anything but "Mr. Lane." When he made a "suggestion," he expected to get results.

Purely by chance, on his way to Altavista from his home near Charlottesville, Edward Hudson Lane ran into a Mr. Loop, who had been his instructor in woodworking during his two years at Virginia Polytechnic Institute. Loop, it seemed, had now moved to Altavista and would be happy to give his earnest young former student some advice on what might be needed at the packing box plant for the manufacture of cedar chests. Upon arriving at the site, they discovered that the packing box plant consisted of a corrugated iron building fifty feet by ninety feet, with two small dry kilns, a boiler, and a small engine. Loop wagged his head sadly. "I'm afraid," he told Edward, "that you're going to need quite a bit of work here."

At the end of the first month, John Edward Lane stepped off the train at Altavista to get a report on Edward's progress.

"We needed some machinery," the dutiful son told him, "and it's all been ordered." John Edward Lane scowled. "How *much* machinery?" "Fifty thousand dollars' worth, Father," said Edward. At that point, Edward Hudson Lane would always recall vividly, "My father hit the ceiling. Before I could explain the credit terms I had arranged, he began to shout that he was ruined."

Until the new machinery arrived, the newly-named Standard Red Cedar Chest Company did most of its sawing by hand, and the chests were nailed together with hammers. "We didn't want to put our own name on that venture," Edward Lane admitted later, "until we knew what kind of a success it would be."

With new machinery, the quality of the chests improved and production inched upward to more than ten chests a day—and now the Standard Red Cedar Chest Company faced a sales problem.

Edward Lane, the tight-lipped young man with the trusting eyes, had been advised that small factories usually relied on commission furniture salesmen, all of whom represented a number of lines. He soon decided he had better get out and learn for himself why that plan did not seem to be working. He asked a dealer in Utica, New York, if he would like to buy some cedar chests. The dealer shook his head. "No, Son, we don't need any." Edward trudged back to his hotel, thinking black thoughts about dealers. Then he switched his thinking to the dealer's point of view. He began to form a mental picture of a window display idea. He would surround a cedar chest with cedar shavings, cedar logs, even small green cedar trees—all topped off with display cards proclaiming the many practical benefits of cedar chests.

While the idea was hot in his mind, he hurried back to see the dealer—and got an order for twenty-five chests. He went next to a dealer who had turned him down in Buffalo, and sold fifty chests. He repeated the perfor-

The original Lane cedar
chest, as produced from 1912
to 1919 by The Standard Red
Cedar Chest Company.

mance in Rochester, Syracuse, Schenectady, Albany, and
Troy—and forever after would advise all his salesmen:
"Along with making a good product, you've got to sell
with an *idea.*"

It would be a while before Edward Hudson Lane
would have his ideal sales force. Meanwhile, as part of
learning everything he could about cedar chests, he
delved into their history, all the way back to ancient
times. And there he found the greatest selling idea of all.

Cedar chests, he learned, were not just utilitarian storage places with the added benefit of protection against
moths. Cedar chests were a symbol of romance—as authentic a symbol of romance as the wedding ring.

The early Egyptians had discovered the unusual protective qualities of cedarwood, and some of their chests
were still on display in the world's great museums. The
chests had become prized depositories for the delicate
garments that would make up a big part of the bride's
dowry. As the custom spread to Europe, makers of the
bridal chests faced a shortage of cedar and had to turn to
other woods; but they compensated by making their
chests more ornate. Such Italian Renaissance artists as
Leonardo Da Vinci and Andrea del Sarto had often been

commissioned to add lavish works of art to the bridal chests of wealthy families. It became a custom, when a new bride went to meet her husband, for her to be carried to the scene atop her trousseau chest—and if she came from a well-to-do family, she would have two or more chests for the dowry. Centuries later, in the United States, there would be "hope chests" with a romantic connotation—and the Virginia colonists would find plentiful supplies of cedar—but very few people would have a full awareness of the cedar chest's ancient, romantic heritage.

The romance of the cedar chest could not have been studied by a more receptive reader. Edward Hudson Lane had recently become the husband of lovely Myrtle Clyde Bell in a marriage that would stand out, for the forty-six years until her death, as a classic example of devotion.

The struggling young Standard Red Cedar Chest Company now had its strong, unique reason for being: it would be the maker of the world's finest cedar hope chests for people in love.

"It was our ambition," Edward Lane recalled later, "to build furniture units so fine that they would be the prized antiques and collectors' items of the future." To that end, he began experimenting with fine mahogany and walnut exteriors for his red cedar chests, and developed new ways of making the construction airtight.

Then World War I came along, and the would-be makers of the world's most romantic chests had to content themselves with the production of pine ammunition boxes.

Toward the close of its first decade, a banker made a careful study of the Standard Red Cedar Chest Company and concluded: "Mr. Lane, we feel obliged to tell you that your company is insolvent." Young Lane was deeply puzzled, and showed it. "What does that mean?" The banker managed a weak, professional smile. "Mr. Lane," he said patiently, "if you don't know what 'insolvent' means, I don't think you should look it up now."

Fortunately for Lane, all the earlier, wide-ranging, trial-and-error efforts seemed suddenly to come together in one purposeful, successful pattern as the company started its second decade in 1922.

Every woman wants a chest of fragrant cedar wood

THE young girl gliding into womanhood, treasuring a store of gifts against Her Day; the radiant wife swiftly fashioning a host of baby things; and mother of mothers fondly dreaming o'er the lace and lavender of a bygone year—each knows the sure protection and the decorative beauty of a lasting cedar chest.

Lane Chests of fragrant red cedar heartwood are moth-proof, dust-proof, damp-proof. Each of the many sizes and designs is as beautiful as care can make it. Each is built to last for generations. Cushioned, there is no more delightful window seat or cosier lounge for the foot of a bed. Always it is as accessible as your dressing table drawer.

Lane processes retain the natural cedar color; accentuate the beautiful graining; keep the moth-killing and refreshing cedar aroma inside. Permanence is insured by a dovetailed panel and interlocked corner construction. Double-plated hardware. Yale locks. The Lane Cedar Chest is as artistic as a jewel box; sturdier than a trunk.

These beautiful chests are made in many different styles and sizes, with trays, to meet every taste. They may be purchased for as low as from $12 to $15 upward. The genuine Lane has the name burned on the inside of lid. Be sure to look for it. If your furniture dealer or department store cannot supply you, write to us and we will tell you who can.

A Whisper to the Gift Buyer
There's pride in giving and joy in having a Lane Cedar Chest. It is the sort of gift that becomes an heirloom.

THE LANE COMPANY, Inc.
Altavista, Va.
Formerly The Standard Red Cedar Chest Co., Inc.

LANE CEDAR CHEST

No. 48207-X—48x19x25½
A massive window seat model in Italian Renaissance.
American walnut veneer is used on the top, front and ends.
All carvings are genuine wood.
The back rest is stationary.

Left: After a close brush with bankruptcy, the company began its second decade with advertisements like this one in the 1922 issues of *The Saturday Evening Post*. It directed its message to "the young girl gliding into womanhood . . . the radiant wife swiftly fashioning a host of baby things . . . the mother of mothers fondly dreaming o'er the lace and lavender of a bygone year," and included an abundance of practical information about the cedar chest that was "as artistic as a jewel box; sturdier than a trunk." **Top right:** A Lane chest of the early 1930's reflected Edward Hudson Lane's ambition to "build furniture units so fine that they would be the prized antiques and collectors' items of the future." **Bottom right:** A Lane inspector checks one of the most recent of more than twelve million Lane miniature cedar chests. The miniature cedar chest operation is now a full-fledged department with its own precision manufacturing equipment.

Edward Lane had decided to advertise his romantic chests directly to the consumer and had found that, by sawing his own cedar lumber instead of depending on suppliers, he could cut his production costs five percent below that of his competitors and thus devote five percent of his cost margin to advertising. In turn, his new advertising agency recommended that he take the money he had earmarked for some newspaper advertisements in several cities and use it, instead, for a national effort in *The Saturday Evening Post*. The advertising agency also recommended that he drop the cumbersome "Standard Red Cedar Chest Company" in favor of "Lane Cedar Chests."

In evolutionary stages, Lane Cedar Chests for young lovers became "Lane Cedar Hope Chests," then "Lane Sweetheart Chests," and finally, "Lane Love Chests." And to this was added the tag line: "The gift that starts the home."

A new sales director not only started developing an exclusively-Lane sales force, but was observant enough to notice that some of the Lane employees had an intriguing after-hours hobby: they were making miniature cedar chests, complete with lock and key, for their girl friends in Altavista, who prized the tiny chests for safeguarding love letters and jewelry. With Edward Lane's enthusiastic approval, the sales office compiled a massive list of girls graduating from high school and sent them all a certificate good for a free miniature chest at the local Lane dealer's store. The response came in like a landslide.

The miniature chest promotion continued to grow, year after year, until nearly two-thirds of all girls graduating from high school in the United States each year became recipients of certificates for the Lane Love Chests—"the gift that starts the home." The latest count on the "Girl Graduate Plan" has now passed the twelve million mark, and company surveys have continued to indicate that approximately half of all girls graduating from high school, every year, are married within eighteen months.

Romance was living up to Edward Lane's fondest expectations as a great selling idea. But the time was soon to come when he would have to wonder if the romantic ap-

Hampton O. Powell, chairman of The Lane Company, Inc.

peal would be strong enough to carry his company through the depression of the early 1930's.

Lane reflected on some of the company's many earlier studies of what cedar chests did for the consumer. By adding some new ideas to an earlier study, he decided he had the answer to depression-time selling. Lane advertisements soon publicized the moth as "public enemy No. 1"—the cause of two hundred million dollars in damage every year—and offered the world's first moth insurance policy, free, with every Lane Cedar Hope Chest. The moth-protection advertisements hit hard with a timely appeal—but Edward Lane still insisted on saving at least a corner of each advertisement to remind the reader of the basic romantic reasons for a Lane Hope Chest.

As the national economy turned upward again, Lane not only resumed all its romantic appeals of old, but added new styling innovations, new choices of cherry, maple, pine, butternut, and other finishes—and then capped it all with an annual Valentine's Day promotion as ambitious as the established Girl Graduate Plan. The Valentine's Day promotion did more than build sales. It also helped to smooth out the year's peaks and valleys in production.

By this time, consumer surveys were indicating that Lane was probably the best-known name in the wood furniture industry—and that it enjoyed the special favor of romantic young women who were dreaming of furnishing their first home. The surveys also pointed out that Lane's appeal was not just to the bride or bride-to-be: more than forty percent of all Lane cedar chests were being ordered by young men for the girls they hoped to marry.

If any Lane people had doubts about the male appeal of a Lane Cedar Chest, World War II quickly put the doubts to rest. GI's flooded the company with requests for information about where to mail an order for a Lane Cedar Hope Chest for that girl back home.

At the close of the readjustment period after World War II, Edward Hudson Lane was ready to act on the consumer findings. But it would not be done in haste. "We feel we should capitalize on our name on other products," he told his management group, "but only to the extent of our ability to properly manage them and consolidate our position after each move. Operating on those standards, we believe we are now in position to move toward diversification."

The company was ready. Far more important, the consumer market of home furnishers was ready to welcome more products from Lane. In 1951, under the direction of Edward Lane, Jr., the company introduced its first collection of Lane occasional tables—a full forty different patterns in modern and traditional styling—and went on to consolidate its position in the table field as one of its top three national names. By 1956, the company was ready to expand its line to include bedroom and dining room furniture. It would all be advertised, of course, as "furniture for lovers."

After careful consolidation in each field, more diversification moves would follow: record cabinets, upholstered furniture, rocker/recliner chairs, and other pieces. By the time of Edward Hudson Lane's death in 1973, his company was operating eighteen plants in five states, with forty-four hundred employees and an annual sales volume of more than one hundred million dollars.

Bernard B. Lane, president of The Lane Company, Inc.

In the mid-1950's, the founder had been succeeded, as president, by Hampton O. Powell, who had joined the company at sixteen, fresh out of high school. In the mid-1970's, Powell moved to chairman, and the presidency was assumed by Bernard B. Lane, one of the four sons of Edward Hudson Lane. Others in the management team include Landon B. Lane and Edward H. Lane, Jr.

Edward Hudson Lane, who often had said that his first concern was not production, or sales, or finance, but *people*, had built a team that could carry his planning forward; and he had installed a company merit system to make certain that ability and performance counted more than kinship.

"The furniture industry as a whole," Edward Hudson Lane once observed, "is made up of family businesses, and many of these families, in one way or another, play out. Younger, more vigorous competitors come along and take their business away from them. I decided, long ago, that I must always consider what's good for The Lane Company first."

MARKETING INSIGHTS

What product could be duller than a wooden box? Even if it is made of cedar, in order to repel moths, a box is prosaicly utilitarian. But if one looks into history, as Edward Hudson Lane did, an abundance of romantic imagery reveals itself. Having done his homework, Lane was ready to offer cedar hope chests to every young woman in love.

His was a large, considered purchase; but he found a way to "sample" it selectively with miniature chests, offered free to female high school graduates—approximately half of whom (according to his surveys) would be married within eighteen months.

Edward Hudson Lane learned early about the vast difference between "order-taking" and "creative selling." He also learned that magazines, selectively distributed, are the best media for a detailed romantic appeal to young females. Today, of course, magazines offer increasingly selective circulation, making it possible for an advertiser to cover not only his best target audiences, but to pinpoint the circulation to the geographical areas where he has dealer representation.

Having established itself among young lovers as the maker of the finest cedar hope chests, The Lane Company was in a strong position to expand into the making of other furniture for the entire home.

LEVI'S JEANS
"The cowboy's tailor"

24 Certain avant-garde members of the fashion world may have been startled when, in 1971, Levi's Blue Jeans won a special Coty Award as America's outstanding contribution to international fashion. Undoubtedly, they were further bemused when they learned that the humble Levi's garment, which began through sheer coincidence, also ranked as probably the only item of American wearing apparel whose style had remained basically the same, totally oblivious to the dictates of fashion, for more than one hundred twenty years.

Levi Strauss, like a motley multitude of others, had been drawn to San Francisco in 1850 by the magnetism of the gold rush. He was just another twenty-year-old Bavarian immigrant, living with relatives in Louisville, Kentucky; but he had two merchant brothers in New York City, and when he asked their advice on the best way to establish himself in California, they outfitted young Strauss with a sample inventory of silks, broadcloths, and fine dress goods—plus a generous amount of canvas duck for tents and Conestoga wagon covers.

It was attractive merchandise. Other passengers on the long voyage around Cape Horn soon purchased everything but the canvas duck. The canvas, Strauss had cautioned them, would be his featured item in frontier California. But when he finally landed and spread out his stock, only one solitary, ragged miner took the time to look it over and then, wagging his head, he observed ruefully: "You should've brought pants."

"Pants?" Levi's brothers had never mentioned pants.

"Yep. Pants don't wear worth a hoot up in the diggin's. You can't get a pair strong enough to last no time."

Levi Strauss promptly headed for the nearest tailor, a roll of canvas under his arm; that first inquirer would soon be on his way to the diggings in a pair of canvas pants; and later visitors from the diggings would be asking where they could find "those pants of Levi's."

Levi Strauss at the time of his arrival in San Francisco in 1850. His stock of tent canvas just gathered dust—until a miner suggested it might make good pants.

Right: Miners were the first to wear Levi's jeans. A harness maker added the first rivets to keep pockets from tearing under the weight of mining tools. **Above:** By the end of the 1850's, American westerners had learned to think of Levi Strauss & Co. as "the cowboy's tailor." A century later, American cowboy movies had created a ready-and-waiting market for the "American folk costume."

Frantically, as he watched his canvas collection dwindle and was turning to local stocks of sailcloth, Levi dispatched letters to his brothers in New York, apprising them of the situation and asking for all available heavy cloth. They responded with a generous variety, out of which Levi selected a heavy cotton of French origin: *serge de Nimes*. In trade usage, the name would soon become "denim." Still later, Levi Strauss would select a special shade of indigo blue dye for the material that made the pants that carried his "two horse brand" label.

He would make only one other modification: copper rivets at the corners of the pockets. A Virginia City tailor, Jacob Davis, told Strauss how he had once taken a pair of pants to a harness maker for riveting in order to end a customer's chronic complaints about pockets ripping loose under the weight of mining tools. Davis had done it as a joke, but the customer had been deeply impressed. So was Levi Strauss. With Davis' cooperation, he obtained a patent on the riveted clothing in 1873.

Levi Strauss, in 1853, had formed Levi Strauss & Company in partnership with his two brothers. In 1890, he incorporated the business. When Levi Strauss died in 1902, nobody seemed to know much about the quiet, industrious, bachelor pants maker, except that he had "always been fair, good at business, and benevolent to his employees and fellow San Franciscans"—and they applied the same evaluation to nephews Jacob, Sigmund, Isaac and Abraham Stern, who carried on the business.

In time, Levi's Jeans would become the "American folk costume" of the West's miners and cowboys, lumberjacks and farmers. The jeans would become known as "the pants that won the West," and Strauss' company would often be called "the cowboy's tailor."

Customers made a family tradition of their Levi's Jeans; they would not tolerate any changes. But the demand, though steady, was not spectacular. In the 1920's, the heads of the company considered liquidation, then decided instead to engage in the wholesaling of underwear, blankets, and other dry goods items to supplement their pants-manufacturing operations. By the time of World War II, three-fourths of the company's revenue came from its wholesaling activities; the remaining fourth came from the manufacture and sale of Levi's Jeans in one model, one color, and forty-five sizes. A total of fourteen salespeople carried out the company's objectives, and not one of them had ever made a call east of the Mississippi River.

During the War, when Levi's Jeans had the status of an "essential commodity, for sale only to persons engaged in

Left: In the 1960's, the company theorized that "Levi's for Gals" could double the market. The success of that move quickly led to a broad expansion of the Levi's line. **Right:** Levi's Sportswear goes far afield from denim, but never forgets its "cowboy's tailor" heritage.

defense work"—and then for two postwar years, when deliveries had to be rationed—Levi's management took a long look at the past and the future and finally decided it was time to rediscover Levi's Jeans.

The wholesaling operations, they agreed, should be phased out. They would concentrate on promoting the Levi's brand, with added diversification in both product line and geographical territories.

Moreover, they would focus their primary marketing efforts on males in what they concluded was the most actively apparel-minded age group: fifteen to twenty-four years old.

Systematically, the company introduced pre-shrunk denim in 1953; light denim casual pants in 1954; a sand shade of the original blue jeans design in 1960; then capped it all in 1964 with the introduction of Sta-Prest permanent press.

During the 1960's, the company also went international, ultimately taking the Levi's brand to seventy foreign countries where American cowboy movies and U.S. servicemen had already made Levi's Jeans a familiar garment.

By 1968, the company decided it was time to double the market by introducing Levi's for Gals—then followed with a Boyswear line and separate line of Panatela sportswear. Each of the major categories was organized under its own Division controls.

Of its recent progress, Levi's management says modestly, "Fashion is a cycle. We can only anticipate what people want to wear; we don't tell them." But all it takes is two sets of figures to indicate how management should evaluate its decision to rediscover Levi's Jeans. In 1950, when Levi's Jeans had been on the market for one hundred years, they had reached an annual sales level of about two million dollars. Within the next twenty-five years, the expanded line of Levi's garments—revolving around the never-changing Levi's Blue Jeans—had grown five hundred times in size to reach the one billion dollar mark, and "the cowboy's tailor" had become the largest apparel company in the world.

MARKETING INSIGHTS

Levi Strauss' extra-tough work pants—made first of canvas, then of heavy denim, complete with copper rivets—became the "folk costume" of the American West and were sold only in the West. Inevitably, the cowboys and miners of pioneer days faded from the scene and the company considered liquidation.

To revitalize the company, the management redefined its markets, decided to concentrate on young males fifteen to twenty-four years old, and expanded from regional to national, then to international distribution. Later, Levi's management improved the product, expanded the variety of its line, and aimed at such new market segments as young females, boys, and adult buyers of sportswear.

But that impressive combination of marketing actions is not a complete explanation of why Levi Strauss soared from relative obscurity to become the largest apparel company in the world.

Levi's Jeans got its major impetus from the company's alert capitalizing on outside forces. Hollywood movies, later joined by television, had made the American cowboy (dressed in Levi's Jeans) a folk hero throughout the world. World War II had accustomed millions of young males to the casual comfort of fatigues and khaki. Still later, the forces of social change cut workweeks back for more leisure time—and also created anti-establishment groups among whom it was fashionable to "dress poor." The makers of Levi's Jeans had the marketing alertness to hitch their wagon to all four of those stars.

MAXWELL HOUSE COFFEE

"Good to the last drop."

25 As one of their first acts this morning, approximately eighty-five out of every one hundred adult Americans made a cup or pot of coffee. Some took the easy way, with instant coffee; but most preferred to begin with roasted, ground coffee and brew it their own favorite way, using a percolator, a vacuum-type coffeemaker, a drip pot, or an "old-fashioned" coffeepot. They left it "black," or added cream and/or sugar, then judged its excellence on the basis of both aroma and taste.

Seldom have so many consumers lavished so much attention on so simple-appearing a food. But seldom has a simple-appearing food been quite so complex.

Coffee begins as a tasteless, odorless bean. Not until it is roasted does it acquire aroma and flavor—both of which, in turn, are greatly influenced by *how* it is roasted. Moreover, the flavor potential of green coffee varies from country to country, and even from plantation to plantation in the same general area, so that a good blend of coffee often requires the precise mixing of six or more different lots of green coffee. As a further complication, coffee defies all known chemical tests for evaluation of quality; it can be judged only by a human tester with highly trained senses of taste and smell.

In the case of Maxwell House coffee, the original tester was Joel O. Cheek, who roamed through Tennessee on horseback in the 1870's as a salesman for a wholesale grocery firm. Joel Cheek wanted a better tasting coffee than was then available, so he began experimenting with new and different blends. When he was satisfied that he had found the ideal combination, he took it to Nashville's distinguished Maxwell House, the hotel that symbolized the very finest in traditional Southern hospitality.

In swift succession, Joel Cheek's subtle blend of coffees became a famous specialty of the Maxwell House, the unique "Maxwell House coffee" was being asked for by an expanded circle of householders, and Cheek's Nash-

Joel O. Cheek

The Maxwell House in Nashville, symbol of gracious Southern hospitality, as it appeared after the turn of the century.

ville roasting plant was on its way to becoming the largest in the United States.

Not until 1907 would a slogan be coupled with the great Maxwell House name. In that year, Joel Cheek proudly served a steaming cup of his coffee to the most distinguished visitor who had ever entered his home, and President Theodore Roosevelt, upon setting down his empty cup, is said to have exclaimed, "That coffee is *good to the last drop.*"

Early in coffee's eleven hundred year history, it became a favorite on its home continent, Africa, among Moslems who wanted to stay alert during their long religious services. Then it became controversial when some of the strict Islamic priests decided coffee was intoxicating and therefore prohibited by the Koran. (Actually, much of coffee's immediate pickup comes from the heat of the beverage; the stimulation of the caffeine comes later.) When coffee made its way into Europe in the early 1600's, it was still regarded as a potion to be used in

On its fiftieth anniversary in 1923, Maxwell House Coffee was still being promoted by the description attributed to Theodore Roosevelt: "Good to the last drop."

religious ceremonies or for medical purposes. It took the early London coffeehouses—the new centers of literary and political influence—to make coffee a popular, everyday beverage.

Even before Joel Cheek began his quest for a new blend, coffee had become such a staple in America that a dried cake form, soluble in water, had been developed for the emergency use of troops in the Civil War. Joel Cheek may have thought it was an atrocious substitute for good coffee, but the concept of an "instant" coffee was destined to reappear in 1910 and again in the late

1930's. By the time America entered World War II, Maxwell House was ready to produce a soluble coffee for the armed forces. At war's end, Maxwell House intensified its instant coffee research and, in late 1949, announced a new instant Maxwell House coffee made up of "flavor buds."

Since the early days when Joel Cheek did all the blending and testing, Maxwell House coffee has been an endless repetition of four basic steps—selecting the right green coffees, blending the proper proportions of the various green beans, roasting under precise time and temperature controls, and cutting (or grinding) to tolerances as fine as a thousandth of an inch—all under the direction of the master testers. The exact procedures, in all four steps, are closely guarded secrets—and what they achieve in aroma and flavor is protected by a fifth step: vacuum packing. The background is the same for both regular and instant coffee; the basic difference is that, for the instant coffee, the percolation or extraction step is done under scientifically controlled conditions in the Maxwell House plant instead of in the home.

The testing of coffee has been called "the most delicate work known to science." Professional coffee testers devote many years to perfecting their sophisticated skills. But the professional testers at Maxwell House have learned how to recruit and train Flavor Panel members from plant and office personnel for the day-in-day-out quality checks on Maxwell House aroma and flavor.

Flavor Panel members first learn that the tongue, the body's taste detector, has highly specialized areas. The tip of the tongue is most sensitive to sweetness; the back of the tongue, near the throat, reacts to bitterness. The top and front sides of the tongue are most sensitive to saltiness; the sides farther back detect sourness.

Panelists also learn how closely the sense of taste is related to the sense of smell, located in special cells (the olfactory area) in the nose. (Typical demonstration: try chewing a piece of potato and then a piece of apple while pinching your nose; you will find you cannot tell them apart.)

Panelists must then learn to recognize the other factors

involved in total flavor sensation: astringency, bite, coolness, warmth, prickliness, and aftertaste. Coffee, they find, has its own special "mouthfeel," and they must follow a uniform vocabulary in describing their reactions to the samples they taste.

All samples must be tasted at between 150 and 160 degrees Fahrenheit. (Hotter, it burns the tongue; cooler, it loses some flavor.) The room is bathed in red light during the tasting so that panelists will not be influenced by color differences among the samples.

Panel members taste the same production samples, usually four to six at a time, including a standard or "ideal" sample—and they do all their tasting during an hour in the midmorning and an hour in the midafternoon, because those are the usual two daily peaks in our sense of taste.

One final point: no dainty sipping is allowed. The coffee must be sharply (and noisily) slurped from a stainless steel teaspoon to make sure it will be sprayed evenly over the entire mouth area. In no other way can all the tastes, aromas, and unique mouthfeel be experienced.

Young Joel Cheek, reining his horse along the Cumberland River trails of Tennessee, had reasoned that, in the largest coffee-using country in the world, anybody who had the skill and persistence to develop a perfect coffee blend—and keep it that way—would be richly rewarded. He was well into his forties before he proved his point; but he proved it with such thoroughness that his Maxwell House blend went on to become the best-liked coffee in the world. At age seventy-six in 1928, he merged his company with General Foods and devoted his remaining seven years to philanthropic activities throughout the South.

The palatial old Maxwell House in downtown Nashville, the favorite home-away-from-home of Sarah Bernhardt, Buffalo Bill Cody, Enrico Caruso, Henry Ford, Thomas Edison, William Jennings Bryan, John Philip Sousa, and at least seven U.S. presidents, finally closed its doors on Christmas of 1961. It had bestowed a distinguished name on Cheek's blend of coffees—and the coffee, in turn, had enhanced its fame.

In a periodic roast test, this quality control man compares the color of beans from the big roaster with the control sample in his left hand. If the beans are too light, coffee brewed from them will be weak. If the roast is too dark, the coffee may taste bitter or burned.

Quite fittingly, when a new luxury hotel was planned as a new landmark in today's Nashville, its developers turned to General Foods for permission to grace it with the historic and respected "Maxwell House" mark.

MARKETING INSIGHTS

Coffee beans vary constantly, from batch to batch, and there are no chemical tests for evaluating the quality of coffee. Only a master coffee tester can control its flavor and aroma.

Joel Cheek combined a distinctive coffee blend with a distinctive image of gracious hospitality—that of the famous old Maxwell House of Nashville, Tennessee—and he never tampered with his successful blend-and-image formula.

The coming of instant coffee introduced a new element: the percolation or extraction step was performed in a processing plant instead of the home. Varying plant percolation methods enabled advertising writers to develop such new appeals as "flavor buds" for Instant Maxwell House and comparable claims of uniqueness for other brands.

Coffee brands fluctuate in tune with the appetite appeal and persuasive spokesmanship of their television commercials. But in the long term, what counts most is how skillfully and steadfastly the master coffee tester lives up to the expectations of the consumer.

PARKER PENS

"Our pens can write in any language."

26 Mankind's first writing instrument was probably a hairy Neanderthal forefinger drawing crude symbols in the dust. Then, over the centuries, came charred sticks for cave drawings, tapered reeds, and later, quills for writing with ink, steel nib pens for still better writing with ink—and finally, in 1884, American L. E. Waterman's basic design for the modern fountain pen. (Earlier attempts to create a fountain pen had been plagued by leakage and irregular ink flow problems for fifty years.)

But even Waterman's design suffered from occasional leakage, and an after-hours pen repairman in Janesville, Wisconsin, spent four years looking for the solution. He found it in a new kind of feed bar, the little part whose upper end extends into the ink reservoir while the lower end presses against the pen nib. The new feed bar evoked such good comments from his repair customers that it persuaded George S. Parker to give up the teaching of telegraphy and organize The Parker Pen Company in 1892. His first model, the "Lucky Curve" pen, remained virtually unchanged for thirty years.

As a teacher of telegraphy, George Parker had delved deeply into the broad study of communications, including man's basic need to express himself. His market, Parker decided, would be every person in the world who wanted to express his thoughts clearly, easily, and with permanence.

"Always remember," he told his associates, "our pens will write in any language." He initiated export operations in 1903, beginning with Scandinavia. The company now has a sales organization in 135 of the world's 198 countries, advertises in forty-two languages, keeps books in one hundred currencies, and does sixty percent of its sales volume outside the United States.

The fountain pen is one of the simplest of all mechanical devices; but George Parker, the meticulous ex-teacher of telegraphy, made a fetish of building it to exacting

George S. Parker

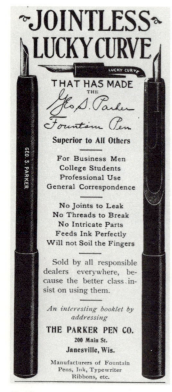

To the concise statement of facts presented in this 1900 Parker Pen advertisement, the copy added: "Sold by all responsible dealers everywhere, because the better class insist on using them."

new standards. He taught his technicians to think in such terms as capillary action and vacuum, surface energy, osmotic pressure, and the synergetic relationship between porosity and viscosity. He insisted on testing, not only for leakage under varying conditions, but for overnight start, proper line width and line intensity, and for checking writing qualities using all handwriting styles: forward slant, upright, left-handed, and back-handed.

But progress was slow. Not until 1918 did World War I give the United States its first real boom in letter writing and record-keeping. Parker moved quickly against the new opportunity, beginning with the Parker Trench Pen for the doughboys—it "made its own ink" out of concentrated ink pellets and plain water. The company chalked up its first million-dollar sales year, planned its first major plant facility—and began to feel the strong influence of George Parker's two sons, Russell and Kenneth. By 1921, the company was ready to revolutionize the fountain pen industry with the spectacular new Parker Duofold.

The Parker Duofold offered double the usual ink capacity. Its large, flexible gold point make it the immediate favorite of penmanship buffs who favored the distinctive Spencerian and Palmer styles of handwriting. Above all, it brought color to an industry that had never known anything but black. Its bright, orange-red color was so unique that Parker became one of the first companies to patent something other than a product. Parker patented the color.

At a time when only about five percent of the literate population of the United States owned fountain pens, the new Parker Duofold was electrifying. Its mass appeal was so enduring that a "Big Red" model would be introduced some forty years later, with great success, during a national revival of nostalgic interest in the symbols of the Roaring Twenties.

Parker Pens was now committed to advanced styling and use of color, as well as to advanced writing qualities—and this led to some surprises in the international market. Green pens failed in India, where green represents bad luck; white pens failed in China, where white

Under Parker guidelines, every advertisement throughout the year is expected to "develop a gift concept" because of the importance to Parker of that market. The Parker Duofold, shown in this 1922 ad, introduced color to pens, was a gift-market breakthrough, and has had lasting mass appeal.

is the color of mourning. On the other hand, the distinctive styling created a brisk market in many foreign countries for Parker pen *caps* (without the rest of the pen) as conspicuous badges of personal success and literacy. And in the Solomon Islands, missionaries made an experimental offer of bright Parker Pens to Natambu tribesmen who would give up "head-hunting" and learn to read and write; the incentive was a spectacular success.

In 1932, the Parker Vacumatic, first of the no-sac pens, gave Parker a timely lift in the depression days—and then went on to become the first pen considered safe on commercial airlines. In the rarified cabin atmosphere, other pens often leaked or even exploded.

When Parker was ready to make its next major new-model introduction, the company decided to avoid any model name that might overshadow the name "Parker." Instead, it would select a designation which would translate into any language. The final choice: "51."

The Parker 51, introduced in 1941, scored such an immediate success that "51," which was supposed to be meaningless, promptly became synonymous with the Parker name. The "51" pioneered new materials and would write with new ease for half a mile between re-fills. But most of all, it represented the Parker family's growing interest in smart design. In an independent poll among leading designers, architects and artists, the Parker 51 was voted one of the five best-designed products of modern times. In another poll, *Time* Magazine would find that Parker Pen, Coca-Cola, Singer, and the Jeep had become the best-known symbols of the United States overseas.

Then came the bombshell: the ball-point pen of 1945. A newcomer to the pen industry introduced it to a seller's market at Christmas with the ringing line, "The pen that writes under water," and it became a sellout at $12.50. By 1951, some two hundred fifty companies were competing for a share of the booming ball pen market, and all the traditional pen makers had jumped on the bandwagon. All but Parker.

Parker decided to continue its research and development, and it waited nine long years. Those nine years became a spectacular acid test of a company's loyalty to its convictions. Parker simply believed that the product was premature from a technical standpoint. "We are committed," Parker has always maintained, "to upgrading both ourselves and the industry."

The first patent on a ball pen had been issued in 1888 to a John J. Loud, but the pen failed because of its coarseness. Not until World War II, with its new techniques in grinding ball bearings for aircraft instruments, did the ball pen become a practical possibility. Even then, it would have to wait until the early 1950's for proper inks to be developed for it.

Parker waited—and watched the competitor's $12.50 price of Christmas, 1945, skid to less than fifty cents.

In 1954, Parker was ready to put its name on a ball pen, the "Jotter," with a choice of point sizes and a large capacity cartridge. At the same time, Parker continued working toward what it called the "truly textured ball," and had it ready for the "T-Ball Jotter" of 1957. The T-Ball Jotter's "truly textured" ball had the porosity of a sponge and hardness approaching that of a diamond. Mean-

while, in 1956, Parker had reaffirmed its quality standing in the fountain pen category with its Parker "61," filled by capillarity, with no moving parts.

The long, grueling battle of the ball-point pens was over. Parker's convictions about quality had paid off in the Jotter and the "61." But the company did not want its proud name to be jeopardized in another such marketing brawl.

Accordingly, in 1957, Parker acquired the Eversharp Pen Company and made it a Parker division. It would be Eversharp's job to meet the low-priced competition, while Parker promoted its own name in the middle and higher price brackets.

Consistently, up through the years, every Parker pen has been priced higher than competitive products. "Added value," the company insists, "not only justifies but commands added payment." The premium price, in turn, not only covers the cost, but serves as a memorable

Left: Despite its glamourous graphics, this early (1903) Parker Pen advertisement promised only that the Parker "Lucky Curve" is a good pen. **Right:** After waiting nine long years for a ball-point pen worthy of its reputation, Parker came back fighting with this ad for the T-Ball Jotter.

Saying "our pens will write in any language," George Parker started exporting his pens in 1903. The company now advertises in forty-some languages.

reminder of the extra value—particularly in the important gift market.

When the company observed its seventy-fifth anniversary, in 1963, by introducing the Parker "75," the prices began at twenty-five dollars. Crafted in solid sterling silver or gold-filled, the "75" offers such features as a rotating, fourteen-karat gold point, which accommodates every angle of writing, and must pass 792 inspections before it goes to market. If something fancier is desired, Parker offers a solid-gold, handcrafted set—fountain pen, ball pen, soft tip pen and pencil—for well over one thousand dollars. Meanwhile, in the middle price range, Parker introduced the Parker "45" cartridge-type fountain pen and would later add the Parker soft-tip pen and a new modular writing system called "Systemark."

By this time, the company was being managed by its third generation of Parkers. George Parker's son Russell had died in 1933 at the early age of thirty-nine, and the founder had died in 1937. George Parker's son Kenneth had served as president from 1933 to 1953, when he moved to chairman and was succeeded by Bruce M. Jeffris. Kenneth's son Daniel resumed the Parker continuity as president from 1960 to 1966, when he became chairman and was succeeded by George S. Parker, son of the late Russell Parker. Within three generations, the founding family advanced the company to a volume level of well over $150 million in writing instruments alone, and to an employment level of about six thousand people. In recent years, Parker has diversified into temporary help services (Manpower, Inc.) and recreational goods, and reports revenues of about $400 million. A new president and chief operating officer, E. William Swanson, Jr., had joined George Parker, now chairman and chief executive officer, in a new management team.

Throughout those years, the goal was always a simple, single-minded one: to be the makers of the "world's most wanted pen."

"Expressing ourselves on paper," says Parker, "is one of the most personal things we do," and each of Parker's "ways to write"—the precision-built fountain pen, the Jotter ball pen, and the soft-tip pen—has its own writing personality. In response to consumer studies, the typical fountain pen owner will say, "This pen has *character*; it writes like *me*." The ball pen owner simply wants a reliable pen that requires little or no attention. The owner of a soft-tip pen likes its bold, flowing line—"especially for signing letters"—and some respondents have added: "It's terrific for writing short, irate notes!"

With a fine sensitivity to the basic differences in "writing personality," Parker advertising assumes the personality of the specific pen being promoted. But in all its advertising, Parker insists on a single format of copy tone and graphics—and further requires: "Every Parker advertisement must offer the reader some reward in return for his time and attention—news, benefits, or service."

And then Parker sums up its entire marketing philosophy by adding: "If a company has a good product, priced right and complemented with convincing, effectual advertising, almost all the other problems in the business diminish."

Wherever important thoughts are being put on paper, Parker wants the writing instrument to be a Parker. Carl

Left: Parker's original objective was to make "the world's most wanted pen," and the company never lost sight of that goal. The Parker "51," introduced in 1941, was honored as one of the best-designed products of modern times. **Right:** Many magazine readers asked Parker, "He isn't mentioned anywhere, but isn't that Carl Sandburg in your ad?" The answer was "Yes." In a no-names-mentioned series, designed to arouse curiosity, Carl Sandburg was joined by such other Parker Pen users as Herbert Hoover, William Holden, Bob Hope, Doris Day, and Charles Coburn.

Sandburg wrote history with a Parker pen, and Edgar A. Guest wrote verse. George Bernard Shaw wrote *Pygmalion* with a Parker pen, and Sir Arthur Conan Doyle used a Parker to write his greatest Sherlock Holmes stories. Artist Charles Dana Gibson used a Parker to draw the legendary Gibson Girl; Italian composer Giacomo Puccini used a Parker to write *La Boheme* and his other great operas; and Robert L. May sat down with a Parker pen to write "Rudolph the Red-Nosed Reindeer."

Some of world history's most important documents were signed with Parker pens in the hands of Presidents Franklin D. Roosevelt and Harry S Truman, and Generals Dwight D. Eisenhower and Douglas MacArthur.

And then there was Beth Brown. She achieved less fame than all those others, but she gave Parker one of the finest of all endorsements after using a Parker pen to write *Hotel for Dogs*. Her book did not make the best-seller list, but its 7.4 million words made it one of the longest books in all publishing history.

MARKETING INSIGHTS

A fountain pen is one of the smallest of all mechanical
devices, but it serves the large and important function of
fulfilling our basic need to express ourselves. Expressing
ourselves on paper—with the light-to-bold line width
that reflects our own personality—is one of the most personal things we do.

But a basic need does not automatically build a market.
Not until World War I brought a boom in letter writing—
and Parker introduced color to the previously all-black
field of pens—would more than five percent of the U.S.
literate population be motivated to own a fountain pen.

Parker made an early commitment to quality: to become the maker of the "world's most wanted pen." In
1945, when the first ball-point pen revolutionized the
pen industry, Parker integrity was put to a spectacular
test—and was spectacularly reaffirmed by the company's
willingness to wait nine long years before introducing a
ball-point it considered worthy of the Parker name.

Parker prices, always higher than those on competitive
products, are a continuing reminder of Parker quality—
and are an important reason for Parker's high standing in
the gift-buying field.

Out of its concern for honest representation of its products, Parker confined an early showcard to the promise:
"Mr. Parker makes good pens." The same discipline is reflected in Parker's creative guidelines for all current advertising: (1) Concentrate on specific and unique product
features. (2) Use a benefit-oriented headline which rein-
forces existing consumer belief or creates a new reason to
buy. (3) Establish a gift concept, emphasizing value. (4)
Create bold, arresting graphics and present the product
in a dramatic and dominant manner. (5) Reflect first-rate
quality; the finished advertisement should be as carefully
executed as Parker products themselves. (6) Be honest—
presenting Parker products in an interesting and persuasive manner, but always in a completely honest, candid
way, without exaggeration, hyperbole or omission.

PIPER AIRCRAFT
"... because air is everywhere."

William T. Piper

27 Among aviation's "greats," William Thomas Piper may well rank as the most vigorous of all crusaders for the rights of the private flyer. He may also rank as one of the unlikeliest of pioneers, and as one who backed into aviation at just about the worst possible time.

It was only at the request of an old friend that Bill Piper had agreed to serve on the board of directors of the small Taylor Brothers Aircraft Company in his hometown of Bradford, Pennsylvania. He developed a curiosity about the business and learned how to fly—just before the company slid into bankruptcy. It was 1931; Bill Piper was fifty; and personal aviation—after a flurry of optimism generated by the Lindbergh flight of 1927—seemed to be doomed by the Great Depression.

With one exception, the Bradford backers of the Taylor Brothers company decided it was time to stop pouring good money after bad. The holdout was Bill Piper. Although he would need a bank loan to keep the company going, Piper bought its assets, gave half of everything to C. G. Taylor, and went into partnership with Taylor in the Taylor Aircraft Corporation. The assets, for which Piper had paid six hundred dollars, consisted of a small hangar-like factory, miscellaneous construction materials, and C. G. Taylor's new design for a small, high-wing, two-place monoplane with the tentative name of "Cub."

To Bill Piper, the Cub held the promise of being the answer to every airport operator's need for a safe, low-priced airplane for student instruction. Bill Piper had started as a construction engineer, specializing in massive concrete structures; now he was busy helping C. G. Taylor build the first Cub mockup out of orange crates. One of their next steps was to arrange with a wholesale grocer to give credit to Taylor employees so that production of the Cub could get under way.

With its little thirty-seven horsepower engine and its open cockpit for two tandem-seated passengers, the origi-

Bill Piper with C. G. Taylor, the designer of the famous Cub. (*Courtesy of William T. Piper, Jr.*)

nal Cub was spectacular in only one way: it had no bad habits. Airport operators, after some early quips about the "little glider with the sewing machine motor," were soon conceding that the Cub was "just about the most forgiving airplane that ever flew."

But days or even weeks would elapse between one Cub order and the next. Within the following six years, the partnership would be dissolved, the Bradford plant would be destroyed by fire, and only Bill Piper's unshakable belief in his "air is everywhere" theory would keep the little company alive.

Piper's missionary message was a simple comparison of the three great revolutions in transportation: the train could go only where its rails led; the automobile could go only where roads had been built; but the airplane needed only the air for its movement, and air was everywhere. Airport facilities, he would add, need not be a major obstacle in the way of this most versatile of all forms of transport, and he would later mount a separate, vigorous campaign for his concept of low-cost air parks.

In 1937, Piper moved his burned-out company from Bradford to an abandoned silk mill at Lock Haven, Pennsylvania. It was at least twice too big for his needs, he maintained, but it was affordable.

What he did not know at the time was that the U.S. Government, with an eye on developments in Hitler's Germany, was about to launch a massive civilian pilot training program. The Piper Aircraft Corporation would

Top: Four out of five World War II pilots got their training in the J-3 Cub. **Center:** General Dwight D. Eisenhower was one of many world famous passengers of the wartime Cub, the L-4. **Bottom:** Piper's postwar "Sky Coupe." It arrived just as the market began to collapse. (*Top and bottom photos courtesy of William T. Piper, Jr.*)

be the only one with enough production capacity to meet the demand for trainer-type airplanes, and four out of every five U.S. pilots of World War II would soon be getting their initial instruction in Piper Cubs.

Then the Cub went off to war. As the unarmed, 65 h.p., L-4 Air Observation Post, directing artillery fire, it soon qualified as "the world's most lethal warplane." It also distinguished itself as the combat-area transport favorite of such history-makers as Winston Churchill and Generals Dwight D. Eisenhower, George C. Marshall, Omar Bradley, George S. Patton, and Mark Clark.

By the end of World War II, a whole nation seemed to agree with Bill Piper that the time of the Air Age had finally come. Wartime pilots, it was said, would never again be content to travel exclusively by automobile; and millions of soldiers, offered GI Bill schooling, would elect to learn how to fly. A national attitudes survey confirmed all this with a mass of glowing statistics. Piper and other established light plane makers were flooded with orders, and hurriedly-formed new companies joined the field. Bill Piper, who sometimes had been criticized as "a grandfather, building a grandfather's airplane," even approved the development of an experimental, futuristic "Skycoupe" as the new second vehicle for the two-car family. The outlook for personal aviation had never been so bright.

Then, in the spring of 1947, the market collapsed. Bankruptcy among light plane manufacturers was epidemic. The nation indeed had "discovered" personal flying—and had decided it was still no substitute for the second family car. The discovery had come with a rush; so had the disenchantment.

The basic problem, marketing analysts would later report, was that the most enthusiastic triers of personal flying—the nation's young people—had found that flying was too rich for their meager budgets. And those enthusiasts lacked something even more important than money; they lacked a basic *need* for personal flying. The marketers were soon concentrating on a prospect who had both the money and the need—the businessman—who, incidentally, often turned out to be as grandfatherly as Bill Piper.

Bill Piper, a man of strong opinions, now had three grown, aviation-wise sons helping to make his views more flexible. William T. Piper, Jr. (who would later become president of the company), Howard, and Tony were persuading him that the flying businessman would not be satisfied until he had a twin-engine, all-metal airplane that could fly above the overcast and move at night without fear of engine failure.

Bill Piper and his three sons.
From left, Howard, Tony, and
William, Jr.

What this meant, in terms of price tags, was traumatic to Bill Piper. A fabric-covered airplane could be turned out with as few as two hundred fifty such tools as milling and welding fixtures, router and drill templates, and dies. Going to an all-metal design meant going to as many as ten thousand tools—or even more.

Piper Aircraft went ahead with the big change and came to market, in 1954, with the Apache. Bill Piper, at the age of seventy-four, took the controls of an Apache and qualified for his twin-engine rating.

Meanwhile, Max Conrad, the "Flying Grandfather," was carrying out Bill Piper's kind of campaign, giving dramatic demonstrations of the safety and simplicity of personal flying with his spectacular, record-setting, over-ocean flights in Piper Aircraft; and lightweight radio equipment was being developed to give personal airplanes the same multiple navigation systems as the commercial airliners.

With the Apache, the Piper company made its big transition. And in the jet age ahead, the galloping technology of the aircraft industry, which once had threatened Piper, would give it a protective umbrella. The giant, fuel-hungry jets of the 1970's would force the airlines to cut back

In 1967, Sheila Scott of England made a solo world flight in a single-engine Piper Commanche 260. She is shown here with Bill Piper (*left*) and Max Conrad, the "Flying Grandfather" and holder of five world distance and speed records. (*Courtesy of William T. Piper, Jr.*)

on service to many cities and to abandon smaller airports altogether. More than ten thousand airports—only about three hundred of them big enough to need a control tower—would invite the business travelers of general aviation, and Piper Aircraft would go on to win a full twenty-five percent of the market, doing about $250 million in sales, with some six thousand employees.

Bill Piper had gone everywhere with his campaign for low-cost air parks, and his influence continued long after his death in 1970 at the age of eighty-nine. In Ohio, by that time, virtually all of the eighty-eight counties had their own paved, lighted airports capable of handling most corporate aircraft; many other states were not far behind; and numerous small communities throughout the country were discovering the advantages of combining airport facilities with new industrial park sites.

In many of those places, and elsewhere in all corners of the world, Piper Cubs are still among the regular visitors. More than twenty-four thousand Piper Cubs have been built, and the Cub (now the "Super Cub") is still in production—making it aviation's longest continuously produced airplane. Given proper maintenance, almost any one of those Cubs—like a graceful, living commemoration of personal aviation's most pivotal period—could aspire to be around for a million miles or more.

MARKETING INSIGHTS

William T. Piper, personal aviation's great crusader, had set out to build a low-cost airplane for student instruction; then the post-World War II enthusiasm for flying persuaded him that his market consisted of "many thousands of young families." It would take his sons to convince him that the market should be defined more precisely as: executives of well-financed companies, who had a business need to travel, and who often traveled to cities and towns not served by commercial airlines. The Piper product and marketing effort had to be changed accordingly.

A widely read, post-World War II attitude survey (not conducted by Piper), which predicted spectacular gains for personal aviation, had violated a cardinal rule of good marketing research: it elicited opinions from *people who did not really understand the subject they were talking about.* Respondents expressed an enthusiasm for flying without having a realistic awareness of its operating and maintenance costs, regulations, and instructional requirements. Young respondents, in particular, failed to recognize that they lacked both a *basic need* and the *money* for personal flying.

Happily, with the help of such dedicated crusaders as William Piper, general aviation made a good recovery from its post-World War II marketing miscalculations. By the beginning of the 1980's, general aviation was the strongest and fastest-growing segment of the aviation market. For every airliner it produced, the industry was turning out about forty aircraft for general aviation.

RALSTON PURINA FOODS & FEEDS

"Find the right foundations and build on them."

28 Among his memories of boyhood, Will Danforth would always recall first that he was sickly—the kid who wanted keenly to be part of the crowd, but never quite made it. There was the vivid recollection of the school teacher who stood him up in front of everybody and "dared" him to become the healthiest boy in the class; and there were grateful recollections of being warmly understood and highly esteemed in Sunday school.

And there were a few bright, comical memories, like looking out from his father's store and watching the Brown kids come to town with their mother for a Saturday of shopping. The village of Charleston, in southeastern Missouri's swamp country, never quite got over the Brown kids. Their frugal mother, unable to resist a special discount on a big bolt of gingham, had taken it to her sewing machine and outfitted the entire family in pants, shirts and dresses of red and white checkerboard brilliance.

"Yep," agreed a customer in the Danforth store. "It may look strange. But you'll never hear of a Brown kid getting *lost*."

At twenty-four, two years out of Washington University in St. Louis, Will Danforth agreed with two church friends, George Robinson and William Andrews, that a "hand shovel horse and mule feed operation" would make a good, year-round business. Will had tried the brick business and knew its seasonal limitations. And he could plainly see that, even though the nation was in the midst of a deep depression, the feed stores on countless corners were kept busy maintaining the county's horse and mule transportation system.

The new Robinson-Danforth Commission Company, formed in 1894, listened carefully to complaints that oats were too costly, and that horses were dying daily from colic caused by bad corn. The new Robinson-Danforth

William H. Danforth

Donald Danforth

feed, mixed with shovels in the back room, was boldly marked: "Cheaper than oats and safer than corn."

Once-sickly Will Danforth, now an early-day "health nut," soon went from bookkeeper to top salesman. He married Adda Bush and settled a home. By the spring of 1896, he had become president of the flourishing new company, had moved it into substantial new quarters, and, on May 26, bought out the interest of William Andrews to become the majority stockholder.

The very next day, at about 4:30 in the afternoon, a balmy spring day suddenly turned black and St. Louis was struck by the worst tornado in its history. Workers in the Danforth-Robinson mill raced to a nearby railroad viaduct and clung to its iron supports as the mill, piece by piece, was reduced to rubble. The loss was total; and tornado insurance, in those days, was nonexistent.

It would be up to Walker Hill, president of a local bank, to decide whether or not the mill would be rebuilt. "I admire what I've seen of you," he told Will Danforth; "but what collateral do you have?" Danforth shrugged. "Nothing." "You have a baby daughter, don't you?" Hill asked. "Yes." "Very well," said Mr. Hill, with a twinkle in his eye, "if you will put up your baby daughter as collateral, this bank will lend you twenty-five thousand dollars to rebuild your mill."

By 1898, the horse and mule feed business was flourishing again, and Danforth was pursuing a new kind of "health cereal" with a Kansas miller who had discovered a way to keep wheat germ from turning rancid. Because of the rancidity problem, the germ was always removed from whole wheat cereals of the day. Nobody in 1898 seemed to know much about the value of wheat germ; but Will Danforth thought it was part of nature's own brand of purity and thus must be important to health. He soon was packaging the miller's cracked wheat for St. Louis grocers and, from his company's slogan, "where purity is paramount," he had coined a new name for the cereal: Purina.

At the same time, Danforth was being deeply impressed by the spectacular success of Dr. Albert Webster Edgerly, who, as "Dr. Ralston," had written an electrify-

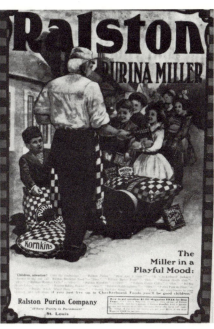

Top left: Early Ralston package used the simple, graphic checkerboard design to win swift national recognition. **Bottom left:** Will Danforth, who seldom appeared at the office without a checkerboard tie, believed the design should appear on all appropriate company surfaces. It can be seen here, not only on the wagon, but on the horses' harness. **Right:** By 1902, the name of the firm had become the Ralston Purina Company, and its checkerboard packaging was a major element in advertising.

ing book entitled *Life Building* and whose followers, now banding together in health clubs, numbered some eight hundred thousand. Dr. Ralston was urging the use of only the pure, whole wheat, complete with germ. Will Danforth was soon discussing his new Purina product with Dr. Ralston, and the two were agreeing on terms under which the product would be renamed Ralston Wheat Cereal and would carry the famous doctor's endorsement. By 1902, the names Ralston and Purina had become so widely known that the name of the firm was changed to Ralston Purina Company.

The new name, Danforth decided, should be backed by a bold new design in all the company's packaging—and a boyhood memory promptly supplied the answer: red and white checkerboard.

In an age when package design was a virtually unknown art, the boldly simple Ralston Purina checkerboard soon enjoyed national recognition. Moreover, with
all the wholesome appetite appeal of a country kitchen
tablecloth, it worked as effectively on cereals for humans
as it did on feeds for animals. The company was soon applying it in every conceivable way—and company headquarters, on the site of the original rebuilt mill, became
"Checkerboard Square."

Will Danforth was now becoming widely known, not
only as a pioneer of commercial animal feeds and human
health foods, but as a sort of lay evangelist who wrote inspirational booklets and preached a philosophy of better
living through the balanced development of the physical,
mental, social and religious sides of a "Four Square Life."
He sponsored an imaginative array of widely-copied employee activities, ranging from theatricals to square
dances to picnics to songfests. Said one incredulous ob-
servor: "He runs that company like a down-home husk-
ing bee!"

Each week, for nearly forty years, Danforth shared his
thoughts with his employees in his "Monday Morning
Message." In one of the last ones, he wrote: "Some folks
are continually making changes. I flatter myself that I
like new ventures and new experiences. But when it
comes to fundamentals, I'm a poor changer. I believe it's
best to find the right foundations and build on them."

Throughout his preoccupation with good works, he
never lost sight of company business. Early in World
War I, for example, he left his company to go to France as
YMCA secretary for the troops of the Third Army Division—and promptly noted, among his first observations
of the military, that soldiers responded with great alacrity to the word "chow." Purina animal rations would
soon be relabeled "chow" instead of "feed."

At about the same time, out of his insatiable curiosity
about health, Danforth established one of the world's earliest nutritional laboratories, opened in 1916. When Danforth's son Donald joined the company in 1920, he was so
impressed by the work of the laboratory that he recommended the purchase of an experimental farm for contin-

uous testing of Purina products. Will Danforth resisted
the idea, arguing that it was not necessary; but Donald
persisted and, by 1926, the company bought a farm, not
only for feed research, but for experiments in management and sanitation.

Will Danforth had become a national symbol of the
power of personal salesmanship. Donald Danforth
switched the emphasis to applied research, out of which
would come knowledge the Purina salesman could share
with his farmer customer.

During the last quarter-century, the American farm
worker has tripled his productiveness, a record un-
matched by any other sector of the economy, and Ralston
Purina has been a key participant in that progress. Purina
Chows, during that period, have reduced the amount of
feed necessary to produce one hundred pounds of pork
by over twenty-five percent, and have played a comparable role in the more efficient production of beef, poultry,
milk, and eggs.

In the midst of its involvement with farm animals, Ralston Purina almost lost sight of an important new customer: the house dog. Shortly after World War II, America's dog population began to climb at a spectacular rate.
Within a decade, the gain added up to an impressive forty-four percent.

Ralston Purina, with long experience in the feeding of
hunting dogs and working ranch dogs, assumed it would
be a simple chore to meet the needs of the house dog. But
the assumption was wrong. The house dog, Purina researchers soon concluded, was the spoiled brat of the animal world. He sulked and he pouted and turned up his
nose. It took a five-year research program covering thirty
different breeds before Ralston Purina went into national
distribution, in 1957, with Purina Dog Chow. Within fifteen months, Purina Dog Chow overtook all the others to
become the nation's leading dry dog food. Cat Chow followed in 1962.

Right up until the time of his death in 1955, at the age
of eighty-five, Will Danforth would be able to relate
proudly that he walked a mile a day, got eight hours
sleep a night with the windows open, and had never lost

Left: In 1916, William Danforth established one of the world's earliest nutritional laboratories. The search for new and better sources of protein is still a major concern of Ralston Purina research and development.
Right: In addition to being a familiar graphic symbol, Ralston Purina's checkerboard inspired the name for an expanding family of cereals: *Chex*.

a day at the office because of illness. But he had agreed, in 1932, when the Depression sent Purina sales plunging, that the time had come to turn over control of the company to his son Donald.

Ralston Purina describes itself as a "protein-oriented food and feed company, building on a foundation of agricultural products and services, and expanding in consumer industries."

In expanding and specializing to meet the needs of its diverse customers, Ralston Purina has become an organization of thirty-seven thousand people, doing more than two billion dollars annually in sales worldwide, all under the Checkerboard trademark. Ralston Purina is the world's largest manufacturer of balanced rations for livestock and poultry. It is also a major manufacturer of breakfast cereals and snack crackers; the largest producer of seafood in the United States; the owner of more than seven hundred restaurants; and a producer and processor of proteins in many forms.

Soy protein is just one example of the protein sources which have preoccupied company researchers for the last quarter-century. The company now produces a full line of soy protein products, some containing up to ninety-five percent protein, which can be used for everything from extending meat to stabilizing puddings.

"Worldwide demand for protein is now at an all-time high," says Ralston Purina, "and available supplies have been stretched to the limit. Protein, the basic energy source and building block of all living things, is the common bond of purpose throughout Ralston Purina Company."

MARKETING INSIGHTS

Given the requirement that every company needs a clear-cut "image" with strong corporate identity, how would you build an appetizing, clear-cut image for a company that makes everything from hog and poultry feeds to cereal for your breakfast table? Will Danforth did it by showing a true concern for healthful nutrition—whether for animals or humans—and then by using, as an identifying corporate umbrella, the simple, graphic, wholesome, red and white checkerboard of a country kitchen tablecloth. Meanwhile, for customer guidance, he reserved the Purina name for his agricultural feeds and the Ralston name for his human foods.

In both the feed and food categories, Ralston Purina products had a common meaning: good health. Danforth backed up that implied promise with one of the world's first nutritional laboratories and other related research.

In his marketing planning, Will Danforth showed a sound, basic sense of direction. Marketing direction, in turn, can be enhanced or hindered by a corporation's overall sense of basic purpose. In the case of the Ralston Purina Company, the present and long-term corporate purpose has been stated in clear and simple—and highly concise—terms: "Protein, the basic energy source and building block of all living things, is the common bond of purpose throughout Ralston Purina Company."

RCA TV/RADIO/STEREO

"It is the use to which the new invention is put, and not the invention itself, that determines its value to society."

David Sarnoff. Colleagues usually called him "General," the military rank he held in Europe during World War II when he was in charge of communications under General Eisenhower.

29 The message had crackled into the earphones that night with the cold, crisp, unmistakable opening every wireless operator hopes he will never hear—and it had kept on coming, in a relentless rush of dot-dash tones that seemed to go on forever, repeating the message over and over again, as operators froze in disbelief. It was the night of Sunday, April 14, 1912, and some alert, land-based operator had picked up and was relaying the faint, desperate "S-O-S" of the White Star liner *Titanic.*

There would be one lone interruption: the White House operator would cut in, during an early pause, to deliver President Taft's order to all but the sending station to get off the air at once.

It was the terrifying night of maritime history's most incredible disaster. Ironically, it was also the night when the world, for the first time, became suddenly aware of the importance of wireless communication.

And in the wake of the first dramatic news flashes, the nation would learn that the faint "S-O-S" from the sinking *Titanic* had been picked up by a twenty-one-year-old operator at the Marconi wireless station atop Wanamaker's Store in New York City, who had then stayed on duty for seventy-two continuous hours, receiving the list of survivors, and other reports, from the rescue liner *Carpathia.* His name was David Sarnoff, and he knew his job. He had been a qualified wireless operator for four years, mostly on ships, and had asked for a transfer to the Wanamaker station because it meant a chance to take a night course in electrical engineering at Pratt Institute in Brooklyn.

Until the Marconi Wireless Telegraph Company of America had taken him on, as a fifteen-year-old office boy, David Sarnoff was just another Lower East Side kid, even poorer than most, whose parents had brought him

David Sarnoff as a young wireless operator at the Marconi station on Nantucket. He had taught himself the Morse code before landing his first Marconi job as an office boy.

to America, at nine, from a tiny village near Minsk, Russia. When his father died, soon after, he became the main support of his family, selling newspapers and working as a delivery boy. By the age of fifteen, he had saved enough money to buy a telegraph instrument, had learned the Morse code, and was on his way to the Marconi office on William Street. Two years later, the company had an opening for an operator at its station on Nantucket Island, an isolated place with only a fine technical library to commend it. With his education in mind, Sarnoff seized the chance—and soon found that Nantucket also offered the opportunity of communicating with the crack operators on the transatlantic liners. It was 1908, a scant seven years since Guglielmo Marconi had received the first successful transatlantic wireless signal.

After the *Titanic* disaster, the new medium of radio began to advance rapidly, and so did Sarnoff. He became Chief Radio Inspector, then Assistant Chief Engineer, then Assistant Traffic Manager. By 1916, he was ready to write a memorandom to Edward J. Nally, then General Manager of the Marconi Company, with the prophetic opening: "I have in mind a plan of development which would make radio a household utility in the same sense as a piano or phonograph. The idea is to bring music into the home by wireless."

His plan, he explained, was for a "radio music box,"

which would make it possible for a home to receive not only music, but lectures—and even firsthand accounts of news events as they were actually happening.

With an eye on business as well as science, Sarnoff concluded his memo with: "It would seem reasonable to expect sales of one million 'radio music boxes' within a period of three years. Roughly estimating the selling price at $75 per set, $75 million can be expected." (Six years later, Sarnoff's "radio music box" was introduced by RCA. Its actual sales during the first three years: $83 million!)

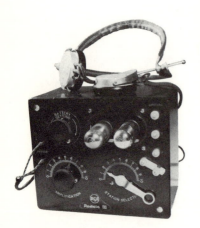

Early model of David Sarnoff's "radio music box," formally named the "Radiola." The first sets were built for RCA by General Electric and Westinghouse.

Wireless, by now, was acquiring its first war experience—in Europe. When the United States later entered World War I, all wireless stations in this country were taken over by the Government as a national defense measure. And suddenly the Government became vividly aware that transatlantic radio communications capabilities here were limited to the Marconi Wireless Telegraph Company of America, which in turn was controlled by the British Marconi Company—which, in 1919, announced plans for expanding its transatlantic service.

The U.S. Navy Department decided it was time to reevaluate the whole wireless situation from a long-range national defense point of view. The official "stop" order came in April, 1919, in the form of a letter to the key radio interests from the then Acting Secretary of the Navy, Franklin D. Roosevelt.

Out of the Navy's swift deliberations came a decision to form a new American company to take over the American Marconi company. The result was the Radio Corporation of America, incorporated in October, 1919, with General Electric holding a substantial interest in the new company because of the many GE radio patents involved.

Radio was now ready to reach out toward the market for the "radio music box"; but the early efforts were frustratingly slow. In the fall of 1920, Pittsburgh's Joseph Horne Company advertised "wireless receiving sets" for home use; a month later, Pittsburgh's KDKA, a Westinghouse station—the first licensed radio station in the world—broadcast the Harding-Cox election returns. On the following July 2, RCA's station WDY in Roselle Park, New York, broadcast the Dempsey-Carpentier fight; and

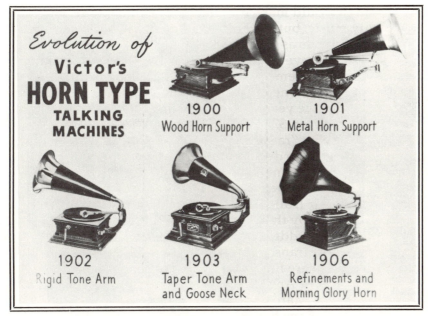

Early Victor horn-type "talking machines."

there was another "program" in the fall on Newark, New Jersey's WJZ.

Not until a year later, in 1922, would RCA market a line of home radios—both crystal sets and tube sets—all built for RCA by General Electric and Westinghouse.

In the midst of all the radio growing pains, David Sarnoff, now RCA Vice President and General Manager, took time the following April to write his Board of Directors another prophetic memorandum: "I believe that television, which is the technical name for seeing as well as hearing by radio, will come to pass in due course. It may be that every broadcast receiver for home use in the future will also be equipped with a television adjunct by which the instrument will make it possible for those at home to see as well as hear what is going on at the broadcast station."

Meanwhile, in that year of 1923, radio pioneers were becoming acutely aware of the chicken-and-egg relationship of radio receivers and broadcasting stations—just as America's automotive pioneers had learned, years earlier,

In 1949, RCA introduced the 45-rpm record and record player as a new system for the reproduction of recorded music in the home.

Right & below: Evolution of a famous trademark: In the early 1890's, London artist Francis Barraud put a record on his studio "talking machine," soon noted the intense curiosity it aroused in his fox terrier, Nipper, and decided to put the scene on canvas with the title, *His Master's Voice.* An executive of England's Gramophone Company saw the painting, decided it had advertising possibilities, and paid Barraud for the painting and all rights to its use. North American rights to the painting were purchased in 1901 by the Victor Talking Machine Company. RCA's 1929 acquisition of Victor included their famous dog-and-phonograph trademark. Nearly a century after he became a trademark, Nipper has been reproduced in sterling silver, bronze, china, and plastic for a wide variety of store displays, advertising and promotion novelties, customer sales incentives and special awards; has served as a three-foot-tall papier-mâché statue in and around thousands of record stores; and is busier than ever, on products and in communications, as the official symbol of RCA.

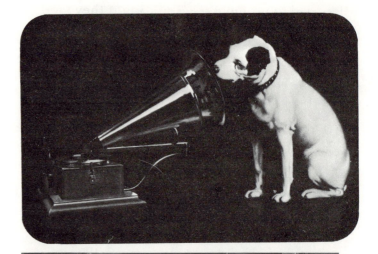

"HIS MASTER'S VOICE"

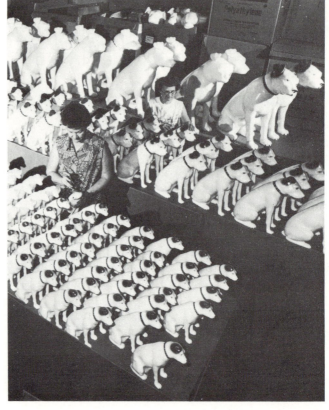

Right: Models of Nipper, shown here acquiring their hand-painted facial features, find immediate homes in RCA promotional activities and among collectors.

that they had to promote roadbuilding if they were going to sell automobiles.

Westinghouse had made a strong start in broadcasting, and American Telephone & Telegraph Company soon followed with WEAF (now WNBC) in New York City. During 1923, WEAF made radio history with broadcasts of the first radio address by the President to the people of the United States (Harding on the World Court); a distinguished religious program (Dr. S. Parkes Cadman); a heavyweight title fight (Jess Willard vs. Luis Firpo); and the World Series (N.Y. Yankees vs. N.Y. Giants)—finally capping the year's progress by establishing the first commercial network, starting with WEAF, New York, and WJAR, Providence. It would be called the "Red Network," simply because the engineers had used red ink to plot the station hook-up, and would lead, in early February of 1924, to the first coast-to-coast broadcasting hook-up.

Sarnoff decided it was time RCA assumed more responsibility for broadcasting, on an established, national basis. In the fall of 1926, he organized the National Broadcasting Company, as an RCA service to the five million homes then equipped with radio.

The public applauded the new broadcasts. But, almost immediately, the new popularity of radio dealt a vicious blow to the important phonograph industry. Sales of phonographs and records were beginning to slide.

There was a period of stubborn deadlock—while phonograph industry leaders, who regarded radio as a passing fad, waited to see if the problem of radio would slowly fade away. Sarnoff broke the deadlock by deciding the two industries should combine to expand communications and entertainment in the home.

In 1929, RCA acquired the Victor Talking Machine Company, adopted a new corporate name, RCA Victor (the double name was used until 1969), and steadily expanded the line of phonographs, stereo equipment, and records. The acquisition also included Victor's historic dog-and-phonograph trademark, entitled "His Master's Voice," first used by Victor in 1901. Ultimately, by the 1980's, Nipper the fox terrier would become RCA's offi-

Early 1960's RCA stereo set.

cial symbol in all corporate identification displays, from product and advertising emblems to stationery, sales literature, truck panels, and shipping cartons.

David Sarnoff, who had started as a Marconi messenger at $5.50 a week, was now tapped for RCA's highest honor, the heaviest responsibility. He became President in 1930—just in time to face two of RCA's most turbulent years. The economic depression was deepening fast; RCA's annual income would drop from $182 million in 1929 to $62 million in 1933. And the Department of Justice, in 1930, would demand the termination of all RCA ties with General Electric and Westinghouse; by 1932, RCA would become a completely independent, self-contained company with its own facilities for the manufacturing, as well as the marketing, of radio products.

Somehow, during this period, Sarnoff also found time to help shape the Rockefeller Center complex in New York City. In June of 1933, RCA moved its executive offices into the seventy-story RCA Building.

Franklin D. Roosevelt, who had triggered the action that led to the formation of RCA, was now using radio to inspire a demoralized nation. His first "Fireside Chat," in March of 1933, explained the banking emergency to the anxious American public. Sarnoff, meanwhile, was deeply involved in the continuing experiments with the newer medium of television.

At the New York World's Fair, on April 30, 1939, David Sarnoff stepped up to a microphone and said, "Now we add sight to sound." RCA was introducing television. "It is a creative force," Sarnoff continued, "which we must learn to utilize for the benefit of all mankind. This miracle of engineering skill, which one day will bring the world to the home, also brings a new American industry to serve man's material welfare. Television will become an important factor in American economic life."

RCA had spent more than fifty million dollars in television research and development, and was yet to receive its first financial return. It was no surprise to anyone when, in 1944, the Television Broadcasters Association selected David Sarnoff for the title of "Father of American Television."

But Sarnoff's most strenuous TV effort still lay ahead.
To Sarnoff, television would not be complete until it
could be received in full color—and the key to color, he
believed, was an all-electronic system, compatible with
black-and-white TV.

Important segments of the industry disagreed. They
had developed a mechanical system for their color TV
receivers and, in 1950, their mechanical system won the
approval of the Federal Communications Commission.
Sarnoff was undaunted. He stepped up work on the RCA
tricolor tube—and, in late 1953, had the pleasure of
seeing the FCC reverse its 1950 decision and approve
standards for color television broadcasting based on compatible signal specifications presented by RCA, NBC, and
others. Compatible color TV is now the only system in
use.

By the end of 1960, RCA had spent more than $130 mil-
lion in developing and promoting compatible, all-electronic color TV, and in providing facilities and color programming. It had been bold planning, but Sarnoff had
trusted his colleagues and his own convictions. Of his
RCA team of scientists, he had said, "I have often had
more faith in these men than they have had in themselves."

By the time of his death in 1971, David Sarnoff had
seen RCA grow into a multinational company, with product diversification extending into virtually every phase
of electronics, from TV receivers to solid-state technology. Ironically, manufacturing of the original RCA product—the radio receiver—had been moving steadily to the
Far East in recent years, and has now disappeared almost
completely from the American scene.

The pace of invention had been so brisk that some of
Sarnoff's favorite achievements received only limited notice. One subject of keen, personal interest to Sarnoff was
national defense. Of the multitude of RCA patents, two
are listed in the name of David Sarnoff. One patent covers a secret signaling system. The other combines the
principles of television, radar and microwave relay in an
"Early Warning Relay System."

But most of all, Sarnoff kept his attention focused on

the American home. In 1916, he had been preoccupied with the promise of the little "radio music box." By the early 1950's, in addition to his championing of all-electronic color television, he was pushing the development of video recording equipment for home use. By the beginning of the 1980's, RCA was placing increasing emphasis on such video-related products as the new VIP hobby computer, the RCA "SelectaVision" video cassette recorder and the RCA "SelectaVision" VideoDisc. The company by then was doing a sales volume of more than $6.6 billion and was employing more than 110,000 people.

In the space of one man's working life, Sarnoff's RCA had revolutionized the lifestyles of the entire world. By the time David Sarnoff observed his sixtieth anniversary in the field of electronics, television had exerted greater impact on social change than any product since the automobile. The time had come when TV-viewing and travel were the nation's two principal ways of using its increasing amount of leisure time.

David Sarnoff was deeply mindful of all the implications. On his sixtieth anniversary, he said: "In the past sixty years, our attentions have been focused primarily on the means to translate scientific knowledge to practical ends. Now I believe we must involve ourselves in the social applications of technology with the same energy and devotion that we give to its development. As the creators of progress, we share a new and fundamental responsibility to the purposes it serves.

"Our chief concern must be with the spiritual, social and political progress of mankind. In the final analysis," the "Father of American Television" concluded, "it is the use to which the new invention is put, and not the invention itself, that determines its value to society."

MARKETING INSIGHTS
David Sarnoff, ex-wireless operator, had an idea for a "radio music box" that could bring music, lectures, and news into the home. Though he did not regard himself as a marketing man, he estimated with remarkable accuracy the size of the market for such an invention and the price

it should carry. His radio sets went to market six years later, carrying the RCA name, but built by General Electric and Westinghouse.

RCA then faced the need to get into the business of broadcasting programs on a regular basis in order to make radio receivers a purchase of more than limited use. The result was the National Broadcasting Company.

While radio was still in its infancy, Sarnoff envisioned the adding of pictures to the radio waves. The dream became reality in black-and-white-television. His next ambition was the development of color TV using an all-electronic system. Beyond that, he urged the development of video-recording equipment for the home.

In a single-minded, evolutionary way, RCA carried out a product development program that helped build today's television industry—an industry whose main product has had greater impact on social change than any other product since the coming of the automobile.

As an industry, the makers of consumer electronics products reflect RCA's emphasis on technical product advances. They market through home appliance and TV-radio-stereo dealers (some of whom handle one brand exclusively), and department stores. In every case, reliable customer service is an important part of the distribution system.

Left: Television's first coverage of a news event was on April 20, 1939, when David Sarnoff stepped before the cameras to dedicate RCA's pavilion at the 1939 New York World's Fair. **Right:** RCA engineer John Konkel compares the chassis of the original RCA color television set of 1954 (*left*) with that of the RCA XL-100 of 1974. The original color set had thirty-seven tubes; the 1974 successor was all solid-state with no tubes.

SHERWIN-WILLIAMS PAINTS

*". . . not just to produce paints, but to contribute
to brighter, more colorful living."*

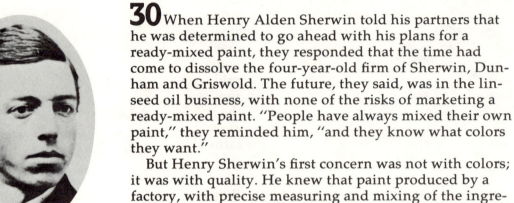

Henry Alden Sherwin

30 When Henry Alden Sherwin told his partners that he was determined to go ahead with his plans for a ready-mixed paint, they responded that the time had come to dissolve the four-year-old firm of Sherwin, Dunham and Griswold. The future, they said, was in the linseed oil business, with none of the risks of marketing a ready-mixed paint. "People have always mixed their own paint," they reminded him, "and they know what colors they want."

But Henry Sherwin's first concern was not with colors; it was with quality. He knew that paint produced by a factory, with precise measuring and mixing of the ingredients, would be consistently superior to the home-mixed paints of that time, and he had a prospective partner, Edward Porter Williams, who shared his convictions. What they wanted would call for ten years of painstaking development work; but when, in 1880, the Sherwin-Williams Company of Cleveland, Ohio, introduced the world's first ready-mixed paint, it was an instant success.

The two partners were a uniquely complementary pair of opposites: shy, meticulous Henry Sherwin, who had been obliged to quit school at thirteen to work in a Vermont general store; brisk, outgoing Edward Williams, who had earned his Phi Beta Kappa key at Western Reserve University. It was Sherwin who developed an advanced formula—and a mill that could grind pigments fine enough to remain suspended in oil—thus making possible the first reliable ready-mixed paint. It was Williams who sold the company to leadership in the house paint market, and then went on to establish the toughness of S-W products on farm implements and buggies, and the beauty of S-W products in that era's palatial Pullman Cars, whose ornate interiors glowed with as many as twenty coats of paint.

As part of their superior product concept, the partners then proceeded to build an integrated company with its

Edward Porter Williams

own smelters, oil mills, chemical units, color-making facilities, can plants—and its own company stores.

Truman Dunham and G.O. Griswold had argued that paint was usually applied by professional painters, to whom the mixing of white lead, linseed oil, turpentine, pigments, and other ingredients was a familiar, routine chore. But the new Sherwin-Williams approach soon created an additional market of "do-it-yourself" painters who learned that, along with providing ready-mixed paint, the Sherwin-Williams store could guide them through the problems of surface preparation, preliminary coatings, color-harmony judgments, and the best choice of brushes and clean-up materials. Encouraged by the helpful advice, home owners gradually learned that paint could do more than protect a surface; it could be the key to brighter, more colorful living.

By the turn of the century, the highly integrated Sherwin-Williams Company enjoyed a wide margin of leadership in its industry. But there was no let-up in the product development pace. When World War I brought raw material shortages, Sherwin-Williams promptly moved into a chemical field formerly monopolized by Germany. And when history repeated itself at the outset of World War II, Sherwin-Williams was ready to move rapidly with two significant developments. The first was a revolutionary type of paint: KEM-TONE®, the first one-coat, fast-drying, water-reducible paint. The second, in response to the scarcity of quality brushes, was a new paint applicator called the ROLLER KOATER®, which evolved into today's familiar paint roller.

When postwar America turned to the job of sprucing up its neglected homes, and do-it-yourself activity became the new national pastime, Sherwin-Williams was ready with KEM–GLO®, a porcelain-like enamel paint, and then with SUPER KEM-TONE®, the first of the modern latex paints. Within two years of its 1950 introduction, more SUPER KEM-TONE® was being sold than any other interior finish ever offered in paint industry history.

One-coat latex paint, smoothly and speedily applied with rollers, launched a revolution in home decorating—

Sherwin-Williams paint rollers helped contribute to the post-World War II do-it-yourself boom in home decorating.

a revolution that was soon being accelerated by the coming of television and its powerful home-centering influence on the American family.

Inevitably, the latex-based, in-home revolution was soon being matched by a revolution in marketing. The new problem-free latex paint became a timely traffic-builder for America's rapidly expanding "discount" stores. The profit in paint manufacturing shrank to a dangerous low as more and more retailers adopted paint as a loss leader—and how-to-paint advice at the Sherwin-Williams store became less and less important to the do-it-yourselfer.

Seldom had any new product created so many problems for its originator. But Sherwin-Williams was not ready to abdicate the leadership of the industry it had pioneered.

By the time the retailing revolution had reached its height, Sherwin-Williams had grown to an industrial complex of seven different paint companies. At that point, in keeping with its vertical integration tradition, the company unified its marketing efforts to match individual product lines with the individual needs of its diverse markets and distribution channels.

For the mass marketers, Sherwin-Williams developed a complete KEM® line. For its independent dealers, the company developed a new line of paints carrying the Martin Senour label. Finally, in the quality-minded Henry Sherwin tradition, the Company made its Sherwin-Williams brand an exclusive to its company-owned stores.

And never, in all this new marketing strategy-making, did the company forget the importance of providing consumers with helpful, how-to-do-it advice. Thus, the Sherwin-Williams paint store was expanded to a complete home decorating center, fully stocked with carpeting, draperies, wallcoverings, and other decorator needs—and carefully staffed with people who know how to advise the customer on the best use of any decorating materials. If the customer, for example, would like a change away from paint—well, Sherwin-Williams is also the

The first thing a typical paint customer needs is free advice. Sherwin-Williams offers it in some fourteen hundred company stores.

leading retailer of wallpaper. "Our purpose," says Sherwin-Williams, "is not just to produce paints, but to contribute to brighter, more colorful living."

Meanwhile, the company and its approximately twenty thousand employees maintain close control over all the materials that play a part in the one-billion-dollar business—including the paint cans. Those humble cans, in the meticulous Henry Sherwin tradition, have now grown into a massive Container Division, the largest volume supplier of containers to the entire paint industry.

MARKETING INSIGHTS

When Sherwin-Williams developed the first ready-mixed paint, the company's sole objective was to create a finer quality product; but the development also helped create what is now called the "do-it-yourself" market.

The company's integrated structure was another quality-oriented idea; but the company-owned stores were soon performing the added marketing function of giving free advice on surface preparation, method of application, and color selection. Without such advice, many do-it-yourselfers would have been deterred from tackling many painting tasks.

When Sherwin-Williams introduced latex paint—and the paint roller—it revolutionized do-it-yourself painting; but it also created a mass of new competition. Latex paint was virtually fool-proof—customers could apply it without much need for the advice they used to get at the Sherwin-Williams store. The nation's new "discount" stores could use latex paints as traffic-builders at loss-leader prices.

To realign its marketing efforts to meet the new competition, Sherwin-Williams created a special line of paints for the discount chains; still another special line for its independent dealers—and then made the Sherwin-Williams brand the exclusive property of its company-owned stores. The company-owned stores, in turn, were expanded to become not just paint stores but home decorating centers, carrying everything from paint to wall coverings to carpet—and staffed, as always, with people trained to give helpful, authoritative advice.

SIMMONS BEAUTYREST MATTRESSES

"Bedding is dull and unappreciated. In fact, no one even sees it; it's usually covered with sheets."

31 Just about everybody in Kenosha, Wisconsin in the 1860's knew Zalmon Simmons. He owned a country store, had become president of both the Rock Island Railroad and the Northwest Telegraph Company, and was now planning to buy a local cheesebox factory for the manufacture of a wood telegraph insulator of his own design. Out of respect and affection, his fellow citizens had elected him Mayor of Kenosha, and they assumed his new manufacturing venture would be an immediate success.

A sleep product then entered the picture in a roundabout way and distracted most of Zalmon Simmons' attention from the wood insulators. As payment for a debt incurred at his store, Simmons had accepted an inventor's patent for a woven wire bedspring. The inventor had admitted candidly that the product had failed because it could not be produced economically, but Simmons did not share his pessimism. He asked a local inventor to re-study the cost aspects and soon brought the cost down from five dollars to eighty cents.

Zalmon G. Simmons, founder of the company and president from 1870–1909. (*Courtesy of Grant G. Simmons, Jr.*)

Retailers were quick to recognize the merits of the woven wire bedspring, but they soon began asking, "Why don't you make bedsteads to go along with the springs?"

Zalmon Simmons pondered the suggestion. It had an obvious negative: bedsteads were just bedsteads, whereas his woven wire bedspring had some uniqueness. But Simmons had decided that his would be a retailer-oriented company, so he promised the retailers a bedstead and asked for their patience while he developed a product that would not be commonplace.

The Simmons response was a bedstead made of gleaming brass. It was sturdy; it would require a minimum of care to keep it looking new; and, by the aesthetics of the

Zalmon G. Simmons, Jr., president from 1909–1929, introduced the Beautyrest Mattress. (*Courtesy of Grant G. Simmons, Jr.*)

time, it was beautiful. Then, to the surprise of the modest Simmons, it also became a status symbol and began to draw orders from all parts of the world.

The Simmons Company began in 1870; but it would take the company another fifty years to get into the mattress business. Why the delay? There were two reasons. The first was that Americans had been long accustomed to sleeping on pads stuffed with hair or cotton, or on "ticks" filled with straw. The second reason was that the innerspring mattress, patented by a Poughkeepsie, New York, inventor in 1853, required handcrafting and was too expensive to interest any marketer. Its use had been confined to a few hotels and to such luxury liners as the *Mauritania*, *Lusitania*, and *Titanic*.

When Simmons finally entered the mattress business, by acquiring several small mattress companies during and just after World War I, it was just a wise investment that also enabled Simmons to provide retailers with a more complete line of related merchandise.

Zalmon Simmons, Jr. had become president of the company in 1909. Now, in the early 1920's, he had bold plans for expansion and, as a man who enjoyed gambling, he was willing to take risks. But he held his father's views about product uniqueness and basic merit and had been dismayed to find that the mattress business was basically a cottage industry, composed of a myriad of local manufacturers who relied mostly on second-hand tailors' cuttings for stuffing their products. Whenever cheaper products were in demand, the makers simply turned elsewhere in the rag field for cheaper filler. Zalmon Simmons, Jr. decided the time had come to develop a machine that would produce innersprings for mattresses on an economically feasible basis. The job would take three years.

By 1925, Zalmon Simmons, Jr. was ready to make some decisions that would cause him, ever after, to be referred to as "The Chief." He decided the company should move from regional to national distribution with the new innerspring mattress, and that the company should take a further step and set the retail price of the mattress at $39.50.

"Nobody called him 'crazy' to his face," a Simmons employee recalled later, "but we thought he was making two very serious mistakes. First, the price was *double* what anybody had to pay for the best hair mattress of that time. And second, it was an unwritten law that no *manufacturer* would ever set a retail price."

Zalmon Simmons, Jr. had listened to the objections, but had closed off the debate with a simple statement: "This time, gentlemen, I'm going to have *my* way."

The name "Beautyrest" had been selected for the new product over such other finalists as "Sleep Comfort" and "Slumber Well," and its introductory advertising carried a cutaway photograph of a mattress, showing the array of individually-pocketed innersprings produced by the Simmons Pocket Machine.

But the long-awaited innersprings and the ingenious Pocket Machine would soon be relegated to a subordinate place in the advertising, because The Chief decided that Simmons would not just sell a mattress; Simmons would sell *sleep*.

In the new project of educating America about the importance of a good night's rest, Simmons advertising people had no difficulty in recruiting the persuasive efforts of some very distinguished spokespersons. Simmons Beautyrest advertisements soon featured such respected authorities as Thomas Edison, Henry Ford, H. G. Wells, George Bernard Shaw, Al Smith, and Guglielmo Marconi.

Later, to provide its advertising people with convincing facts, the Simmons Company would initiate the first scientific sleep research program. Among its findings: "People do not sleep like logs; they move and turn from twenty-two to forty-five times a night to rest one set of muscles and then another." Ultimately, the sleep researchers would use specially-designed electronic devices that measured and correlated brain waves, heartbeat, respiration rate, muscle tension, skin temperature, and body movements.

The Simmons Beautyrest Mattress, at $39.50, was first advertised in 1926. By the end of 1927, sales had soared to three million dollars a year; by the end of 1929, sales had tripled to an annual nine million dollars. So bright was

H.G.Wells disagrees with Napoleon on sleep

An Interview with the famous English Author

by Audrey Scott

REMEMBERING how greatly most people differ on the subject of the amount of sleep a human being requires, my first question to Mr. Wells was:

"How much sleep do you need?"

The answer was quite definite. "I don't mind," said Mr. Wells, "what Napoleon said about six hours for a man, seven for a woman and eight for a fool—I want eight hours of dreamless, motionless sleep and I cannot do without it!

"If I do not get that allowance, then in a few days my nerves and mind are threadbare. In addition to my regular sleep I can snatch a little nap in the train with my mouth shut—on a sofa in the afternoon—on the grass under olive trees. And I wish I could sleep through some plays as a certain wellknown dramatic critic used to do. I slept once through the reading of an author's play, but that was one of my less fortunate slumbers."

"Do you ever suffer from insomnia?" I asked.

"Some twenty years ago I began to come awake about three in the morning. Lots of people do. It is champagne, coffee, cigars, stimulating talk, nightingales and distant dogs that set this habit going. After a time I got that right again without renouncing the normal life of over-eating, over-assembling, minor excitements, etc., which is so amusing and so unavoidable in our world.

"Whenever I found myself awake I tumbled out of bed, made myself tea, and went on with my work. Far better that than counting sheep for tranquilizing the mind. After an hour or so my bed and,I were friends again.

"Nowadays these nocturnal spells of work are rare.

"I'd rather slave than go sleepless."

Copyright, 1928, The Simmons Company

Clear thinking men recognize the tremendous advantage of a well-rested mind and body. Simmons, largest makers of beds, springs and mattresses, have developed scientifically the sleep equipment which gives complete relaxation and induces healthful sleep. This extraordinary comfort, embodied in their Beautyrest Mattress and their Ace Spring, is within reach of every income. Simmons Beautyrest Mattress $39.50; Simmons Ace Spring, $19.75 (slip cover additional). Rocky Mountain Region and West, slightly higher. Look for the name "Simmons." The Simmons Company, New York, Chicago, Atlanta, San Francisco.

Simmons Beautyrest—Hundreds of small sensitive coil springs, each cloth-encased to insure independent action and greater resiliency. Over these, thick layers of soft, luxurious upholstering—covered with beautiful new damask, an exclusive Simmons innovation. Two patterns—six lovely colors.

Simmons Ace Spring—The perfected modern coil spring. Light weight, yet with the coils in close together, so skillfully reinforced that maximum comfort and wear are assured. Smartly tailored slipcover at slight extra cost protects the spring and gives it a finished appearance.

SIMMONS
BEDS · · SPRINGS
MATTRESSES
[BUILT FOR SLEEP]

H. G. WELLS,
Author of the famous OUTLINE OF HISTORY. *Mr. Wells is one of the world's best known living writers. His works include a great number of popular romances, fantasties, sociological fiction, and articles on contemporary English life and manners.*

Soon after going to market with his new innerspring mattress, Zalmon Simmons, Jr.—"The Chief"—decided to subordinate the mattress features and put the spotlight on the importance of sleep. H. G. Wells, Henry Ford, Thomas Edison, George Bernard Shaw, and other notables were happy to participate, providing their views on sleep for a 1928–29 series of advertisements in *The Saturday Evening Post*.

the Simmons business outlook that in 1929, The Chief acquired three companies in related fields, including the distinguished Grand Rapids furniture firm of Berkey and Gay. Zalmon Simmons, Jr. enjoyed risk-taking; he was reputed to have played golf on one occasion with a bet of an automobile a hole, and he was accustomed to winning his bets. But he could not anticipate how his fortunes would be affected by other risk-takers in the stock market.

Within three days after the Crash of 1929, Simmons stock plummeted from $188 per share to $98—and continued dropping until it reached a 1932 low of 2 7/8.

The Chief's son Grant had assumed the presidency in 1929, just in time to see his company face disaster. One of his first official responsibilities was to go out and arrange

for a fifteen-million-dollar loan. One of his next moves
was to liquidate the 1929 investment in Berkey and Gay
and another furniture company, liquidation so painful
that it lived on as a "horror case" at the Harvard Graduate
School of Business Administration. By 1933, operations
were brought back to a break-even point, and by 1935
were profitable. In the long history that began in 1870,
the family-run Simmons Company would later note that
only during the 1930–1934 period did the company operate at a loss.

After the years of World War II, when Simmons had
turned from mattresses to such items as shells, para-
chutes, and tents, Grant Simmons was ready to revive his
father's interest in related furniture products. To a new
postwar market, far behind in housing facilities, Simmons introduced the Hide-A-Bed sofa. By 1957, when
Grant Simmons retired and the presidency moved to
Grant Simmons, Jr., the corporate net worth was double
what it had been before The Crash.

Grant Simmons, Jr. promptly reaffirmed his company's
determination to maintain the Beautyrest Mattress as its
number one product. In 1958, guided by the continued
findings of the sleep research program, Simmons
launched its Beautyrest Supersizes. Among the new generation of "super-sized" Americans, Simmons contended
that the long-standard fifty-four inch by seventy-five
inch mattress was now obsolete.

Grant G. Simmons, Sr., president from 1929 to 1957.

"Bedding is dull and unappreciated," Grant Simmons,
Jr. once observed. "In fact, no one even sees it; it's usually
covered with sheets. Only when you move to another
house do you think about it. Then you say, 'Am I going to
pay to move this dreary old thing?' Then, you might buy
a new one."

With its Supersizes, and such companion products as
extra-firm orthopedic mattresses (including one with a
built-in bedboard), Simmons was giving the consumer
some good reasons for buying a new mattress *now*, instead of waiting until he moved to another house.

Also, as it moved through the 1950's, the Simmons
Company got a giant boost from a product developed in a
field outside its own. The television receiver suddenly re-

Grant G. Simmons, Jr., president from 1957 until the 1978 acquisition of the company by Gulf + Western.

Opposite: As other mattresses began to look more and more like the Beautyrest, Simmons advertising pointed out, at regular intervals, that the Beautyrest Mattress was "the one mattress with individual coils." This ad shows that the Beautyrest Mattress gives individual support to the individual parts of the body.

kindled a national interest in the home. The new number one national pastime became TV-viewing, including TV-viewing in bed.

Grant Simmons, Jr. expanded his management team and kept up with the new opportunities for diversifying his company's operations throughout the home furnishings field. To provide retailers with a more complete line, Zalmon Simmons, Sr. introduced a brass bedstead. To the retailers of today, the Simmons organization offers mattresses, bedspreads, Hide-A-Bed sofas, a wide selection of furniture, wallcoverings, metal art sculpture for walls and tables—and many other related products. In the specialized health care field, the Simmons Hausted Division provides special coronary and intensive care beds. In the hotel field, the Simmons National Contract Studios can deliver a fully integrated furnishings package. Wherever and whatever the needs may be in the future, says Simmons, "we expect to be where the action is in home furnishings and the contract furnishings fields."

By thus concentrating its attention in and around the world of sleep, Simmons—now a division of Gulf + Western Industries, Inc.—has grown into an organization with seventy-two manufacturing plants operating throughout the United States, Canada, Mexico, England, France, Italy, Algeria, Morocco, Senegal, the Ivory Coast, Australia, and Japan. Employees now number more than thirteen thousand; sales are approximately $440 million.

The factories are geared to volume. A modern Simmons Pocket Machine demands a feeding of four miles per minute of high-carbon wire. On any one working day, Simmons plants can turn out more than twenty thousand mattresses.

At the same time, the advertising concentrates on pushing the top of the line, the very best of Simmons quality. And that, says Simmons, is the way it ought to be. "It's the wage earner, not the rich man, who is the best customer for Beautyrest and the Supersizes," the company notes, "because it's the hardworking wage earner, more than anybody else, who needs a good night's sleep."

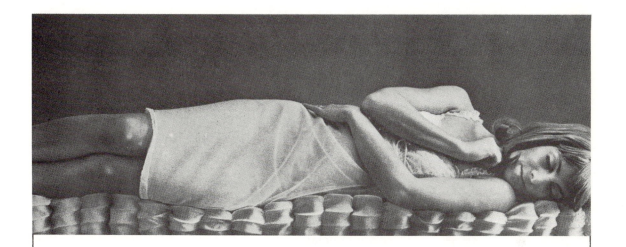

She measures 18-22-17-29-38.

When she sleeps, her statistics are in pounds. Her head weighs 18 pounds. It needs 18 pounds of support. Her shoulders 22, her arms only 17.

Her mattress either supports her the way she's built or treats her like a lump. Most all mattresses go the lump route. They're made with all their coils wired together. So they all sag together. The support each part of your body needs is compromised into one spot. The result is your whole body sleeps in a hollow.

There is a mattress that treats you like a human being. The Beautyrest. Made only by Simmons.

Beautyrest coils aren't wired together. Each coil is in its own pocket. Each is free to work individually. To give individual support to each part of your body. Arm support to arms.

Head support to head. Leg support to legs. No matter how you turn or move, every part of your body gets the individual support it needs.

Two bodies also get the same individual support. And without disturbing each other's sleep. They aren't affected by each other's weight or movement. There's no rolling together.

You can't get more comfort than that.

Try sleeping on a mattress that treats you like a human being.

Try a Beautyrest. Regular, Queen or King size. Give every part of your body a good night's sleep.

Be our guest on Beautyrest for 45 nights. If 45 nights don't convince you it's all we say, we'll take it back and your money will be refunded. Limited time offer, only at participating stores.

Beautyrest by Simmons

MARKETING INSIGHTS

The Simmons Company, maker of bedsprings and bedsteads, entered the mattress business only because it wanted to offer its department store and specialty store retailers a complete line of related merchandise. The mattress business was then a cottage industry with few, if any, standards, and the American public had long been accustomed to sleeping on hair pads and straw ticks.

Developing the Simmons Beautyrest Mattress meant first developing a machine to make innerspring construction affordable. Then, to develop a market for this unique mattress, Simmons took the long view and embarked on a series of advertising campaigns selling the importance of a good night's sleep. To generate provocative information for the advertising, Simmons initiated an ambitious program of sleep research.

Simmons was among the first manufacturers to set a retail price and give it national advertising support. The Beautyrest price of $39.50—double that of the best hair mattress of the times—was an important element in the Beautyrest image of innovation and quality.

After establishing the importance of a good night's sleep on an innerspring mattress, Simmons expanded its product appeals with supersize mattresses, then with extra-firm orthopedic mattresses.

An outside force, television, stepped up the momentum of the Simmons effort by introducing the national custom of TV-viewing in bed.

For the typical American family, the purchase of a mattress is an event that occurs only two or three times in a lifetime. On that infrequent occasion, Simmons wants you, the consumer, to think first of Simmons as the maker of the most desirable of all mattresses; hence Simmons advertising always features the top of the line, the Beautyrest.

Meanwhile, to offer its retailers a complete line of related merchandise, Simmons produces a broad spectrum of items ranging from furniture to wallcoverings, and even metal art sculpture to put on the tables it manufactures. "Our purpose," says the company, "is to be wherever the action is in home furnishings."

SINGER SEWING MACHINES

"If the purchase price is a problem, why not let her buy the machine with monthly rental fees?"

32 Not long after Mahatma Gandhi had issued a sweeping ban against the use of Western machinery in India in the early 1920's, he decided to make one exception: the sewing machine. "The sewing machine," he explained, after learning how to operate a Singer during a jail term, "is one of the few useful things ever invented."

Ironically, in the beginning, the sewing machine was a dreaded instrument no honest, god-fearing person wanted to invent.

France's Barthelemy Thimmonier completed a workable machine in 1829; but when eighty of the machines were later put to work making uniforms for the French Army, an infuriated mob of tailors promptly smashed the machines to pieces. When, around 1832, New York's Walter Hunt perfected the first sewing machine which contained all the elements of practicality, his fifteen-year-old daughter persuaded him to abandon the project because it could throw so many seamstresses out of work. At least two American ministers of the gospel turned their backs, for the same moral reason, on near-perfect models they had built.

Boston's Elias Howe, Jr., however, was not thus deterred and proudly demonstrated in a clothing factory, in 1845, that his new machine could out-sew the five best seamstresses in the place. He was granted a patent the following year, and other inventors soon entered the field.

The coming of Isaac Merritt Singer to the sewing machine scene was purely accidental. A machinist by trade, he was in Boston in the summer of 1850 to arrange for the sale of a wood-carving machine he had invented, and happened to visit the machine shop where Orson Phelps was trying, without much success, to manufacture a sewing machine under license from one of the early inventors. Singer, suddenly curious about the workings of a

Isaac Merritt Singer

Edward Clark, the marketing-minded lawyer who turned Singer's invention into a successful company. (*Courtesy of the Museum of the City of New York*)

sewing machine, studied the malfunctioning of the model in the shop and suggested three fundamental changes: the shuttle, he said, instead of moving in a circle, should move back and forth in a straight line; the needle should be straight instead of curved; and the needle, instead of moving horizontally, should work up and down.

Phelps was incredulous; how could so brief an examination lead to such revolutionary recommendations? But Phelps was also desperate enough to be open-minded, and finally encouraged Singer to try his hand at the development of a completely new machine. The result— finished in just eleven days—was soon acknowledged to be the first truly practical sewing machine and is now preserved in the Smithsonian Institution. Its name, Singer had decided, should be "The Perpendicular Action Belay Stitch Machine."

To manufacture and market the new machine, I. M. Singer & Company was formed in 1851. Isaac Singer would be the designer; Orson Phelps would provide the machine shop facilities; and one George Zieber became the financial backer with an initial advance of forty dollars. Because Isaac Singer had once worked briefly as an actor in a traveling Shakespearean troupe, he also drew the assignment of lugging his machine around to county fairs and church suppers for dramatic demonstrations of its prowess. Before long, some garment manufacturers visited I. M. Singer & Company and placed substantial orders.

Then came a highly unwelcome visitor; Elias Howe, Jr. arrived to demand payment of twenty-five thousand dollars for infringement of the Howe patent. Isaac Singer was still barely making expenses; but he decided the crisis warranted the help of one of the very best law firms in the City of New York. He wound up talking with a junior partner, Edward Clark. With some reluctance, Clark finally agreed to fight the legal battles in return for an interest in the company.

The new principal partners were a strangely contrasting pair: truculent Isaac Singer, son of poor German immigrants, a rough-hewn man of lusty appetites who had

The first practical sewing machine, invented by Isaac M. Singer in 1851 and now preserved as a relic in the Smithsonian Institution, Washington, D.C. Singer built it in eleven days and described it as a "Perpendicular Action Belay Stitch Machine."

left home at the age of twelve; soft-spoken, shy Edward Clark, a graduate of Williams College with a broad interest in financial and marketing as well as legal affairs.

While Singer tended to designing and manufacturing, Clark worked with competitive-company lawyers to organize the Sewing Machine Combination, America's first patent pool, and thus end the "sewing machine war." Manufacture was licensed at fifteen dollars a machine, divided among the four organizers, with Howe and Singer receiving more than the others. Ultimately, twenty-four companies were licensed, and the industry began to make rapid gains.

Clark then turned his attention to marketing and soon

concluded that the outlook was more bad than good. The sturdy Singer machine was selling well to tailors and garment makers, but was being badly outsold in the home market. Furthermore, the entire market was being stalled by the suspicious attitude of the numerous owners of early-day, defective machines. Those pioneer buyers were wary of being stung a second time and were very vocal about it.

Clark aimed first at the industry-wide problem of distrust. To clear the way for new Singer machines, he offered to pay fifty dollars for any used machine, regardless of make, in exchange for a new Singer. He thus became the originator of the trade-in allowance, and had the immediate satisfaction of watching Singer sales triple during 1856.

In his second big problem area—lagging sales to housewives—Clark decided most housewives would feel guilty about spending $125 for a Singer sewing machine at a time when the average breadwinner was earning barely $500 per year. "If the purchase price is a problem," he told his sales people, "why not let her buy the machine with monthly rental fees?" Clark's "Hire-Purchase Plan," introduced in late 1856 with terms of five dollars down and three dollars a month, pioneered installment selling and was credited with doubling Singer sales during the following year.

Meanwhile, Clark continued to press the advantage the rugged Singer machines enjoyed in a growing variety of industries. To maintain close control over his marketing activity, Clark elected not to follow the competitors who sold through wholesalers, jobbers, and retailers. Clark preferred having his own agencies in key markets, and his own salesmen in outlying districts; and he followed the same policy overseas. The benefits of this policy were sharply enhanced when the Civil War broke out, bringing with it a war sales tax on manufactured goods. If a company made an article from its own raw materials and sold direct to the consumer, the tax was paid once; if a manufacturer bought his materials, and the product then had to pass through a distributor, a wholesaler, and a retailer, the sales tax had to be paid five times. Singer

responded by stepping up the integration of its manufacturing facilities. By 1867, the company had become
virtually a maker-to-user manufacturer and in several
plants has followed that tradition ever since.

The Civil War, with its depreciation of the dollar, also
gave Singer a memorable demonstration of the importance of foreign trade. Singer had begun marketing its
products internationally in 1853, and by 1861 was selling
more machines in Europe than in the United States. By
1867, the company was ready to take the next step and begin manufacturing operations overseas.

Edward Clark, all this while, was guiding the destiny
of the Singer sewing machine. Since the incorporation of
the company in New York, in 1863, as The Singer Manufacturing Company, inventor Isaac Singer had been
spending most of his time in Europe, catching up on the
pleasures he had missed in his youth. He died in England
in 1875. The company, by then, was selling nearly as
many sewing machines as all other manufacturers combined.

Modest Edward Clark, to whom public appearances
were almost painful, was persuaded to assume the official
title of President and he held it until his death in 1882. In
the already well-established, hard-working, no-frills Singer tradition, Clark was succeeded by George Ross
McKenzie, who had arrived in America as a young immigrant from Scotland.

And the Singer sewing machine was well on its way to
becoming what it now claims to be: "The best-known and
most widely used product in the world."

With a level of zeal and ruggedness that would have
done credit to any nation's explorers, Singer salesmen
carried their machines to virtually every inhabited spot
on earth, from igloo settlements above the Arctic Circle
to Pygmy kraals in Equatorial Africa; from South America
to the Turkish Empire; and from old Imperial China to
Russia, where, at one time, Singer sold more sewing machines than it was selling in any other country in the
world, the United States included. Singer sold to the
household market and to industries ranging from textiles
to shoemaking to bookbinding. In pursuit of their duties,

Right: Singer sewing machines moving to market in Thailand via elephant transport. **Below:** A lady in the Philippines helps show why the Singer sewing machine is claimed to be "the best known and most widely used product in the world."

Singer salesmen over the years have been held for ransom by bandits, attacked by mobs, and jailed during revolutions—serving all the while as mechanics, collection agents and sewing teachers, as well as salesmen. Singer always gave them staunch engineering and advertising support (Singer believes it was the first company to spend one million dollars a year to promote its products); but it was usually up to the individual salesman to solve the problems he encountered, whatever they might be.

It was in Japan that the early Singer salesmen met one of their most perplexing challenges: the kimono. For centuries, Japanese housewives had sewn kimonos loosely, with simple basting stitches—all of which they would remove and replace every washday. The early Singer machines made only short, tight stitches that were intended to be permanent.

The Singer salesmen promptly called for engineering support, and a new machine was developed especially for the Japanese household market. It sewed a quarter-inch basting stitch. But the Japanese refused to trust it with kimonos.

Company management now took a special interest in the problem and endorsed a bold plan of action: it would convert an entire nation to Western-style dress. In Tokyo, Singer built a sewing school big enough to enroll one thousand day pupils and five hundred boarders; it offered, for a modest tuition, a three-year course in how to sew the latest Western styles. The school was soon turning away applicants, and Western styles went on to win a permanent place in Japan—but the kimono went its ancient way untouched.

The experience in Japan was an early lesson to Singer about the importance of respecting local customs. Later, in a Moslem country, Singer people were careful to "Mohammedanize" one of the store mannequins in elaborate detail—and then were completely baffled when a shouting mob smashed the store windows. The Singer mannequin-dressers had forgotten just one detail: the veil.

Ultimately, Singer would provide its far-ranging salesmen with instruction books printed in more than fifty languages—plus some books that are entirely pictorial.

And in its-sales organizations throughout the world, Singer believes it employs a higher percentage of nationals than any other major international company.

If Singer seemed at times to be over-emphasizing foreign trade, it was for three very logical reasons. First, the United States sewing machine market was considered saturated by the early 1900's. Second, the ready-to-wear dress—like early-day home appliances—had become part of the national trend toward lighter housework. Finally, more and more American women were going out to work, turning their backs on sewing and other domestic work.

In 1922, Singer management was shocked when a marketing study revealed that the nation's schools—which always had been supplied with Singer machines at a discount—had no up-to-date sewing textbooks and had almost ceased to teach the subject. Singer responded with a modern textbook for home economics teachers and a condensed version for students. Wall charts followed, along with instructional films. At about the same time, Singer stores began to offer sewing courses for adults.

The depression of the 1930's, with its tighter household budgets and fewer jobs for women, brought a strong revival of home sewing—and Singer made the most of it with new machines, including a new portable electric, made of aluminum and weighing only eleven pounds. Singer educational efforts were steadily increased, and Singer stores began a changeover to Singer Sewing Centers.

During and after World War II, Singer Sewing Centers became so much a part of community life that many women who enrolled said they were as much interested in becoming acquainted with their neighbors as they were in making new dresses, draperies, or slipcovers. A Singer Sewing Book, published in 1949, sold a quarter of a million copies and went on to become an offering of the Book-of-the-Month Club.

Home sewing had become fashionable again, and Singer was a major beneficiary of the boom. But Singer's gains were soon being undercut by the onslaught of post-war machines from Japan and Europe, all with highly attrac-

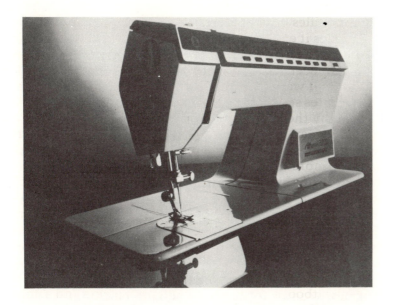

In 1975, Singer introduced the Athena 2000, the world's first electronic home sewing machine. With an electronic system replacing over 350 mechanical parts, the Athena 2000 enabled the user to sew any of twenty-five different stitches at the touch of a button.

tive price tags. Singer fought back by redesigning its entire line and by overhauling its production and marketing facilities. By the late 1950's, Singer had neutralized the threat and had increased its share in the United States market.

During that turbulent period, Singer also decided it was time for a major diversification program. Beginning in 1958, Singer moved into business machines, furniture, aerospace systems, and other products.

But the home sewing machine continued to be The Singer Company's best newsmaker. To its burgeoning post-World War II market, Singer had offered such improvements as zigzag stitching for more sophisticated work—and the slant needle, push-button bobbin, and speed basting for easier work. By the mid-1970's, Singer was ready to zoom beyond all previous improvements by offering the world's first electronic sewing machine for the home, the Athena 2000.

Singer now sells its household sewing products through a worldwide network of more than thirty-four hundred retail outlets, and has operations in over one hundred countries. Total corporate sales exceed two billion dollars; employees number some eighty thousand.

The machine that was once dreaded—as a threat to the livelihood of every seamstress—is now in use in about seventy percent of all U.S. households; and today's woman who sews is no longer a pitied "seamstress." Singer surveys of the American market indicate that today's home sewers are predominantly young (seventy percent under forty-five), well-educated (eighty percent have finished high school), and well-off financially (two-thirds have incomes of more than seventy-five hundred dollars per year).

Economy, of course, is still one of the reasons for home sewing; but it is now one of the minor ones. Easier fashion styles, easier-to-sew fabrics, and new teaching methods with greater emphasis on "results" are among the major new reasons for buying a sewing machine.

And there are two additional reasons which might be the most significant ones of all: the creativity of sewing and the desire for individuality.

MARKETING INSIGHTS

The fact that an invention will serve an important consumer need is no guarantee of success. The sewing machine was bitterly opposed on the grounds that it would throw many poor seamstresses and tailors out of work.

Nor is a technically-fine invention any guarantee of success. Isaac Singer invented the first practical sewing machine; but it took Edward Clark, a lawyer with a marketing flair, to turn the Singer invention into a viable business.

To purge a market glutted with defective, other-brand machines, Clark offered the first trade-in allowance: fifty dollars for any used machine, regardless of make, in trade on a new Singer.

To enable the housewife to buy a product whose price represented about twenty-five percent of an average family's annual income, Clark originated installment buying with his "Hire-Purchase Plan": five dollars down, three dollars a month.

To maintain better quality and cost control of marketing and production, Clark set up his own sales force and integrated his manufacturing facilities.

To inform the public of its new products and their advantages, Singer became an early advertiser and probably was the first company to budget one million dollars a year for advertising.

To educate the public in the use of a new machine, Singer organized schools with enrollments of up to fifteen hundred students and courses lasting up to three years, and maintains a network of Singer Sewing Centers. The company prints instruction books in more than fifty languages—plus some books that are entirely pictorial. One Singer Sewing Book became an offering of the Book-of-the-Month Club and sold a quarter of a million copies.

Throughout its more than a century of marketing, Singer has felt the forces of social change in bad, good, and sometimes strange ways. By the early 1900's, more and more women were going out to work, wearing ready-made clothes. The Depression of the 1930's brought a major revival of home sewing. During and after World War II, Singer Sewing Centers attracted many women who were even more interested in meeting new neighbors than in learning how to sew.

During that long history, the company also observed a slow but sweeping change in customer demographics. Originally, Singer sold primarily to the low-income housewife to whom a sewing machine was an economic necessity. Singer buyers are now predominantly young, well-educated, and relatively affluent, with such major new reasons for sewing as creative expression and the desire for individuality.

When the time came for Singer to consider diversification, the company moved naturally—on the basis of its mechanical expertise and its high level of homemaker respect—into such new and diverse products as business machines and home furniture.

SPALDING SPORTING GOODS

"Spalding has gone into the baseball business."

Albert Goodwill Spalding

33 A grim hush spread slowly through the stands at the prestigious Washington baseball park. Before the unbelieving eyes of a crowd glittering with congressmen and other notables, the National Club—"the best baseball team in the United States"—was going down to certain, humiliating defeat at the hands of a ragtag team of unknowns: the Forest City Club of Rockford, Illinois. Out of the undercurrent of grumbling came a recurrent question: "Who's that Rockford pitcher—who is Albert Spalding?"

Back in Rockford, Harriet Spalding, a widow, gave careful consideration to her son's reports of the offers he was now receiving to play baseball as a career. The famous clubs in Washington, Cleveland, and New York already had made firm offers, and others were still arriving. The figures ranged from $1,500 to an incredible $2,500. To a boy of seventeen, then earning $5 a week as a grocery clerk, it was almost beyond belief. In 1867, $2,500 was a fortune.

At length, with the strong support of her daughter, Harriet Spalding announced her decision: "No, Albert," she said, "it would not be right. It would turn your head." Albert Goodwill Spalding agreed that the judgment was reasonable. After all, he had completed his studies at a Rockford commercial college and was a qualified bookkeeper. Perhaps he should look for better-paying work in Chicago.

Within a five-year period, he was destined to work for seven different firms—all of which failed soon after his arrival. The experience was traumatic. Was he "jinxed" as a businessman? By 1871, he decided it was time to disregard his mother's wishes and sign as a pitcher-outfielder with the Boston Red Stockings. In his first season, he pitched his team to a pennant victory.

Between 1871 and 1875, first with Boston, then with the Chicago White Sox, Spalding pitched 301 games and won 241 of them. Along with the distinction of becoming baseball's first 200-game winner, he clinched his spot in the Hall of Fame by leading American baseball teams on their first foreign tour to England and on their first around-the-world tour.

Now, he decided, the time had come to return to business, not as a bookkeeper, but as a hero. When in March, 1876, he opened his long-planned sporting goods emporium in Chicago, he saw to it that a large sign was painted over its doorway proclaiming: "Spalding has gone into the baseball business."

His featured product was a baseball he had made originally for his own use. During his final months as manager and pitcher with the Chicago White Sox, he had used the Spalding ball in sixty-one complete games and had won forty-seven of them.

In the following year, with Albert Spalding's active participation, the National Baseball League was organized in Louisville with eight member clubs, whose owners agreed that the official ball for League use should be the Spalding.

To keep pace with business generated by Albert Spalding's reputation and the National League endorsement, the A. G. Spalding Sporting Goods Company soon moved to Chicopee, Massachusetts, a city known as the manufacturing hub of the United States. The man who had become known as baseball's "hardest-throwing" pitcher was now broadening his line of baseball equipment and looking for additional products to manufacture. During the 1880's, he introduced the first U.S.-made tennis balls and footballs, and a new Spalding-designed tennis racket.

In 1891, the now-prominent Spalding company received an intriguing but vague inquiry from the YMCA College in nearby Springfield. One of the instructors, Dr. James Naismith, was trying to devise a new kind of indoor game—something more exciting than calisthenics and gymnastics—to keep his athletes in good condition between the football and baseball seasons. Spalding offered to develop whatever kind of ball would be needed.

Dr. Naismith, reflecting on the games of his Canadian

Albert Goodwill Spalding as a pitcher-outfielder with the Boston Red Stockings. He became baseball's first two hundred-game winner.

Some of Spalding's past and present advisors (*from left to right*): Bobby Jones, perhaps the greatest golfer of all time; Wilt Chamberlain, usually named center whenever all-time basketball teams are chosen; "Pancho" Gonzales, one of the all-time greats of tennis.

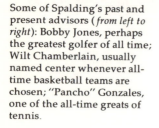

boyhood, favored the player positions of lacrosse, and the ball-tossing (rather than hurling) of "duck on a rock." The goal, he thought, should be high, with a horizontal opening, so that the ball could not be slammed through it; the ball should be soft enough not to hurt the players, and large enough not to be concealed; and the ideal number of players would be nine to a side.

When he was ready for the first practice session, in mid-December of 1891, Dr. Naismith selected two teams of nine men each, gave them a soccer ball, stationed a man in the balcony at each goal to retrieve the ball after each score, and dispatched the school janitor to find two fifteen by fifteen-inch boxes to be used as goals. Finding no boxes, the janitor appeared instead with two half-bushel peach baskets, and suddenly the new game had a name.

A new Spalding-designed ball was soon in production, and the official rules of basketball would later state: "The ball made by A. G. Spalding & Bros. shall be the official ball."

From left to right: Carl Ya-strzemski, with three thou-sand hits, four hundred home runs, and going after more; Rod Carew, perennial batting star of the American League; soccer's incompara-ble Pelé.

Albert Spalding now turned his attention to golf. In his earlier work with tennis products, he had noticed that players did not blame poor scores on the ball; they blamed it on the racket. Thus, he decided to enter the golfing field in 1894 by becoming the first U.S. maker of clubs; the balls would follow later.

By 1900, the one-time pitcher for the Forest City Club of Rockford, Illinois, had become the logical choice of President William McKinley to serve as Commissioner of the Olympic Games in Paris; and his company was established as the leader in the two separate worlds of sporting goods.

In the world of balls, Spalding had learned to manufacture to highly exacting tolerances, and thus become the official choice of various leagues and associations. In the world of baseball gloves, tennis rackets and golf clubs, Spalding had learned the art of custom designing to obtain the personal endorsements (in return, of course, for a fee) of famous players in every field of sport.

Beginning with the organization of the National

League in 1877, and the American League in 1901, Spalding was the official supplier of baseballs for both—ultimately thirty thousand dozen baseballs for each new season—until the termination of the League agreements, in 1977, to buy exclusively from Spalding. Each of the balls begins with a center of cork wrapped with two layers of soft rubber, with a finished weight of seven-eighths of an ounce. The cushion-cork center then receives four windings of yarn: 121 yards of rough gray wool; 45 yards of fine white wool; 53 yards of fine gray wool; 150 yards of white cotton. The cover is then applied and a hand-stitcher, using two needles, each threaded with eighty-eight inches of waxed twine, makes exactly 108 stitches. To be stamped "Official," the ball must then be within 9 and $9\frac{1}{4}$ inches in circumference, must weigh between 5 and $5\frac{1}{4}$ ounces, and must be backed by proof that it has an initial velocity of eighty-five feet per second and a rebound velocity of 54.6 percent of the initial velocity; that it retains its roundness after being pounded two hundred times all over its surface by a force of sixty-five pounds; and that it is hard enough to distort less than 0.3 inch when compressed between two anvils. Comparable specifications apply to Spalding tennis, golf, basketball, volleyball and soccer balls.

And all the Spalding *non*-specification equipment is designed by and for the heroes and would-be heroes of the world of sports. Spalding makes a special-design baseball glove, for example, not only for each of the six player positions, but also in a Professional, Collegiate, Youth and Youngstar series—and every single one of them carries the personal endorsement, complete with signature, of a baseball superstar. To maintain this kind of "hero authority" in all its fields, Spalding employs a Sports Advisory Staff of more than two hundred fifty athletes, all of whom—in return for their fees—are expected to use and evaluate the equipment and suggest improvements when needed. In many cases, the stars have also been the originators of new equipment.

In addition to the Sport Advisory Staff, Spalding maintains close working relations with top teaching and playing professionals in all its chosen fields. Before Spalding marketed the V-throat Speedshaft tennis racket, for example, samples of the racket were given to a national group of professionals to be played with, taught with, competed with, and then evaluated.

Products carrying the Spalding name are sold only through retail sporting goods dealers and through the shops of professionals. To cultivate such other markets as discount stores, premium and incentive operations, and private-brand sellers, Spalding develops special product lines.

Albert Goodwill Spalding, the one-time bookkeeper turned baseball hero, pioneered a simple combination of athletic hero authority backed by exacting workmanship. Before his death, in 1915, he was rewarded by abundant proof that baseball, his first love, would continue to grow as "the national pastime," and that basketball—the first wholly American sport—had all the makings of what it ultimately became: the most popular sport in the world. He also knew that he had established good traditions for a company that now operates a dozen plants throughout the world, with a work force of more than thirty-five hundred people.

MARKETING INSIGHTS

On his way to a place in baseball's Hall of Fame, pitcher Albert G. Spalding decided that "hero authority" was the key to success in selling sporting goods. He earned those endorsements by conscientiously custom-designing his equipment for final testing and approval by the heroes he selected.

Beginning with a baseball of his own making—which he had used in achieving an extraordinary single season record of forty-seven wins and fourteen losses—Spalding swiftly expanded to cover every major sport in which balls were used. Baseball gloves, of course, followed naturally. Also, he had noted early that tennis players blamed low scores on the racket, not the ball; so he became a maker of rackets, and would later become a maker of golf clubs as well as balls.

In applying today's market segmentation principles, the Spalding company aims at all market segments through retail sporting goods dealers and pro shops, and makes special lines for such other distribution channels as discount store and private-brand sellers. As an example of the segment-serving breadth of the product line, Spalding—in baseball gloves alone—makes gloves for all player positions in separate Professional, Collegiate, Youth and Youthstar series. And every single one of those gloves carries the endorsement, complete with signature, of a baseball superstar.

WRIGLEY'S CHEWING GUM

"Restraint in regard to immediate profits."

34 If and when our present age of tension tonics comes to a close, scientists may concede, in retrospect, that the safest and cheapest of tranquilizers, all along, has been the humble stick of chewing gum. They also may note that no simple, harmless product ever had to work so hard to win a modicum of social acceptance.

No less a behavioral scientist than Columbia University's H. L. Hollingworth concluded, in *Psycho-Dynamics of Chewing* (1939), that the act of chewing reduces muscular tension and helps people feel more relaxed. This, in turn, helps explain why chewing gum is included in Armed Forces field and combat rations and why GI's in combat chew it at a rate about five times greater than the national average.

The first makers of chewing gum in America were the Indians. They used the resin from freshly-cut spruce bark. But not until the late 1860's did chewing gum become a commercial success, after Staten Island inventor Thomas Adams noticed that his visiting neighbor from Mexico seemed to derive a lot of satisfaction from chewing on what turned out to be lumps of chicle. The visiting Mexican had every right to feel tensions: he was deposed dictator Antonio Lopez de Santa Anna, best remembered as the hated target of the Texas battle cry, "Remember the Alamo!"

Inventor Adams decided chicle was better than the limp paraffin sometimes chewed in those days, and went to market with "Adams New York Gum—Snapping and Stretching." Later he tried adding flavors, found that licorice lasted best, and still later invented a gum-making machine.

At about this time, the future king of the chewing gum business, William Wrigley Jr. (who never used a comma in his name), was running away from his comfortable Philadelphia home, at age eleven, to play hookey from school among New York City's Park Row newsboys and

William Wrigley Jr.

bootblacks. William Wrigley Jr. had enjoyed selling soap in the street market for two years; but school was something else. Ultimately, after the boy returned from New York, only to get into trouble at school again, his soap-manufacturer father voiced the great understatement, "Your school life hasn't been a success," and put Junior to work in his factory.

But young Wrigley was not to be denied his chance to sell. At thirteen, he persuaded his father to let him go on the road as a soap salesman, complete with a wagon and a four-horse team with jingling bells in the harness. People who had seen him in action were not surprised when William Wrigley Jr. was later called "the greatest salesman since John H. Patterson of National Cash Register and the greatest showman since P. T. Barnum."

At the age of twenty-nine, he headed west to check out Chicago as a market for soap. He liked what he found—liked it so well, in fact, that he decided to start his own company. He had a wife and child by that time, and thirty-two dollars in cash.

His plan, in Chicago, was to sell soap to the wholesale trade, with baking powder as a premium. He was a staunch believer in premiums: "Everybody likes something extra, for nothing." When the baking powder showed signs of being more popular than the soap, he promptly switched to the baking powder business and added chewing gum as a premium. When the chewing gum drew more enthusiasm from his customers than the baking powder, Wrigley's Chewing Gum was born. It was 1892 and his first two brands were Lotta Gum and Vassar, soon to be followed by Juicy Fruit and Wrigley's Spearmint—with a spear of his own design on the label.

Twenty-seven years later, on a visit to California, he would say to his family, "You know, I've got an interest in an island somewhere out here. Why don't we go out tomorrow and see if we can find it?" They would find it without difficulty, because Catalina is more than three times the size of Bermuda. Ada Wrigley would say it looked like a wonderful place for a home, and Wrigley would respond, "All right, we'll keep it." He had bought his interest in Catalina Island during a casual meeting with an old whaling captain in a dockside lunch room. Later, to protect the island's natural beauty, he would buy out his partners and own it outright.

An old business associate used to say of William Wrigley Jr., "I've never seen Mr. Wrigley flustered; I've never even seen him act worried. He just seems to approach everything in an easy, uncomplicated way."

At a time when he was acclaimed as America's greatest salesman, Wrigley would sum up his whole philosophy on selling in these words: "To be always pleasant, always patient, always on time, and never to argue."

His philosophy on advertising was even more concise: "Tell 'em quick and tell 'em often."

Wrigley credited advertising for his company's first big breakthrough, when it zoomed, within weeks, from a relatively small local business to a national one. He chose the depression year of 1907 for that bold move, reasoning that, with competition quiet, his advertising would have a bigger voice. Also, he counted on getting some advertising bargains, and he did. With $250,000, at depression rates, he bought well over $1.5 million worth of advertising in New York City—and did it all in three days time. Simultaneously, to build strong distribution in support of this consumer effort, he sent every prospective dealer a coupon good for a free box (twenty packages) of gum when presented to the Wrigley jobber. Within a year, his sales soared to nearly ten times their former level.

William Wrigley Jr. enjoyed being called the master of the spectacular. But all the while, he was indoctrinating his young son, Philip K. Wrigley, with the humble, basic belief: "We are a five-cent business, and nobody in this company can ever afford to forget it."

When asked, in 1921, what single policy had been his most profitable one, William Wrigley Jr. said thoughtfully, "Restraint in regard to immediate profits. That has not only been our most profitable policy, it has been pretty nearly our only profitable one. It has been the inspiration of every distinctively successful method we have used."

He elaborated, on that occasion, on the importance of holding the line on his five-cent price. It had built dealer confidence and had eliminated cancellations and negotia-

Philip K. Wrigley

tions on rebates. It had been a deterrent to price rises on raw materials. But the most important thing of all, he concluded, was the impact of the stable low price on consumers: "Not only did we hold our old customers by avoiding a higher price; we also got a great many new ones by the *virtually lower* price."

When Philip K. Wrigley took charge of the company after his father's death in 1932, he faithfully applied what he had learned about running a "five-cent business."

Inevitably, in an age of inflation, the Wm. Wrigley Jr. Company would have to yield a little in its determination to hold the price line. In 1960, it announced its first price increase in forty-three years—a quarter of a penny a pack. When, in 1972, the company went to a seven-stick package to sell for a dime, it was only after painfully long and detailed analysis of other possibilities which included a five-stick package for a dime, a four-stick package to sell for a nickel, and an eight-stick package to sell for a dime. Inevitably, other increases followed.

Along with holding the line on price, Wrigley had long concentrated on just three main brands: Wrigley's Spearmint, Doublemint, and Juicy Fruit, plus a limited amount of "P.K," mostly for export—a significant streamlining since the early years, when the company also marketed Blood Orange, Lemon Cream, Pineapple, Banana, Licorice, Pepsin, and "Sweet 16." (Wrigley's P.K, incidentally, got its name from its early slogan, "Packed tight, Kept right"—not, as often rumored, from the name of Philip K. Wrigley.)

There was still another brand name in Wrigley history, used at different times on two separate products. The first product did not last long, but it made a point about Wrigley's attitude toward keeping faith with the consumer. The product was the original wartime Orbit, produced for the civilian market during the closing years of World War II, when quality ingredients were in short supply and the full output of Wrigley's Spearmint, Doublemint, and Juicy Fruit was being turned over to the U.S. Armed Forces overseas and at sea. The company frankly told the public that wartime Orbit was not good enough to carry a standard Wrigley label. Before World War II ended, pre-

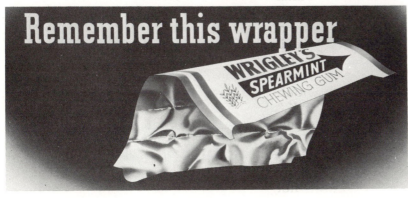

Above: William Wrigley Jr. advised his advertising people: "Tell 'em quick and tell 'em often." The company also believed in not straying from simple, effective themes. The "twin" graphics of this Doublemint poster, for example, were used with only slight changes for more than twenty years. **Left:** During two years of World War II, when no regular Wrigley gum was available, the company continued its advertising—but featuring an empty wrapper. When the regular Wrigley brands returned to the market, they soon exceeded their pre-war sales volume.

war quality gum was not available, even for the Armed Forces, and Orbit became Wrigley's only representative for two years. (Many years later, the Orbit name was revived for the company's sugarless gum.)

During that two-year wartime period, the company's advertising featured a picture of an empty Wrigley's Spearmint wrapper with the slogan, "Remember this wrapper." When regular Wrigley brands returned to the market, they not only regained but soon exceeded their pre-war volume.

Behind all this wartime Orbit and "empty wrapper" advertising was a little-known fact: reticent Philip K.

William Wrigley

Wrigley, so quiet compared with his flamboyant father, was an equally effective salesman in his own way. Advertising was the way. Until his death in 1977, Philip K. Wrigley regarded the company's advertising as his personal province. He followed his father's precept, "Tell 'em quick and tell 'em often," and added many refinements of his own.

In 1975, the Wrigley company began a major expansion of its product line with the introduction of Freedent gum for denture wearers. A year later came Big Red, Wrigley's challenge to Dentyne, the only other major brand with a cinnamon flavor. Within another year, the Wrigley company entered the sugarless gum market with a new Orbit sugar-free gum in three flavors—and then made a major bid for the youth market with nonstick Hubba Bubba bubble gum.

The company has declined to diversify into other types of confectionery or related products. "It's not that we have a closed mind on diversifying," William Wrigley, grandson of the founder and current president, has said. "It's just that you're better off doing what you know how to do best. As long as there is room for expansion within your field, you can diversify into new markets. That's what we do." With that uncomplicated philosophy, the company has moved its volume up past the $450 million mark, employs more than fifty-five hundred people, has factories in nine other countries, and enjoys worldwide distribution.

For many years, chewing gum was just not socially acceptable in the right places—even though America's roster of gum chewers included such distinguished names as Harry Truman, Dwight Eisenhower, and Henry Kissinger. Emily Post finally gave the practice a qualified approval when she wrote that it was allowable "whenever formal standards of behavior are not in force. Certainly not in church, during recitation periods in school, or when wearing formal clothes."

Opposition to gum chewing in England was even stronger. It was almost an official national prejudice—but that did not seem unreasonable to Philip K. Wrigley, a man who had inherited all his father's sensitivity about the feelings of the consumer. "We decided," he said later, "that there was a time and place for chewing gum, just like there is a time and place for eating bananas or anything else. So, in 1962, we ran a print campaign in England that was headed, 'Certainly *Not!*' We showed places where you were not supposed to chew gum—a barrister in court, a businessman at a conference, and so on. This started a controversy. People started writing letters saying, 'Tell us, then, when *can* we chew gum?' Then we changed the campaign to tell them when they could chew it."

William Wrigley Jr. had been fond of observing that "nothing is so much fun as business." He rose every morning at five to give his business a long, full day, and he never took a vacation that was not combined with a business trip.

"My father," Philip K. Wrigley once recalled, "was never particularly interested in making money, and neither am I. He always said that if you do the right thing, and build your bridges strong, it will come automatically.

"My father also taught me that if you haven't built an organization that can run without you, then you haven't done anything. That's been my real ambition: to build an organization that can carry on. When I pop off, I'm sure things will keep on going following the same principles that they always followed, through my son Bill."

MARKETING INSIGHTS
Successful marketing begins with knowing what the *consumer* wants. Based on consumer reactions to what he was selling, William Wrigley Jr. switched his business from soap to baking powder, then to chewing gum.

Lastingly successful marketing calls for the continuous earning of consumer trust. To keep faith with the consumer, during an extended, two-year shortage of quality ingredients, Philip K. Wrigley took the standard Wrigley label out of the market, explaining candidly that his temporary substitute gum was not good enough to carry the Wrigley name.

Holding the line on price has been another important

In England, where it met stiff social opposition, Wrigley ran a "Certainly *Not*" advertising campaign, featuring situations where gum was taboo, until it drew letters asking, "When *can* we chew gum?" Wrigley then responded with this "Certainly not . . . however . . ." approach.

Wrigley way of keeping faith with the consumer—and, for Wrigley, it had these additional benefits: it built dealer confidence, eliminated cancellations of dealer orders, served as a deterrent to price increases on raw materials—and attracted new customers when competitors raised prices.

Wrigley's chewing gum is a family brand covering various flavors; but the flavors (e.g., Doublemint) are promoted individually. In applying the principles of market segmentation, the company in recent years has introduced a sugar-free gum, a special nonsticking gum for denture wearers, and bubble gum.

Diversification? The Wm. Wrigley Jr. Company plans no diversification into related confectionery fields or into unrelated categories, saying, "As long as there is room for expansion within your field, you can diversify into new markets."

William Wrigley Jr. made advertising history when he chose a depression year for his boldest spending effort. His reasons for the timing: with competition quiet, his advertising would have a bigger voice; also, he counted on getting some bargain buys. He was right on both counts. Within one year after the advertising campaign was launched, his sales were up ten times their earlier level and his company had soared from local to national status.

In creating advertising, Wrigley has long followed a basic rule, "Tell 'em quick and tell 'em often," and has always maintained a high standard of integrity, good taste, and restraint.

MARKETING INDEX

INDEX

A

B

ABOUT THE AUTHOR

David Cleary is a professional communicator who believes that American business ingenuity is not just a lot of smoke. The great American brands, he feels, tell us something about our character, our energy, our success as a nation. So, he set out to document the story.

His very special background surely prepared him for the task. At Young & Rubicam, he climbed the agency ladder, and had, as vice president, creative or account management responsibility, at one time or another, for the likes of Birds Eye Foods, Eastern Airlines, Goodyear Tires, Lincoln Automobiles, Safeguard Soap, and Time Magazine, to name a few.

In a warmup for the current work, he wrote a series of pamphlets on important brands for The Dartnell Corporation. He has been helped greatly in preparing this work by his wife, Virginia, who is also his business partner in their opinion and marketing research company in Tampa, Florida.

Essentially, David Cleary has been a writer. An exception was his stint as company commander with the 9th Armored Division in World War II. He made news then, too. The 9th Armored crossed the Remagen Bridge and helped shorten the war.

6-84

DATE DUE

JUL 1 4 1984			
JAN 8 1987			
MAR 0 1 1988			